WITH MY OWN EYES

With My Own Eyes

A Lakota Woman Tells Her People's History

Susan Bordeaux Bettelyoun
and
Josephine Waggoner

Edited and Introduced by
Emily Levine

University of Nebraska Press
Lincoln and London

© 1998 by the University of Nebraska Press
All rights reserved
Manufactured in the United States of America
⊛ The paper in this book meets the minimum
requirements of American National Standard for Information Sciences—
Permanence of Paper for Printed Library Materials, ANSI Z39.48-1984.

Library of Congress Cataloging-in-Publication Data
Bettelyoun, Susan Bordeaux, 1857–1945.
With my own eyes : a Lakota woman
tells her people's history /
Susan Bordeaux Bettelyoun and
Josephine Waggoner ; edited and
introduced by Emily Levine.
p.   cm.
Includes bibliographical references and index.
ISBN 0-8032-1280-1 (cloth : alk. paper)
1. Brulé Indians—History.
2. Bettelyoun, Susan Bordeaux, 1857–1945.
3. Brulé Indians—Biography.
I. Waggoner, Josephine, 1872–1943.
II. Levine, Emily, 1956–   .   III. Title.
E99.B8B473   1998
973'.04975—dc21   97-37884
CIP

SECOND PRINTING: 1998

DEDICATED,
on behalf of
Susan Bordeaux Bettelyoun
and Josephine Waggoner,
TO THE LAKOTA NATION
and
TO MY MOTHER

Contents

Illustrations

Acknowledgments

During the ten years I worked on this book, I often felt that I was working alone, laboring through a seemingly impossible task. Nothing could be further from the truth. It is my pleasure, finally, to give thanks to all those whose time, skill, insight, and generosity helped bring this volume to fruition.

First, I'd like to acknowledge CD Ybarra, who initially told me of the manuscript.

Staff members at numerous libraries and archives were invaluable during my research, both in person and through extensive correspondence. Mary S. Rausch of the Western History Collections at the University of Oklahoma Libraries; Ellen L. Sulser at the State Historical Society of Iowa; Michael Pilgrim at the National Archives; Shirley A. Koeppel, lay coordinator at Saint Mary's Church in Hamburg, Iowa; Harry F. Thompson at the Center for Western Studies, Augustana College; and the staffs at the Saint Charles County Historical Society in Missouri and the Anoka County Historical Society in Minnesota all provided important information. I owe thanks to Ted Hamilton, Julie Lakota, Mary Little White Man, and especially Jeanne Smith, all at the Oglala Lakota College. Likewise, Marcella Cash of the Lakota Archives and Historical Research Center at Sinte Gleska University provided valuable assistance. The staff members at the Wyoming Department of Cultural Resources were especially helpful in unearthing material. I'd like to thank Ann Nelson, Senior Historian; LaVaughn Bresnahan, Photographic Historian; and Judy West for all their assistance at Cheyenne.

James A. Davis, at the State Historical Society of North Dakota, was persistent in his search for material written by Josephine Waggoner, and Mark Thiel, of Marquette University Libraries, contributed biographical information on various Lakotas and background on the Catholic missions in the Dakotas. At the State Veterans Home in Hot Springs, secretary Nancy Mileusnich diligently searched old records for Bettelyouns' and Waggoners' files.

I spent wonderful days at the Fort Laramie National Historic Site; the entire staff was welcoming. Shawn Wade, Park Ranger, answered a number of questions by mail, and special thanks are due Sandra Lowry, Librarian, who during two hot days personally helped me with voluminous material at the archive on the second floor of the old barracks. Thomas Buecher, Nebraska State Historical Society Curator at Fort Robinson, spent an afternoon clearing up nagging questions for me. Special thanks are also due Ane McBride of the Library/Archives Division at the Nebraska State Historical Society. At the Museum of the Fur Trade in Chadron, Nebraska, director Charles E. Hanson Jr. talked with me for hours about the early fur trade and its cast of characters. His knowledge is a treasure chest. Thanks to Donna Cordier-DuBray at the Buechel Memorial Lakota Museum for generous assistance in researching that institution's extensive photographic collection. Thanks also to the people of the Hollow Horn Bear sundance, who provided much more than a place to stay during those days on the Rosebud.

Of particular help was Mary Lou Hultgren, Curator of Collections at the Hampton University Museum. Ms. Hultgren's work with the files of the first Indian students at Hampton, including her own interest in Josephine Waggoner and research on the Standing Rock students, was invaluable. Finally, a special thank-you to LaVera Rose, originally from Rosebud and now a Curator of Manuscripts at the South Dakota State Archives, for her professional assistance and personal friendship. LaVera researched endless queries from me, and when I got to Pierre, she opened her home to me for a two-day stay and had a great turkey dinner waiting for me. Her research skills, intimate knowledge of the archives' holdings, and personal interest in the subject of Lakota mixed-blood women were an incalculable aid to my research.

For lending me their computers or for providing financial assistance so I could get my own, I am grateful to Pat Dean, Gina Matkin, Jane Levine and Randy Signor, and June Levine. I suppose I could have done it without you, but it would have taken at least twenty years! For additional financial assistance I thank numerous friends and family members.

Although I utilized a Lakota-English dictionary to help with the translation and spelling of Lakota words, having the help of native speakers was essential. I'd like to thank Kenneth Bordeaux, great-grandson of James Bordeaux and Supiwiŋ, for his help with translations, his wonderful stories, and his support throughout the project. A special thank-you to Anne Keller, raised on the Rosebud and now living in Lincoln, for her diligent hours of translating and so much more. For compensation, I was

Acknowledgments

only able to offer Mrs. Keller rides home from work; because of our wonderful conversations it never seemed like payment at all.

For assistance in answering seemingly small but crucial questions, I wish to acknowledge James Gibson, Arthur Amiotte, Robert Utley, and Father Peter J. Powell. David Wishart provided editorial assistance. In Saint Francis, Rose Bordeaux offered hospitality and information on the Bordeaux family. Bruce McIntosh opened his home to me at the edge of the beautiful Nebraska National Forest while I conducted research at the Museum of the Fur Trade. Special thanks to Bruce for the trip up West Ash Creek. The entire research trip would have been impossible without transportation. When it was clear that my old Datsun pickup wouldn't be up to the task, Barbara DiBernard lent me her car for two weeks. Thanks to her for support and generosity beyond the call of duty.

The staff of the Center for Great Plains Studies at the University of Nebraska, under the auspices of John Wunder, provided indispensable technical support. I'd especially like to thank Linda Ratcliffe. Sharon Bays keyed a majority of the notes, and both she and Gretchen Walker printed numerous drafts for me in the days before I had a printer.

Early in my work, Joy Harjo read the introduction and some original sections of the text. Her enthusiasm and advocacy meant a great deal to a novice like me.

This book would not exist without the guidance and sustaining faith of two women: my professors, mentors, and friends Fran Kaye and Susan Rosowski. Their trust in my ability to undertake this project let me think I could; their hours of diligent reading and suggestions made it a better work.

Serious thanks to Mary Lou Meier for helping me get back so I could finish the work.

Betty Orr kept me going with emotional and spiritual support and true grace. Thanks for all those walks that winter.

Finally, my mother, June Perry Levine, Professor Emerita of English at the University of Nebraska, not only provided the kind of support only a mother can give, but gave me the finest editorial assistance available. No one reads a manuscript with such a careful, critical eye.

Mitakuye oyasiŋ

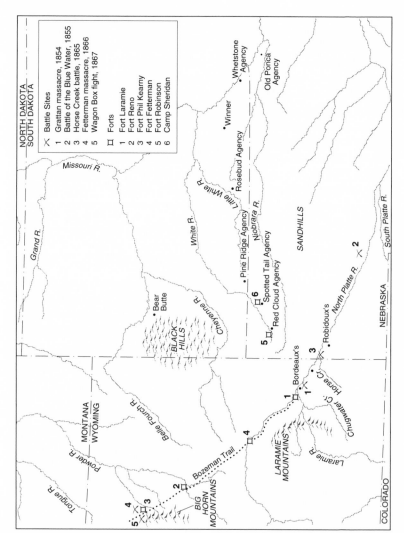

The Northern Plains

Introduction

During the winter of 1933, two mixed-blood Lakota women met and agreed to collaborate on writing what would eventually become a history of the Oglala and Brulé Lakota during the last half of the nineteenth century. Susan Bordeaux Bettelyoun and Josephine Waggoner spent their winters in the warmth of the Old Soldiers' Home at Hot Springs, South Dakota, and it was here that their productive friendship and working relationship was formed. For the next three or so years the two women worked together: Josephine Waggoner carefully recorded Susan Bettelyoun's words, filling tablet after tablet with her penciled script. Together, they produced a manuscript that expresses a distinctive view of Indian/white history on the Plains. With this document the voice of Native American women rises to tell history, rises to speak for itself—and rises to be heard.

Susan Bordeaux Bettelyoun was born on Sunday, March 15, 1857, at Fort Laramie—at the time, one of the most important military posts on the Plains. Her father, French-American fur trader James Bordeaux, had been an employee of the American Fur Company at Laramie until that organization sold its post to the United States in 1849. At the time of Susan's birth, he operated a trading post and road ranch just east of Laramie on the North Platte River. Susan's mother, Huŋtkalutawiŋ, or Red Cormorant Woman, was a Brulé Lakota of the Tiśaoti or Red Top Lodge band, a group formed by the intermarriage of Sissiton Santees and Brulés. An honored woman in her band, Huŋtkalutawiŋ was a sacred banner carrier, a pipe bearer in the White Buffalo ceremony, and a member of the *Huŋka* order. James Bordeaux and Huŋtkalutawiŋ met on the North Platte River where the Red Top band and other Brulés often camped, trading with the growing number of Euro-Americans. The two were married in 1841 and Huŋtkalutawiŋ subsequently moved into Fort Laramie where she was known as Marie.

James Bordeaux and Huŋtkalutawiŋ had eight children, Susan falling in the middle. Susan's early years were spent at her father's trading post eight miles downriver from Fort Laramie. A few years before her birth, this post and her father had played an important role in the first major military encounter between the U.S. military and the Brulés. In 1854, the so-called Mormon cow incident resulted in the deaths of Lt. John L. Grattan and his men. It was James Bordeaux who, to no avail, had tried to stop the brash young officer from entering the peaceful camp of Conquering Bear and it was Bordeaux who later buried the slain soldiers. Susan grew up practically on top of the battle site.

Living near Laramie on the "Platte River Road," Susan saw firsthand the onslaught of white migration and the growing conflict between the Lakota and the military. One incident seems to exemplify this conflict for her: when she was eight, Susan witnessed the hanging of a Cheyenne and two Lakotas at Fort Laramie; seventy years later, she was still able to recall in detail the sight of the bodies swaying in the High Plains breeze.

A few weeks after the hanging, the Brulés were sent east on a forced march, under military escort, in order to receive their treaty annuities. Because of the enormous difficulty and expense of freighting, it was easier for the military to transport the people to the goods than vice versa. Bordeaux and his family, along with other traders' mixed-blood families, joined the Brulés on the journey. The march came to an abrupt halt at Horse Creek when the full-blood members of the band killed the commanding officer, turned on their escort, and escaped. The soldiers and mixed-blood families—including Susan's—retreated. One of Susan's brothers raised a rifle to the attacking warriors, but Bordeaux knocked it from his hands. Many of the escaping Indians were Susan's close relatives; indeed, it was her uncle Swift Bear who had helped to plan and lead the revolt. This critical incident, when "friendlies" turned on the military, is often neglected in histories of the period. Susan Bettelyoun gives us a gripping eyewitness account.

As tension mounted around Laramie, Susan was sent to join her brothers at school in Hamburg, Iowa, where they were the only Indian children. In Iowa, Susan lived in a white world, which, for a girl of nine, must have profoundly affected her sense of identity at the same time that it provided her a new perspective and the education with which to express that identity. In 1870, after four years in Iowa, Susan joined her mother and father at the town of Wheeler, in present-day South Dakota. Wheeler was near the Whetstone Agency, where Spotted Tail's Brulés had been moved. Here, thirteen-year-old Susan taught in the band's first school.

In her manuscript, Bettelyoun often criticizes the constant moving of the Brulés and their agency. She clearly understood the absurdity and counterproductivity involved. By tracing the agency's movements, we can follow Bettelyoun's own life over the next few years. In 1871, at the pleading of the Brulés, who had despised living along the Missouri and the influence of liquor there, the Whetstone Agency was moved to the White River country in northwest Nebraska. For the next six years the agency—soon renamed Spotted Tail—moved around the area between Big and Little White Clay Creeks, finally settling on Beaver Creek. Susan moved to the White River, but apparently spent some of her time at Bordeaux's place near Wheeler.

In 1874, at the age of seventeen, Susan Bordeaux married mixed-blood Charles Tackett at White Swan back along the Missouri, and on October 5, 1876 she gave birth to a daughter, Marie. The child was born near the Niobrara River in Holt County, Nebraska, where Susan's sister Louise had settled. The Tackett family returned to the Brulé agency on Beaver Creek, but, according to the manuscript, Susan spent some of the next year at nearby Camp Robinson. In the fall of 1877, the Brulés were again moved east, this time to the recently vacated Ponca agency in northeast Nebraska. Once more, Susan went with her people. Within a year, the tribe persuaded the government to allow them to return west and the Brulés finally settled at Rosebud in present-day South Dakota. Although she makes no mention of it in her manuscript, on one of these moves Charles Tackett left her and took up with a daughter of Spotted Tail. (Additional information on this episode, as well as more detailed biographical information about Bettelyoun, can be found in the notes.)

In 1884, Susan took Marie to Anoka, Minnesota, where she worked as the matron of the girls' building at Saint Anne's, a Catholic school. Four years later she returned to Rosebud, but left Marie in Minnesota so that the girl could continue her education. At Rosebud, Susan found employment in the Field Matron program. Marie joined her in 1891, but died within the year at the age of fifteen.

That same year, Susan married Isaac P. Bettelyoun, a college-educated mixed-blood almost twelve years her junior. Isaac, an interpreter and guide for the army, also worked for the Rosebud Agency as a clerk and farmer. Susan continued her job with the Field Matron program; records indicate she was employed as a Female Industrial Teacher from at least 1889 to 1901.

Sometime during the 1890s, Isaac and Susan adopted a full-blood girl named Rose. Whether or not this was a formal, legal adoption is unclear. She is listed with the Bettelyouns on the 1900 federal census of the

Rosebud Reservation (enumerated by Isaac) as "Rosy, adopted daughter," born in May 1894. Bettelyoun makes no mention of the child in her manuscript, stating both there and in her Old Soldiers' Home application that she had only one child, her deceased daughter Marie.

In 1909, the couple moved to Winner, South Dakota, where Isaac got a job as a bank cashier. When the bank failed, they moved to Saint Francis where they farmed, dealt in cattle, and received income from leasing their allotment. In 1933, when their health deteriorated and they were unable to continue managing their ranching operation, Susan and her husband moved into the Old Soldiers' Home at Hot Springs.

It was here that Bettelyoun met Josephine Waggoner. Waggoner, a generation younger than Bettelyoun, was also a mixed-blood Lakota—Irish on her father's side and a member of the Kiglaśka band of Huŋkpapa on her mother's. While the stories told here are Bettelyoun's, Josephine Waggoner, a great Lakota historian, was the catalyst for this book. Perhaps in the future, scholars will examine her career and she will attain the recognition she deserves.

Josephine Waggoner was born in October 1872 at her grandmother's camp near the Grand River Agency, Dakota Territory. Her father, Charles H. McCarthy, drowned two years later while on duty as the sheriff of Burleigh County. Her mother, Itatewiŋ, or Wind Woman, left behind McCarthy's savings and property and took the infant Josephine and her half sister Marcella to her people on the Standing Rock Reservation. When Catholics established a school at the agency in 1877, Waggoner was sent behind its stockaded walls and permitted to see her mother only through small cracks between the palisades. After a few years, Waggoner was sent east to the Hampton Normal and Agricultural Institute in Virginia, a school for African Americans that had recently begun an educational experiment in accepting Indian children.

Student files at Hampton reveal a somewhat contradictory record. Upon entering the school, Waggoner was described as "a very amiable little girl, of more than average promise, and of an unusually even and happy temperament." In 1893, a Hampton publication remembered the former student differently: "Her career here was not promising and her career at home . . . was not above reproach. In dress, general bearing and accomplishments, she was an example to the more uncivilized, but her helpfulness too often ended there." A form in Waggoner's student file lists her Record of Character as "very good" and her Industry and General Influence as "fair." Whatever the teachers and administrators thought of her, in later years Waggoner could not praise Hampton enough. For decades she kept up a correspondence with staff members, writing such accolades as, "There is never a day passes in my life but what I think of Hampton. I can never forget, and never shall until I lay down my life forever. . . . When I think of Hampton I think of everything that is pure, good and holy. When I am troubled, impatient or worried, I think of Hampton and peaceful thoughts come to me" (Hampton University Archives, Waggoner student file).

Waggoner spent three years at Hampton, returned home for a year, went back to Hampton for an additional three years, and finally settled back on the reservation in 1888 at the age of sixteen. There young Josephine worked for the Episcopal and Congregational missionaries, often interpreting sermons from beside the pulpit. While working at the Congregational mission hospital near Fort Yates, she met a white soldier, Pvt. John Franklin Waggoner. The two were married on Thanksgiving Day, 1889.

Throughout the next year, educated Josephine was called upon by Huŋkpapa chiefs, including Sitting Bull, to read the letters they received from the Pine Ridge Reservation concerning the spreading Ghost Dance movement. In December, her husband's troop accompanied Indian police part of the way when they went to arrest Sitting Bull. Private Waggoner later testified that the policemen were drinking. During the arrest action, Sitting Bull was killed. Josephine helped to lay out the great leader's body.

After a few years at Fort Yates, John Waggoner left the army and the couple set up ranching on Four-Mile Creek. In 1905, they moved with their growing family to an allotment of four sections at Keldron, South Dakota.

Josephine Waggoner's married life was hard. While helping with the ranch, keeping house, and growing food for the family, she raised nine children and provided them all with higher education. Later she helped raise a number of grandchildren as well. Throughout these busy years, Waggoner found time to paint and to write poetry and stories. In the early 1920s she filled fourteen newsprint tablets with the story of her mother's first husband, Benjamin Monroe Connor. Lewis F. Crawford of the South Dakota Historical Society obtained these manuscripts of Connor's exciting life on the plains and from them published *Rekindling Camp Fires: The Exploits of Ben Arnold (Connor)* (1926). Although Crawford does acknowledge Waggoner in his introduction, he refers to the fourteen tablets simply as "some data taken down just before Arnold's death." Additional study could reveal just how much *Camp Fires* is based on Waggoner's work.

By the end of the 1920s, her children grown, Josephine Waggoner turned her attention to seeking out and recording the history of her people. Despite her age, illnesses, and daily struggles during difficult economic times, she was a prolific writer. In 1929, she wrote author Stanley Vestal (Walter S. Campbell): "It is very hard for me to write. My daughters and son leave their children a great deal with me. I do all my own housework and try to sew for myself and others so the only time I have is when everyone is asleep—The light disturbs my husband so I write in the kitchen" (December 5, 1929).

Waggoner felt herself on a mission to create a written record for her people: "My work is for the Indians. They don't study history much are not interested, but I believe they would be from someone they know" (Waggoner to Campbell, October 20, 1929). She realized too that "the old people are dying off so fast a person must work fast or their stories will be like a closed book" (January 4, 1930). Throughout the 1930s, Waggoner was called on by white historians to provide information she knew firsthand or that she could obtain from the Lakotas she spoke with. Her voluminous correspondence with Frank Herriott of Drake University concerning Iŋkpaduta for his *Annals of Iowa* articles and with Vestal concerning Sitting Bull for his biography of the chief attest to her eagerness to provide these white scholars with invaluable eyewitness information. In September 1933, she wrote Herriott: "I am always glad to help if I can to those who are interested in Indian history. I have been corresponding with several writers who have been wanting to know historical facts. There has been so much fictitious and misleading stories written about the Indians. I am always anxious to see the truth about these stories brought before the public." Waggoner knew that without the Indians' input, white historians' accounts would not be complete or accurate. She provided information to numerous writers, including Doane Robinson and Charles Deland, both of the South Dakota Historical Society. Of the former, she wrote Herriott: "I know Mr. Robinson thought and wrote different, but he knows the truth now, I think. He heard what the white people told, I am writing what I heard Indians said" (January 19, 1933).

The historians who obtained information from Waggoner gave her varying degrees of consideration, compensation, and credit for her work.

Frank Herriott was solicitous in his requests, not wanting to use in his articles work that she intended to publish herself. Stanley Vestal sent Waggoner extensive questionnaires to complete; she wrote to him in 1930: "We have had a hard year and times have been hard. I am on the verge of losing my home but I have worked hard to fill your needs in your book with hopes of a substantial payment when your book is published as you promised me" (March 23, 1930). The same year, in the hospital with diabetes, Waggoner asked Vestal for money for insulin saying, "I have done a pretty daring thing to give you so much information" (February 24, 1930). What compensation she received from Vestal is not clear; their correspondence indicates that Vestal sent her only a few dollars now and again. In 1941 he offered her one dollar "for the Indian story of the 'Race Track' around the Black Hills" (March 19, 1941).

While Waggoner was providing information to a number of white historians, she proceeded with her own work. This included poetry, autobiographical sketches and reminiscences, the recording of traditional Lakota culture learned from her mother and grandmother, and a large manuscript concerning her life and the history of the Lakota people and their chiefs. She tried throughout the 1930s to get this latter work published, asking Herriott, Vestal, the North Dakota Historical Society, and others for assistance. Herriott had a typing class at Drake produce a typescript of the manuscript free of charge, and the Federal Writers Project staff at the historical society read the work and offered their help. Although the manuscript was at one time with the society, it is no longer in their collections. In 1994, the Waggoner family self-published this major work of Josephine's life, *My Land, My People, My Story*.

All through the 1930s Waggoner sought to procure eyewitness accounts from the old-timers at Standing Rock and, after she began spending winters at the Old Soldiers' Home in 1932, she continued her work there and at nearby Pine Ridge and Rosebud as well.

For years, Susan Bettelyoun had been angered at the way white scholars had presented the times she had lived through. In the foreword to her manuscript, she writes: "I have read many books on Indian lore, none of which have entirely reflected the facts as I know them from my own observations and from statements made to me by my parents and other relatives. The reading of these books has stirred my ire, because of a lack of understanding of the plains Indians by the authors" (NSHS MS185 typescript). Bettelyoun was determined to set the record straight, but her severe rheumatism prevented her from extensive writing. Fortunately, Josephine Waggoner entered her life.

When Susan Bettelyoun and Josephine Waggoner met in 1933, each had witnessed the dispossession of the Lakota from her own unique perspective. One woman wanted to correct the accepted history of the times but couldn't write and the other wanted to record the stories of the old people. It is not surprising that within a few months of meeting, Bettelyoun and Waggoner had decided to collaborate on the writing of Susan's stories.

In June 1934, as their work began, Waggoner wrote to Addison E. Sheldon, director of the Nebraska State Historical Society. She explained their project and asked for help in determining certain dates that Bettelyoun could not remember (Waggoner to Sheldon, June 19, 1934). Realizing the importance of securing their work, Sheldon replied enthusiastically. He provided the information they needed, encouraged Waggoner and Bettelyoun to continue their work, and went so far as to offer to have the manuscript typed and to help in getting it published.

Over the next two years, Waggoner and Bettelyoun wrote their manuscript. When a section was completed, it was sent off to Sheldon, who first made corrections and then had it typed. The typescript was then returned to the women at Hot Springs for any further corrections.

The question arises of how the manuscript was created. Waggoner described her role by saying, "I wrote the words just as they were spoken" (Waggoner to Sheldon, March 1, 1937). The manuscript supports her description, as its style and tone make it appear that, for the most part, Waggoner wrote down word for word what Bettelyoun said.

That Waggoner was the recorder, not the source, does not mean that authorship should be attributed solely to Susan Bettelyoun, for Waggoner was not simply an amanuensis. The two women were collaborators; they worked as a team. Waggoner invested over six years of her life in the project and was as determined as Bettelyoun to get the stories told and see them in print. It was Waggoner who carried on the necessary correspondence with Sheldon. Waggoner wrote, "She and I are pardners in that story" (Waggoner to Sheldon, June 30, 1936). Bettelyoun also understood Waggoner's role as one of great importance. In the foreword to her manuscript she wrote: "Mrs. Waggoner is now my good friend and I am deeply indebted to her for her assistance and for her interest in my well-being. My hand is now so infirm that, in my judgement, it would have been impossible for me to place this material on paper. I regret that, in so far as this material life is concerned, I will never be able to repay her" (NSHS MS185 typescript).

During the time that Waggoner and Bettelyoun worked on the manuscript, they corresponded regularly with Addison Sheldon. The letters are almost entirely in Waggoner's hand, although some appear to be written for, if not actually dictated by, Bettelyoun. These letters, now housed in the Nebraska State Historical Society, reveal that a warm, mutually beneficial relationship developed between the women and Sheldon while the manuscript was in progress. Early in 1935, the first handwritten installments arrived in Lincoln. In April, after correcting them and having them typed, Sheldon wrote Waggoner praising her for a job well done. Sheldon had shared their work with society employee Mari Sandoz (who had just won the *Atlantic Monthly* award for *Old Jules*) and he told Waggoner that they both agreed that the material had the makings of a "first class book." He also explained that, even though he and Sandoz were well acquainted with frontier history, much of the information was new to them (Sheldon to Waggoner, April 30, 1935). This pattern continued for the next several years: installments were sent to Sheldon, he wrote his praises, and he continued to suggest that the publication of a book was in the future.

As time wore on, however, and the work remained unpublished, Waggoner and Bettelyoun's letters grew first impatient and, eventually, angry. During this time, Bettelyoun was receiving requests from historians—both amateur and professional—for information and even copies of the manuscript. Bettelyoun and Waggoner wrote Sheldon of these requests, hoping it would hasten the date of publication. By 1937 the women's impatience was becoming obvious. After four months with no word from Sheldon, Waggoner wrote Mari Sandoz, explaining that, "Mrs. Bettelyoun is quite discouraged. . . . She is afraid she will pass on before anything is done" (Waggoner to Sandoz, April 5, 1937). Throughout the remainder of the year, most of Waggoner's letters expressed concern about the manuscript; she repeatedly asked what was being done and when their work would be published. Then, in November, she wrote to Sheldon, "I am afraid it will never be published. [Mrs. Bettelyoun is] very anxious about it and suggested I write and inquire. . . . Please let us hear from you soon." Waggoner went so far as to ask, "Could she get this published at her own expense—and where?" (Waggoner to Sheldon, November 15, 1937).

Again, Sheldon did not respond. Frustrated, Waggoner wrote to Mari Sandoz a second time. Apparently it was upon receipt of this letter that

Sandoz took her first good look at the manuscript and got the slow moving wheels to spin a little faster. On December 21, she sent her opinion of the manuscript to Sheldon: "I think this contains invaluable frontier material and should, of course, be in print. And yet it lacks the continuity requisite for the regular reader. . . . [T]here are some vaguenesses, ambiguities, and even contradictions that should be carefully checked, altered or cared for by footnoting. . . . I wonder if it is salable as it now stands." She suggested that if Sheldon had the time, he should edit the manuscript himself, "clear up the bad spots and get more light on many things Mrs. Waggoner . . . cannot appreciate, not being a historian" (Sandoz to Sheldon, December 21, 1937).

In early January of 1938, Sheldon sent the manuscript to Edward Weeks, Sandoz's editor at *Atlantic Monthly*. Sandoz, trying to keep the process moving, had spoken to Weeks about the manuscript and he was eager to see it. It is curious, in light of Waggoner's insistent letters, that Sheldon did not let her know of this development. When John Walcott of *Atlantic Monthly* responded to the manuscript in April, he said he had come to the same conclusions that Sandoz and Sheldon had. He wrote: "[W]hile the material is interesting and sometimes valuable it is not in proper form for publication under our imprint" (Walcott to Sheldon, April 22, 1938).

Sheldon forwarded Walcott's letter to Waggoner and said he had discussed the matter with Sandoz and that they had agreed on two main points:

> 1st The manuscript has important historical material in it
> 2nd The only way it can secure a publisher is by having someone with literary ability and a thorough knowledge of the west take the manuscript, rewrite it completely, check the statements in it by the historical record, so that it shall harmonize with them; provide illustrations for it, use footnotes to supplement and explain its story and then offer it to some well known publisher. (Sheldon to Waggoner, April 22, 1938)

Soon after this, Federal Writers Project staffers began editing the manuscript. As Sheldon predicted, their editorial work was extensive. In many places the manuscript was entirely rewritten; it was crowded out by footnotes, and the compelling first person voice was sometimes replaced by "she" and "Mrs. Bettelyoun."

Throughout the next year, work continued on the manuscript and

Waggoner and Bettelyoun continued to write impatient letters. By the spring of 1939, Sheldon had decided that the historical society would publish the manuscript itself. He informed Waggoner of this, telling her: "We have pending in our appropriation request for the Nebraska legislature, the hope of securing some money which would enable us to publish the manuscript" (Sheldon to Waggoner, March 21, 1939).

Ten months later Waggoner was still asking Sheldon to "Please let us know if there is a chance to get her work published" (Waggoner to Sheldon, January 8, 1940). At the end of January, Sheldon received a letter from Bettelyoun pointing out that it had been seven months since they had heard from him. It had also been five years since the first installments had been sent and she wanted to know when their book would be published. She wrote that she realized many changes had been made during the editing process and, because she "was most desirous that anything historical that I am connected with should be authentic in every respect, I would like to have you send me the entire work . . . that I may personally go over it to check for errors of all kinds," effectively turning the tables on Sheldon (Bettelyoun to Sheldon, January 31, 1940). The correspondence files at the historical society contain no reply to this letter. Bettelyoun's March letter to Sheldon (in Waggoner's hand) reveals her increasing anger. In it, she demands that the manuscript be returned to her—the society had not succeeded in securing a publisher and she had found a possible buyer (March 6, 1940).

This is the last known correspondence of Susan Bettelyoun or Josephine Waggoner with Addison Sheldon. It is not known whether Sheldon ever returned a copy of Bettelyoun's manuscript; it is known that the society never published it. Two factors may have contributed to the delays and lack of publication: by 1940 serious illness affected Sheldon's work, and a lack of funding and the loss of the Federal Writers Project employees in the early forties hampered the day to day work of the society.

Yet, even during this period, Sheldon's interest in the manuscript continued, apparently now beyond the involvement of its authors. Fully a year after his correspondence with Waggoner and Bettelyoun ended, Sheldon was working with Florence Poast of the Writers Project concerning details for publication of the manuscript in a format "similar to that for the Project's state guides" (Poast to Sheldon, June 4, 1941). In a memo to Sheldon, Poast asks, "if you still desire me to edit the manuscript as it is" (Poast to Sheldon, June 4, 1941). It seems there was some dissatisfaction with the editing done by Walter Mahlon Herbert and others a few years earlier and additional editing was planned. Of particular interest, Poast continues with an "unsolicited suggestion" in which she describes the manuscript as "unique" and "worth anybody's money" and is a lone voice ahead of her time in recommending: "Would it not be a greater contribution to the literature of the American Indian to publish her manuscript as she submitted it making only such editorial changes as are absolutely necessary from a point of view of good English (which she would undoubtedly want you to do). If you desire to include the historical notes, could they not form an appendix at the back?" (Poast to Sheldon, June 4, 1941). How Sheldon responded to Ms. Poast's suggestion is not known, but no edited version of the manuscript aside from the one housed at the Nebraska State Historical Society has been located and it certainly does not reflect her proposals.

As Bettelyoun and Waggoner feared, Susan died before seeing the society publish her work. She died on December 17, 1945, and is buried at the Saint Francis cemetery. (Inexplicably, her tombstone gives the year of death as 1946.) Josephine Waggoner had died three years earlier on a visit home to Keldron on February 14, 1943. She too did not live to see her own historical manuscript, *My Land, My People, My Story*, published.

Nearly twenty years passed before another attempt was made to publish the Bettelyoun/Waggoner manuscript. In the late 1950s, Bruce Nicoll, director of the University of Nebraska Press, developed the Bison Books paperback series. Primarily set up as an imprint for reissues of out-of-print books about the West, Bison Books was also intended to include original manuscripts.

During this period, Mari Sandoz, whose works were to be reissued under the Bison imprint, suggested many possible titles to Nicoll. It was undoubtedly Sandoz who first told him about the Bettelyoun/Waggoner manuscript. While visiting Lincoln in the spring of 1959, she wrote Nicoll: "Correspondence files of the Society, say 1935–1937, ought to tell what the arrangements about the Bettelyoun book were. There must have been some kind of arrangement about the rewriting" (Sandoz to Nicoll, April 17, 1959). Later in the month, Nicoll sent Sandoz a memo regarding possible Bison titles they had been discussing. Topping the list was the Bettelyoun manuscript, of which Nicoll wrote with definite intent: "We have the . . . manuscript and when it is checked with the original it will become part of the Pioneer Heritage Series" (Nicoll to Sandoz, April 27, 1959).

Unfortunately, Nicoll ran into problems when he approached Bill Aeschbacher, then director of the Nebraska State Historical Society. Nicoll had hoped that if the press did the editorial work on the book, then the society could find someone to do the historical research that was needed. Apparently Aeschbacher was not pleased with Nicoll's assumptions about publishing the manuscript. Writing to Sandoz about their initial meeting, Nicoll explained:

> To make an hour long conversation short, he said that the Bettelyoun [manuscript was] . . . of course, historical property and that naturally the society would have to work out a formal arrangement with us as to [what] we could publish, and somewhat as to the form. . . . I had the impression that perhaps he felt I had been a little pushy. . . . In the meantime he will consider devoting staff time to preparing the . . . manuscript for us. (Nicoll to Sandoz, May 22, 1959)

In a postscript to a letter dated August 7, Nicoll informed Sandoz, "Mr. Aeschbacher has stopped work on the Bettelyoun manuscript and I am not entirely sure why, despite a letter and a phone call." Sandoz replied: "I don't understand the trouble about the . . . manuscript. I had it once, perhaps I should have kept it. Anyway, good luck" (Sandoz to Nicoll, August 11, 1959).

Correspondence over the next two years between Nicoll and Sandoz reveals that Nebraska continued to pursue publication of the manuscript and that Sandoz was still trying to get the work into print (UNLA, Mari Sandoz Collection, correspondence files). Regrettably, the files that the University of Nebraska Press kept on the Bettelyoun manuscript have been discarded, so it is difficult to ascertain why they never published it. However, Kay Graber, longtime employee of the press, recalls that the decision not to publish had to do with the amount of work necessary to get the manuscript into acceptable form. Although Nicoll's philosophy on these matters was, "When you try to slick 'em up, and footnote them to death the basic feel and purpose of these writings is lost," the holograph would still have required considerable editorial work (Nicoll to Sandoz, June 6, 1960).

Whatever the reasons, the Bettelyoun/Waggoner manuscript once again sat on the shelves of the Nebraska State Historical Society's archives. It sat but, as in the previous twenty years, it did not collect dust. When historians of the West traveled to the society to conduct research, they found the manuscript to be a gold mine of information. The manuscript is listed as a source for such books as Merrill Mattes's *The Great Platte River Road*, Sandra Myres's *Westering Women and the Frontier Experience: 1800–1915*, and, of course, numerous books on Lakota-white history. Historian George E. Hyde, who was unable to obtain the manuscript from Bettelyoun in the 1930s, used her work for his books, including *Spotted Tail's Folk: A History of the Brulé Sioux*. There are also instances where certain passages from the manuscript appear in historical works with little change and no direct credit (compare, for example, Remi Nadeau's *Fort Laramie and the Sioux*, 184, with Bettelyoun's account of Green Plum's experience after the Horse Creek Fight, and Mari Sandoz's *Crazy Horse*, 159, with Bettelyoun's description of the bodies hanging at Fort Laramie in 1865).This work by two Lakota women, which had been called "priceless," "unique," and "worth anybody's money," was not published, but eminent western historians used—and misused—it for their own books which have been published and have shaped our interpretation of Indian-white history.

Why was this manuscript not published—neither in 1940 nor in 1960? The answer seems to lie in the problem of "history" and, in turn, with the problem of editing.

It was taken for granted, by both the Nebraska State Historical Society and University of Nebraska Press, that the manuscript could not be published as it stood. To begin with, the language had to be cleaned up, as Poast explained, "from a point of view of good English." Unfortunately, at the historical society, this led to a wholly reworked edition with alterations in the sentence structure that caused substantive changes in meaning and destroyed the overall tone of the work.

The editors at the historical society also set about to rewrite the manuscript in a strict chronological order. Their pursuit of linear, progressive time and the elimination of repetition resulted in a wholly reworked edition. The original manuscript was, for the most part, an oral telling of memories by a woman whose tribal background caused her to perceive time in a much different way from Euro-American historians. Because "the story" is also the "telling of the story," the reworked edition inevitably altered the essence of the work. (See Martin and Drinnon in Martin for discussions of the effects of Western concepts of time on the academic interpretation of native history.)

A different conception of time is only one of the problems academic historians face when dealing with Indians telling their own story. Another is authenticity. Regrettably, when an Indian writes history, many of these historians demand "verification." They want to check the "story" against the "facts": military reports, Commissioner of Indian Affairs reports, books by eminent white historians. One factor in the need for verification stems from the oral nature of much native history. The reliance on memory is often suspect in a culture that relies on the written word, but members of oral cultures pride themselves on their ability to record history in their minds. (See Berkhofer for a discussion of what he terms "formal history" and its relation to other forms of Native American history.)

Susan Bettelyoun told the truth as she knew it. As Josephine Waggoner wrote, "All this is true history Mrs. Bettelyoun saw with her own eye and what her father, mother and relatives [saw]—I mean to say it is not fiction" (Waggoner to Sheldon, April 13, 1936). Regardless of this, Addison Sheldon was determined that the manuscript be "check[ed] . . . by the historical record, so that it shall harmonize with [it]." And so the Historical Society's researchers checked everything Bettelyoun said against "the historical record," and, to verify or dispute her words, they quoted extensively from these records in their footnotes. The nature of many of these footnotes suggests that Bettelyoun's words were not taken at face value, were not trusted to represent "the truth." This reliance on government—often military—records gives credence to the view, to paraphrase Paula Gunn Allen, that the time before the soldiers came you call myth, the time after they came you call history. The contradictions to the "historical record" that Sheldon was so intent on "harmonizing" are themselves one of the reasons this manuscript is important. They give us another history. As Berkhofer asks, "From whose categories of reality should the facts of history be derived?" (41).

The argument the editors and annotators would make is that some of the things Bettelyoun says are simply inaccurate and her dates are wrong, confused; therefore, everything she says must be taken with caution. The answer to such assertions is that the manuscript expresses a reality other than—and perhaps more important than—facts and dates, a reality in which "pertinence replaced dates as the index of utility" (Berkhofer, 40). In the remembering and telling of such a history, a person might "subordinate facts to the essential truth of the subject's life" (Bataille and Sands, 13). Waggoner herself realized this when she wrote Sheldon, "Some of the dates were not exactly right I know, but the stories told were true" (August 11, 1938).

Ironically, the one place Bettelyoun falters dramatically, where her chronology and facts truly fall apart, is when she relies on the published work of a white historian. A large part of the confusing original section titled "Annuities" (now divided between chapters twelve and thirteen) turns out to be based on G. W. Kingsbury's *History of Dakota Territory*— a book with serious problems regarding names, dates, and more substantive issues. I have retained the Kingsbury-based material, dealing with its inaccuracies through the use of notes.

Fortunately, editorial attitudes are changing with regard to historical works by native peoples. Editors are now interested in allowing the voice of the Indian to be heard and in maintaining the oral quality of that voice. Undermining, intrusive footnoting and excessive rewriting are absent in most recent scholar-edited narratives. Explanations, when needed, are now placed at the beginning or end of the text, as Florence Poast incisively suggested they be. For examples of these changing attitudes one need only look at the editorial policies and supplemental material of such scholars as Kathleen Sands, Nancy O. Lurie, Margaret Blackman, Kathleen Weist, and others in their recordings of Indian narratives.

This new, more sensitive editorial policy is articulated by Brian Swann and Arnold Krupat in the introduction to their book *I Tell You Now: Autobiographical Essays by Native American Writers*. They write:

It is our belief that Native American autobiographies—if not texts by Native Americans generally—have been more often overedited than underedited. . . . Editing, especially when done by non–Native Americans, tends to work for a kind of surface polish that is, usually unthinkingly, felt to be the fixed and unchanging attribute of "good style." . . . Our own notion is that "good" style can be judged only rhetorically and functionally, in relation to the context in which it appears and the effects it seeks to achieve. The Euro-American tradition has been a written tradition used to dealing with textual objects. The Native American tradition, however, has been oral, presenting not objects but acts, not pages but performances. The question, therefore—and this question must be faced directly by any readers unused to having it posed—is not whether language appears "good" according to some conventional model of textbook goodness but whether it *works* to good effect, whether it communicates to us, moves us, makes us see. Thus, we have held to our belief that Native American writers should speak *for* themselves while they speak of themselves, regardless of whether their speech seems polished . . . or whether instead it seems to adhere to some very different manner that we ignore to our impoverishment (xiii–xiv).

Kathleen Sands has been a major contributor to this new approach to editing native American autobiography; she explains, "The editor's principal duty is to establish an accurate text and to preserve the integrity of the narrative within the bounds of publication requirements. This requires not only a thorough knowledge of the narrator's culture but also a sensitivity to Indian perceptions of language, landscape, time, reality, and the nature of the cosmos" (59). (See also Gretchen Bataille, 1983, on this subject as it relates specifically to native women's autobiography; and Brumble, 1988; Krupat, 1985; and Wong, 1992, for discussions of the editing of native autobiographies in general.)

These new approaches to history and editing require taking a fresh look at the Bettelyoun / Waggoner manuscript. As has been pointed out, much of the knowledge we have of the Lakota–Euro-American conflict of the late nineteenth century comes to us from some sort of military or Commissioner of Indian Affairs source; it is, therefore, primarily white and male. Those Native American sources that do exist are usually in the form of interviews conducted by white men (such as Eli S. Ricker), or as-told-to histories. The "as-told-to" invariably means "as told to a white person" (for example, Black Elk as told to John Neihardt) and again are colored by Euro-American perception and interpretation. Almost without exception, historians traveling to the reservations to record information concerning the military conflict or tribal politics did not interview or record the stories of women. (See Theisz for a discussion of "as-told-to" works, which he terms "bi-autobiography.")

White audiences have had little access to Lakotas' own interpretation of their history. Only a handful of books have been written by Lakota men, often by those educated at off-reservation boarding schools (for example, Charles Eastman, Luther Standing Bear, and even Bettelyoun's nephew, William J. Bordeaux). Even more inaccessible to a general audience—and even to scholars (perhaps especially scholars)—is Lakota oral history, which carries on the stories of tribal dispossession.

What of the voices of Indian women? Historical works by Indian women are, not surprisingly, rare. Of the works "by" Indian women, most are as-told-to reminiscences or life histories. The "as-told-to" in these cases often refers to white women anthropologists and, although many of these works are edited with a new sensitivity to the native woman's voice, they are still solicited and edited by white academics. Examples of this collaboration between native women and white women include *Belle Highwalking: The Narrative of a Cheyenne Woman*, edited by Katherine M. Weist; *Mountain-Wolf Woman*, edited by Nancy O. Lurie; *The Autobiography of a Papago Woman*, edited by Ruth Underhill; and *During My Time*, edited by Margaret B. Blackman.

And what of native women speaking for themselves, of their own volition? The past twenty-five years have given rise to a growing number of such works. Maria Campbell's *Halfbreed* is an engrossing autobiography with no white "as-told-to." Similarly, Beverly Hungry Wolf's *The Ways of My Grandmothers* is a book that records tribal legends and preserves women's traditions of the Blood people of the Blackfeet Nation without academic, anthropological intrusion. Native poets and novelists like Leslie Marmon Silko, Paula Gunn Allen, Linda Hogan, Joy Harjo, Elizabeth Cook-Lynn, and Chrystos are creating a rich, expressive body of work. Still others, like Jaune Quick-To-See Smith, find their "voice" through the visual arts. Beatrice Medicine has contributed invaluable work in the overwhelmingly white field of native ethnography. Finally, "common" women have found their voices and published their work in such groundbreaking anthologies as *This Bridge Called My Back* and *A Gathering of Spirit*.

Over the years the words of native women have become increasingly available. The question arises, then, of how the Bettelyoun/Waggoner manuscript fits into this growing body of work. What are its merits? How does it fill the gaps of native women's writing? How does it differ from that writing?

Two important points stand out: the nature of the collaboration and the intention of the authors to record history rather than personal reminiscence.

The relationship of the narrator to the recorder/editor is a crucial one, and, as far as I can determine, no as-told-to form of autobiography or history has been published in which both the narrator and the recorder are native women. Susan Bettelyoun's stories were not solicited by a white anthropology graduate student, not recorded by a white fieldworker of the American Bureau of Ethnology; she was not interviewed by a white historian looking for eyewitness accounts of the frontier—

indeed, it was the shortcomings of those historians that prompted her to record her stories.

Susan Bettelyoun not only had her own stories to tell, she had her own voice with which to tell them. And to help her to accomplish her task she enlisted the help of another like her—a mixed-blood Lakota woman. Although almost twenty years younger and a Huŋkpapa, Josephine Waggoner was not "other" to Bettelyoun as a white collaborator would have been. The importance of this collaboration cannot be overstated. As Bataille and Sands point out, "the quality of the working relationship determines in large measure the impact and validity of the work as both story and literary text" (11–12). Here were two Lakota women who, decades before the second wave of feminism and the "new Indian history," realized the inadequacy of established white history, knew that theirs was a voice that needed to be heard. Certainly the "quality of the working relationship" between two old Indian women living together will be different from that between white ethnographers doing summer fieldwork on the reservation and their "informants."

The second major difference between the Bettelyoun/Waggoner manuscript and other works "by" Indian women lies in the intention of its authors: they saw themselves as recording the history of a people and a time, not simply a personal reminiscence. Unlike most writing "by" native women, the Bettelyoun/Waggoner manuscript is not conventional autobiography, for, even when recording incidents of her own life, Bettelyoun almost always focuses on the historical context of an event rather than her personal responses to it. When Bettelyoun moves to Whetstone Agency and teaches school, for example, we are told the historical significance of the experience: "it was the first school among the Brulés;" and when whiskey peddling at that agency disrupts life there, we do not get personal reactions, but, rather, the historical consequence of the Brulés asking that their agency be moved to a more isolated locale. Yet Susan Bettelyoun is such an interesting woman that one sometimes wishes she had included more personal reaction or revealed more of her own life.

But for native cultures the distinction between "autobiography" and "history" is itself often superficial. Speaking to the concept of the individual in a tribal society, Kathleen Sands points out: "The American Indian autobiography centered on personal experience, but the subject, no matter how dominant within the culture, is a participant in his or her own family history and in the events of the tribe. Isolation of the subject from the history, traditions, and the practices of the tribal culture is not only impossible but also highly undesirable" (57). (See also Brumble, Krupat, and Wong on this subject.)

The historical society decided to reconcile the problem of individual versus tribal history by titling the manuscript "The Autobiography of Susan Bordeaux Bettelyoun: A Story of the Oglala and Brule Sioux." This is not simply a matter of semantics: the belief voiced by native Americans, "You have history, I have memories" (Nabokov, 145), is making a distinction that reveals not only a different concept of the past, but the place of the individual in that past. Addison Sheldon requested an autobiographical sketch of Bettelyoun ("Susan Bordeaux Bettelyoun"), apparently feeling that not enough information about her life was included in the manuscript. He requested such a sketch of Waggoner as well.

The manuscript differs from most writing by native women before the 1960s, which was almost exclusively autobiographical. As Bataille and Sands point out, "female autobiographers in general tend toward the tradition of reminiscence with a focus on private relationships and examination of personal growth. . . . [They] generally concentrate on 'domestic details, family difficulties, close friends,' . . . everyday events and activities. . . . They are private lives, allowing the reader to glimpse into the intimate working of an individual woman's experience" (8). Obviously, this was not Susan Bettelyoun's intent. If one looks at the manuscript as a whole, only a small portion recounts the personal history of Bettelyoun and her family. We get no insight at all into "domestic details" or "personal growth"; what we get is a history of the Lakota-white conflict of the nineteenth century.

One reason for the difference between the historical Bettelyoun/Waggoner manuscript and the personal reminiscences of other native women is directly related to the nature of the authors' collaboration. The ethnographers who solicited and recorded life histories of Indian women were concerned with recording, from a woman's perspective, the rapidly diminishing life-ways of a dispossessed culture. They were interested in documenting marriage customs, puberty rituals, food ways, and women's crafts before they were lost. Some recent books initiated by Indian women themselves, like Hungry Wolf's *The Ways of My Grandmothers*, may focus on the same subjects, but they have a different motivation. Instead of documenting dying customs, native women are preserving those customs for future generations of their tribes.

Bettelyoun was not working with a white historian or ethnographer; she was working with another mixed-blood Lakota woman who wanted to record history from an Indian perspective. In the Bettelyoun/Waggoner manuscript, personal reminiscence merges with history, reflecting, in many respects, the lack of this division in the Indian world. The difference in the writing is one of intention. Most Indian women did not write or dictate with the intention of publishing history. Susan Bettelyoun did. This is a profound difference in intention and it speaks to the confidence and self-concept of the women involved, women who saw themselves as perfect for the job.

One of the reasons that Bettelyoun's perspective is so interesting is that she lived in a complex world—not fully traditional Lakota, not fully white. It was a society made up mostly of French-American men, their Indian wives, and mixed-blood children. Unfortunately, the literature concerning this important subculture and the role it played is practically nonexistent. These families often acted as liaisons between the Lakota and the military or government. The French men, especially in the early days, were accepted by the tribe; they and their sons often acted as interpreters. The Lakota word used to designate a mixed-blood is *ieska*, literally "an interpreter." These families were included on the tribal rolls and in later years lived at the various Lakota agencies and reservations. Today, their descendants can be found at Pine Ridge and Rosebud, evidenced by such names as Bissonette, Robidoux, Bordeaux, DuBray, and others.

As a member of this intermediary society, Susan Bettelyoun was able to see, at close hand, the important events going on around her. As she says, "I was in a position to learn and see about all that went on, on both sides." Bettelyoun was well aware that her unique position gave her the ability, if not the obligation, to tell her stories.

How did Susan Bettelyoun see herself, identify herself? Certain clues can be found in her manuscript. She uses the terms "mixed-blood" and "half-breed" to refer to the children of the French traders and Lakota women. Beyond this, there is an identification with Lakota as opposed to white culture; Bettelyoun often refers to both herself and Waggoner as "Indians"—but never as "whites." And when she speaks of "her people," she invariably means her mother's people, the Brulés.

It was Susan Bettelyoun's sense of identity, her awareness of her special perspective, coupled with a strong belief that white history spoke from a limited perspective, that drove her to share the things she knew.

Similarly, Josephine Waggoner's mission to record the stories of the old people grew from her Lakota identity and the sense of responsibility afforded her by her education at Hampton.

Although some of the dates may be confused or names forgotten, Susan Bettelyoun's words, recorded by Josephine Waggoner, are vital if we wish to obtain a full, rich picture of what happened on the Plains in the last century. This is what they wanted, what we owe to them—and to ourselves.

WORKS CITED

Bataille, Gretchen M. 1983. "Transformation of Tradition: Autobiographical Works by American Indian Women." In *Studies in American Indian Literature: Critical Essays and Course Designs*, edited by Paula Gunn Allen. New York: MLA.

Bataille, Gretchen M., and Kathleen Mullen Sands. 1984. *American Indian Women: Telling Their Lives*. Lincoln: University of Nebraska Press.

Berkhofer, Robert F. 1987. "Cultural Pluralism Versus Ethno-centrism in the New Indian History." In *The American Indian and the Problem of History*, edited by Calvin Martin. New York: Oxford University Press.

Blackman, Margaret B., ed. 1982. *During My Time: Florence Edenshaw Davidson, A Haida Woman*. Seattle: University of Washington Press.

Brant, Beth. 1984. *A Gathering of Spirit: Writing and Art by North American Indian Women*. Rockland ME: Sinister Wisdom Books.

Brumble, H. David. 1988. *American Indian Autobiography*. Berkeley: University of California Press.

Campbell, Maria. 1973. *Halfbreed*. Toronto: McClelland and Stewart.

Crawford, Lewis F. 1926. *Rekindling Camp Fires: The Exploits of Ben Arnold (Connor)*. Bismarck SD: Capitol Book.

Drinnon, Richard. 1987. "The Metaphysics of Dancing Tribes." In *The American Indian and the Problem of History*, edited by Calvin Martin. New York: Oxford University Press.

Hungry Wolf, Beverly. 1980. *The Ways of My Grandmothers*. New York: Quill.

Hyde, George E. 1961. *Spotted Tail's Folk: A History of the Brulé Sioux*. Norman: University of Oklahoma Press.

Krupat, Arnold. 1985. *For Those Who Come After: A Study of Native American Autobiography*. Berkeley: University of California Press.

Lurie, Nancy O., ed. 1961. *Mountain Wolf Woman, Sister of Crashing Thunder: The Autobiography of a Winnebago Indian*. Ann Arbor: University of Michigan Press.

Martin, Calvin, ed. 1987. *The American Indian and the Problem of History*. New York: Oxford University Press.

Mattes, Merrill. 1969. *The Great Platte River Road*. Lincoln: Nebraska State Historical Society.

Moraga, Cherríe, and Gloria Anzaldúa. 1981. *This Bridge Called My Back: Writings by Radical Women of Color*. Watertown MA: Persephone.

Myres, Sandra L. 1982. *Westering Women and the Frontier Experience: 1800–1915*. Albuquerque: University of New Mexico Press.

Nabokov, Peter. 1987. "Present Memories, Past History." In *The American Indian and the Problem of History*, edited by Calvin Martin. New York: Oxford University Press.

Nadeau, Remi. 1967. *Fort Laramie and the Sioux*. Lincoln: University of Nebraska Press.

Sandoz, Mari. 1942. *Crazy Horse: The Strange Man of the Oglalas*. New York: A. A. Knopf.

Sands, Kathleen Mullen. 1983. "American Indian Autobiography." In *Studies in American Indian Literature: Critical Essays and Course Designs*, edited by Paula Gunn Allen. New York: MLA.

Swann, Brian, and Arnold Krupat, eds. 1987. *I Tell You Now: Autobiographical Essays by Native American Writers*. Lincoln: University of Nebraska Press.

Theisz, R. D. 1981. "The Critical Collaboration: Introductions as a Gateway to the Study of Native American Bi-Autobiography." *American Indian Culture and Research Journal* 5:1.

Underhill, Ruth, ed. 1936. *The Autobiography of a Papago Woman*. American Anthropological Association, Memoir 46.

Weist, Katherine M., ed. 1979. *Belle Highwalking: The Narrative of a Northern Cheyenne Woman*. Billings: Montana Council for Indian Education.

Wong, Hertha Dawn. 1992. *Sending My Heart Back across the Years: Tradition and Innovation in Native American Autobiography*. New York: Oxford University Press.

ARCHIVAL SOURCES

Hampton University Archives. Collis P. Huntington Memorial Library. Hampton, Virginia. American Indian Student Records.

Nebraska State Historical Society. Lincoln, Nebraska. MS185, Susan Bordeaux Bettelyoun Manuscript and RG1, Directors' Records.

State Historical Society of Iowa. Des Moines, Iowa. Frank Herriott Papers.

University of Nebraska Archives. Love Library. Lincoln, Nebraska. Mari Sandoz Collection, Correspondence Files.

University of Oklahoma Libraries. Western History Collections. Norman, Oklahoma. Walter Stanley Campbell Collection.

Editorial Policy

In editing the Bettelyoun/Waggoner manuscript, I have followed the basic tenet discussed in the introduction: editing should be unintrusive and should preserve the integrity of the text. Therefore, I have made only those changes necessary to produce a readable, accurate text.

The first step in the editing process was to produce an accurate transcription of the holograph—a task complicated by the fact that "corrections" had been made directly on the document by former historical society employees. Once these "corrections" had been excised, spelling and punctuation were standardized, something the women's correspondence with Addison Sheldon implied was their desire. In a handful of instances, punctuation alone could not render a sentence easily comprehensible. In these few situations, a minimum number of words were added, deleted, or altered. For Lakota words and translations I have referred to Eugene Buechel's *Lakota-English Dictionary* as well as having received the invaluable assistance of Anne Keller, a native speaker from the Rosebud Reservation, and Kenneth Bordeaux, great-grandson of James Bordeaux and Supiwiŋ.

The second part of the editorial process involved putting the manuscript in some sort of order. Waggoner and Bettelyoun sent sections of their writing to the historical society over a period of years; some were dated, others were not. Because there is no way to determine the order in which the pieces were written or how the women wanted them ordered, an artificial order has been created.

The autobiographical sketches that Addison Sheldon requested of Waggoner and Bettelyoun have been placed at the beginning of the text to provide the reader with some background for the two women. I have retained the original "sections" as chapters and have organized them—as much as possible—chronologically. Two page-long sections concerning Enoch Wheeler Raymond and the Bettelyoun brothers have been added to the chapter "At Laramie," and two paragraphs sent to Sheldon as corrections have been incorporated. A chronologically confusing section called "Annuities," dealing primarily with events after 1868, has been divided between two chapters: a portion of it has been added to the chapter "Crazy Horse," while the remainder has been retitled "On the Reservation."

Additionally, certain pieces of the original holograph have been left out of this edition. A long, fictional account of Crazy Horse—which Bettelyoun prefaced by saying it was an example of the sort of absurd romanticized tales being written about the chief—has been omitted. A page concerning Bettelyoun's niece, Winnie Bordeaux; two poems, probably by Waggoner; and a winter count of undetermined origin have been omitted as well. Seven short biographical sketches of noted Brulés and Oglalas were included in the holograph. I intended, originally, to place these pieces at the end of the text. Unfortunately, five of these sketches had to be omitted due to copyright concerns. Of the remaining two, "White Thunder" has been incorporated into chapter 2, and "Rain in the Face, a Brulé" has been divided between chapters 5 and 12.

Finally, explanatory notes have been added at the end of the text. These notes offer additional information concerning people, places, and events mentioned in the text as well as directing the reader to other useful sources of information. Notes have also been used to discuss inaccuracies and inconsistencies in the text.

Throughout the years that I have worked on this project, I have questioned the ethics of a non-native such as myself editing the manuscript. The advice, support, and blessings of native friends—including relatives of Susan Bettelyoun—have convinced me that it was appropriate for me to accept the privilege of being the vehicle for Bettelyoun and Waggoner's work to come to publication.

PART I. AUTOBIOGRAPHIES
OF THE AUTHORS

CHAPTER ONE

Susan Bordeaux Bettelyoun

I was born at Fort Laramie, Wyoming, in 1857 on the fifteenth of March on a Sunday morning, within the fort in one of the quarters of the garrison. My father, being an interpreter for the military, had been allowed quarters, as well as the scouts. The scouts and interpreters lived in long quarters divided into rooms. I grew up near and around Laramie amid its swift-changing scenes. The westward bound people were still traveling by Laramie by the thousands as I grew old enough to remember what was going on about me. As a small child I was not talkative but very observant and could remember well incidents and faces and names. Any stories or tragedies related to me was never forgotten.

Laramie, which had been a center of trading for many years for the French fur traders, suddenly turned into a military post, and a warlike attitude was shown at once by the hanging of Indians, and from this military seat expeditions were made against the tribes in all directions. There were many events that were not reported correctly to the War Department. The eastern people had a hazy idea of what all the struggle was about; that it was the struggle for existence on the part of the Indian was little realized. It was a battle for the empire of the Sioux, as the military built garrisons in the midst of the Sioux domains and built roads across the best hunting grounds. It took skillful fighters like Red Cloud, Crazy Horse, Sitting Bull, Iŋkpaduta to try to save the Sioux dominion at great odds.

I was a small girl during those troublous times, but I was in a position to learn and see about all that went on, on both sides. There were many happenings that escaped my attention which would have been interesting, but I could not authentically place names and dates of the different important military officers who visited Laramie while I was there.

Another thing that was never reported was that soldiers often went out in groups and attacked traveling Indians, whose heads were scalped as war trophies, when they were only passing by, not disturbing anyone. It was not long till the Indians retaliated when they caught soldiers out on the hunting grounds. Many Indians, even the friendly ones, who went hunting never returned. Indian scouts saw scalps in the soldiers' possession, but such was the terror and dread of the soldiers that the scouts did not even whisper of the things that were done against their race. They knew that the least pretext given the soldiers would lead to great disasters like the Fleming and Grattan cases.[1] Although no one complained openly of these mysterious disappearances, the news reached the hostile camps as quickly as wires. However, the Indians could not make an attack on these reports till it was done in a body against garrisons and posts. Most Indians could not believe that the white race wanted a treaty and peace. They thought it was some kind of a ruse to deceive them. Most of the food given to them they threw away, believing it was poisoned to destroy them.

I witnessed the hanging of a Cheyenne and two Sioux chiefs by the name of Two Face and Black Foot; I saw my father bury Lieutenant Grattan and his soldiers on the prairie; I was in the battle at Horse Creek. Most of the Indians who fought in this battle were my mother's relatives and her friends of the Brulé bands. Most of the scouts, interpreters, and mule drivers were French men with Indian families; these remained with the soldiers. Most of the French men did not take up their arms. My father was right with them and tried to keep peace. My brother Louis Bordeaux was the only one who fought, but my father soon took the gun away from him as I have related in another chapter of this story.

I was at Pine Ridge Agency when the Cheyennes made their escape under Dull Knife, Red Bird, and Tangle Hair from Fort Robinson, where they had been held prisoners all fall and winter. These were Northern Cheyennes who had been exported to Oklahoma, who had left that country without permission from the government. There were 150 men, women, and children with five chiefs who had given up their guns and surrendered to the U.S. government. After the hardships and escape from the imprisonment at Fort Robinson under Captain Wessels, there were about fifty-eight who reached Pine Ridge. It made many of the Indians cry to see them so sick and starved. Many of those who escaped were never seen or heard of again. Some were shot down by the soldiers as they fled, while others died from hunger and exposure from the cold, as it was cold with heavy snow.[2]

I have been in the different agencies of Spotted Tail and Red Cloud as they were moved about from place to place.[3] My father was a subagent at times and other times he was interpreter, and, being always in close contact with the Brulés and Oglalas, I was aware of all the dealings by the government and the misunderstandings of the tribe. Although my father's sympathy was for the Indian, he was a law-abiding man and was for the government with his sworn allegiance.

In 1866, my father started to send us to school. My oldest sister, Mrs. Louisa Lamareaux, was then living at Hamburg, Iowa, in Fremont County. Two of my brothers were already at that place going to school. My mother accompanied us to Iowa and stayed with us a couple of winters. My brothers and I attended school at Hamburg for four years.[4]

We came back to Whetstone Agency, where Spotted Tail's camp was. The Indian agent there had two well-educated daughters who were able to teach school in a new schoolhouse that was put up there for that purpose. But the girls could not speak a word of Indian and the Indian children could not understand them, so I, being able to speak both languages, was employed to help teach at Spotted Tail's first school.

Major Poole was very much interested in the school and visited our classroom many times, which was very encouraging; but as I have written in another chapter, Whetstone Agency was a very unsuitable place to try to begin the education of the young Indians. While both of the Miss Pooles and I tried to hold the young minds interested in their advancement in educational lines, Whetstone Agency was just across the river from white settlements where whisky was made and peddled to the Indians. It became worse after the river froze over; it was hauled right over in wagons and sold down in the timber where the Indian camps were. There was terrible debauchery and carousing among the older people. Any time of the night one could hear gunfire, shouting, and singing; murders happened between drunken people. Many times, when excitement ran high outside, we were unable to control the students. Some of the parents came with their children and stayed all day till school was out. And many times women took refuge in the schoolroom as conditions grew too terrible. We had a janitor who kept up the fire with plenty of fuel. It was always a warm and comfortable place; we always had hot coffee and bread for dinner, which Mr. Poole allowed to the school. Our noon hour was kept for dinner and recess. All those who were at the school got their bread and coffee along with the children.

It was during this winter at Whetstone that the drinking and lawlessness caused the people to want the agency to be moved back into the interior away from the border. An appeal was made to the Indian Department which was granted. So, when summer came, Spotted Tail's agency was moved to Beaver Creek at Chadron, and from there to Camp Sheridan, Nebraska. It was not long till the Brulés and Oglalas were moved to Ponca Agency, the Poncas having been removed to Oklahoma. The following year, the Sioux trekked back to Rosebud, where the agency still remains.

At Whetstone Agency, Chief Big Mouth was killed by Spotted Tail in a duel. At Rosebud, White Thunder was killed in May 1884. This trouble was brought about by jealousy: Little Spotted Tail enticed White Thunder's wife away. In revenge, White Thunder took away all of Spotted Tail's horses; his relatives shot every horse belonging to Spotted Tail. White Thunder was my mother's cousin, was of the Wajaja band.[5]

White Thunder was born in 1838, the year called *caŋhasaŋ wakpala el titaŋka waŋ kaǥapi*—"when the Sioux built a dirt lodge on White Cottonwood Creek" (a tributary of Rapid Creek).[6] White Thunder was an unusually handsome man: tall, straight, and handsome, with long wavy hair; his skin was lighter than general among Indians. He was courageous and brave; he was in all the war parties with the young Sioux. It fell to the lot of young Sioux warriors to keep the enemies off of Sioux hunting grounds. The Brulés kept the country guarded to the south. They met the Pawnees, Omahas, Poncas, and the southern tribes like Comanches, Kiowas, and Apaches in a constant conflict.

In the year 1857, a Sioux war party went down to the Loup River, south to find a Pawnee village. Now, the Pawnees were always in possession of very fine horses; they traded with the Mexicans, who had been breeding up their horses for years, prize horses and mules. The Sioux coveted these spirited horses and would go a long way to steal some of them, although they were always carefully guarded. This Sioux war party succeeded in getting some of these Pawnee horses and were on their way north when they met some Omaha who had been hunting on the Elkhorn River and were camped for the night. The Sioux crept up to the Omaha village, they unloosened their hobbles and drove the herd away; only those that were picketed were left. The Sioux were pursued by the Omahas; two of the Sioux were wounded. They stopped to fight and a very noted Omaha was killed by White Thunder at this fight, Logan Fontenelle.[7] There were many noted men also in this fight. Big Turkey, who afterward became a faithful adherent to the Catholic church at Saint

Francis, was in this fight.[8] There were also Yellow Hair, Left Hand Bull, Brown Blanket.

White Thunder was in the battles for the defense all the time. He was in the battle at Horse Creek and was shot in the foot by my brother Louis Bordeaux.[9] At Horse Creek, the Indians could not fight the soldiers because the mixed-bloods were used as shields. Many a surprise attack was led by White Thunder.

In 1884, he was murdered at the mouth of Scabby Creek, ten miles west of Rosebud Agency, South Dakota. He was shot by the Brulé Thunder Hawk and Young Spotted Tail Jr. White Thunder enlisted under General Crook in 1871 and served as a scout for several years before his death. Just before his death, there was a tribal war between Spotted Tail Jr. and White Thunder. White Thunder took all of Spotted Tail Jr.'s horses away from him. The trouble arose over young Spotted Tail eloping with Mrs. White Thunder. Long Punkin tried to make peace between them, but White Thunder was killed in the trouble.[10]

In 1884, I was at Anoka, Minnesota, at a Catholic institution.[11] For four years, part of the time I was matron of the girls' building. After I returned to Rosebud, I received an appointment to fill a field matron's position. I worked in this capacity for eight years, from 1898 to 1906.[12]

I was married to my first husband, Charles Tackett, at White Swan, near Wheeler in 1874. My daughter, who was my only child, was born in 1876. She died at fifteen years of age after returning from Anoka, Minnesota, where she had been attending school.[13]

My second marriage, to Mr. Isaac Bettelyoun, took place at Rosebud in 1891. I resigned from my work as my husband was interested in farming and ranching. Mr. Bettelyoun was a well-educated man and worked in the Indian agent's office as chief clerk for many years, till we were married. At the time of our marriage he had a large herd of cattle, horses, and hogs. He did quite a lot of farming besides. After Tripp County was thrown open for settlement in 1909, we sold out and moved to Winner, South Dakota. He worked in the bank as cashier. He had quite a large interest in the bank there, but several years of drought and hard winters went hard on the bank. We lost our investment when the bank became insolvent and George Mitchell, one of the bank officials, absconded with the money from the bank through the mismanagement of the Jackson brothers. These fellows were caught down in Texas, served a short term, and returned to Tripp County.

In later years, we lived at Saint Francis on the Rosebud Reservation. We had lost heavy in dealing in cattle and farming, but we still had our home to live in near the mission and we still had considerable land which brought us an income through leases.

During the earlier days I was a small child but could remember well what terrible things happened. Slade, the notorious outlaw, often stopped at our house as he went back and forth from Denver to Julesburg as a mail carrier.[14] One of father's places or fur-trading posts was on a small branch of Horse Creek, Wyoming. I believe the place is still called Bordeaux. Slade had a white wife in Denver, but he also had an Indian woman. At the time that Slade made a raid on my father's place, my brother-in-law Lamareaux was running the place. Slade made the remark in Denver that he was going to make a raid on the Bordeaux post and kill Lamareaux. My folks put all the most valuable things in an ox team, such as blankets, dry goods, and ammunition, and hauled them away from the place to a tent in the woods. Now, my father's buildings on the branch of Horse Creek in Wyoming were built of stone, or Slade would have burned them down as he threatened to do. My father and Slade were always good friends; in fact, he stayed at our place many times. As time went on, Slade and other outlaws got worse; they came and demanded what they needed. So my father left the buildings and moved all his goods to Rawhide Creek and set up a store there, north of the Platte in Wyoming. It was my brother-in-law Clement Lamareaux who had dealings with Slade in Denver. The outlaw claimed that he was cheated, and was going to have revenge.

Slade had an Indian wife; in fact, he had been living with Indian women whom he bought in different places, but there were never any offspring from any of them. The last was a Sioux woman who was related to my mother. This woman had a brother staying with her; he had quite a large family. Slade was disappointed because his woman did not have any children. In a drunken state he got abusive. The brother tried to interfere and Slade shot him dead, also his wife and another. Four of the children ran away to the timber and froze to death that night. There was a five-year-old boy asleep at the time; this one Slade took with him. He next married a Cherokee woman who brought up the boy. The boy was called Mato Hiŋsma by the Sioux. He grew up. I never heard of him again after I came north.[15]

After Slade destroyed everything in my father's store in 1862, he afterward came and paid my father two thousand dollars. The same year, after destroying my father's store, Slade shot Jules at Cold Springs, and from then on he seemed worse in his thirst for murder and robbery.[16]

All the men dealing in the fur trade moved to the Platte, where most of the traveling was done along the river road. At other times, when the roads were bad, the traveling went on higher ground back of Scotts Bluff at Robidoux's place; this was on a branch of Horse Creek. My father's place was eight miles below Laramie. Here, he ran his store and ranched. It was a stopping place for all travelers on account of a large spring we had there. My father was attacked by some traveling Mormons and would have been killed but for my grandfather, Lone Dog, who happened to be there just at that time to save him, but he bore the knife scars all his life.

Nearly all my people on my mother's side died of the smallpox as they were on their way north, at the mouth of Sand Creek (this is a branch of the Keya Paha). White Thunder was killed by Young Spotted Tail soon after old Spotted Tail was killed. White Thunder would have been the next chief. Turning Bear, a Brulé, was the cause of this killing. He told Young Spotted Tail that he was being cheated out of his rightful heritage. Young Spotted Tail was killed three years later by a train running over him in 1896.

In the earlier days, during the later fifties, my mother had an aunt by the name of Pretty Woman. It was in those days when love and romance cost the lives of warriors. The bravest man won the prettiest woman and hero worship ruled the heart and hand of the most particular sweethearts. Pretty Woman was promised to be a concubine to her sister. The husband of her sister was cruel and mean, but the brother-in-law, Touch the Cloud, was waiting patiently for Pretty Woman to come into his home as his wife. Pretty Woman avoided this as long as she could by staying with her aunt and taking care of her. Now, Pretty Woman was a tall, active, and a very good looking woman; there were many who would have sought her, but Touch the Cloud claimed her. No one would dare to attempt to court her under the circumstances. It was an age-old custom with nearly all tribes of Indians: women were a property of the parents and male children of the family; they had to be obedient and go wherever they were sold or given. In this case the oldest sister was bought by Touch the Cloud; she bore several children and needed help in her care and work. Pretty Woman would have been glad to help her sister if it were not for her hatred of Touch the Cloud. Her sick aunt postponed what Pretty Woman dreaded; in the meantime her brother-in-law guarded her and watched her so that she did not go where there were any gatherings or dances.

The old aunt was very sick and the woeful thing was about to happen. What would Pretty Woman do when her aunt was gone? There would not be a living soul to protect her from the most dreadful life. The more she thought about it the more distracted she got; if she could only die and go with her aunt. Indeed, she contemplated killing herself.

The old aunt passed away. Kind friends dug a grave and buried her on a high knoll. Pretty Woman remained long at the grave crying, sometimes singing. Touch the Cloud sat outside of his tent smoking and keeping an eye on her. This was in Nebraska, near Chadron. As she gazed around on the other side of the hill, she could see a man coming. He was riding a beautiful pinto horse. The man had on a chieftain's buckskin coat; a single white eagle plume dangled from his jet black hair. This could not be Touch the Cloud; he was not a chief. She looked toward camp and saw Touch the Cloud still sitting beside his tent waiting for her and watching her even as she was mourning. She bowed her head and kept silent. When the man reached her he said, "Get on the back of my horse. I am prepared to travel a long distance and I will take you with me." It seemed as though her heart's desire had been answered. She looked up to see a tall, handsome man with brave and daring features and she knew his face: he was the greatest warrior and hero of the Oglala band. How could this be, she thought. But the chance she had not even dreamt of came to her and she quickly got on behind.

From his tent, Touch the Cloud could see what had happened. He recognized Red Cloud's horse as he rode back and forth along the ridge to show that he had taken a human trophy. As the sun was sinking low these two fled; he picked up robes, food, and a horse that he had picketed. They reached Powder River, where the western tribes were camping, in a few days. Touch the Cloud did not pursue the lovers.

Pretty Woman was happy and loved her husband. She had three children when she died from pneumonia. Red Cloud mourned for her many months. There were other women who came into his life, but Pretty Woman was the one of his choice.[17]

My late husband, Isaac Bettelyoun, went to school at Springfield, an Episcopalian mission. From there he went to Peoria, Illinois, to Jubilee College. He taught at Genoa Indian School two years.[18] He clerked at

Rosebud for Mr. Jordan.[19] After this he enlisted as a scout in 1888. He clerked at the agency office twenty years. After the banks failed at Winner, my husband's health failed, so we went to the Black Hills in the Soldiers' State Home. He received a pension. He died July 28, 1934.[20] I still remain in the Home, leasing our places. I am more contented here as I meet many people who came here to regain their health the same as we did.

CHAPTER TWO

Josephine Waggoner

I was born October 23, 1872, at Grand River Agency, Dakota Territory.[1] The agency was still at the mouth of Grand River and a garrison was also there. My mother was a Huŋkpapaya of Kiglaśka band.[2] She had been married before to a white man and had one child—my half sister was Marcella Arnold Conner.[3] A year after I was born, the garrison and agency were moved sixty miles further at Standing Rock Reservation and the garrison was called Fort Yates after Captain Yates of the 7th Cavalry.[4]

My father's folks emigrated from Ireland about the year 1846 or near there. They came with the first Irish emigrants who settled South Saint Paul. My father's name was Charles H. McCarthy. He was nine years old when he came over the sea. There were several in the family, five boys and four girls. My father enlisted in the Minnesota Volunteers during the Civil War. He was wounded at the battle of Chickamauga; he marched with Sherman through Georgia. When he was discharged because of his wounds he came back to Minnesota, then went to California for a year and returned to Dakota. He was engaged in the fur trade when he met my mother and was married to her legally by a Catholic priest. My father gave me the name of his favorite sister, Josephine McCarthy.

When Buffalo County was first organized, its county seat was Gann Valley. My father was recommended for a County Commissioner. He had been a member of the Dakota Legislature in 1866 and '67. He was elected first sheriff of Burleigh County when it was first organized at Bismarck. He lost his life in the Missouri River while he was on duty. Burleigh County was at that time called Buffalo County and took in quite a large territory, being east of the Missouri River to the Minnesota line and up to Devils Lake. My father also held the office of County Judge at Interior. At Bismarck, my father took a claim at Apple Creek and started a land organization for the purpose of surveying of public lands. After my father and his deputy drove into an air hole and drowned, my mother took my sister and I and went down to Standing Rock, leaving all of my father's property that he had invested in. Almost all the lots and land went back and sold for taxes.

In 1874, my mother was living at the agency in a log cabin. We were there in time to see a great many changes come over the country. The Fort Yates garrison was built and the agency; schools and churches were in the process of being built. Miss Louisa Picott started to teach at a little log school house. In 1876 we heard of Custer's battle, only a day or two after the tragedy. Swift messengers rode day and night to bring in the news, but it was only whispered among the Indians in secrecy. Then we heard that Sitting Bull had escaped into Canada. One day, we followed Mother as she, with others, climbed the hill at Fort Yates to view something. All I could see was great clouds of dust. Then, on nearer approach, I saw thousands of head of horses being driven by soldiers. Every Indian was disarmed and horses were taken from them.[5] I was old enough to remember the terrible famine, hardships, and the awful death rate among the Indians during the surrender. The first issue of annuities was given out by acting agent McTagart. The issue was made in January, nearly thirty below zero. In my mother's cabin were Indians by the score, who came in for shelter.

In the winter of 1876 and '77 a priest by the name of Father Jerome and six sisters came. They occupied a row of four large log rooms that had been used by the working men who built the agency. There were about fifty girls enrolled as students. This place was enclosed by a stockade. The boys' quarters was outside in a long four room log cabin where the priest and the brothers dwelt.[6] The beds in all the students' quarters were homemade and built one over the other, with three boys in a bed, straw ticks and straw pillows. In the dining rooms were long rows of tables with tin plates and cups. We were first taught the Latin alphabet so we could read our own language. This came natural and was easy. Then came lessons in English—it was surprising how quickly some of us learned. The following year, better school houses were built; we moved into these. Father Stephan was agent until Mr. James McLaughlin came.[7] McLaughlin's wife was part Indian of the Santee tribe. She had a fine education, but could speak fluent Sioux. She did wonderful work among the Indians to Christianize us, going from camp to camp, forming religious societies. She, whose life was spent, while she was able to work, in religious work—her influence among us was very uplifting.[8]

13

In the fall of 1881, Major McLaughlin started gathering children to send to eastern schools—those that had a little training were preferred. I was among these. Mrs. McLaughlin started with us; when we got to Bismarck, we met other children there from Fort Berthold. They were Rees, Mandans, and Gros Ventres. We journeyed till we reached Hampton, Virginia. I was there three years and returned home for a year, then went back and stayed three more years.[9]

When I returned to Standing Rock, I was interpreter in the church and performed Sunday school work at Saint Elizabeth Mission near where Wakpala is now. I often interpreted for Rev. Bishop Hare when he came once a month to speak to the Indians.[10] In his audience were Gall, John Grass, Iron Star, Bone Club, and many other prominent Indians.[11] The minister was Mr. Weddell, who was a young graduate from Minnesota—an Episcopalian. I worked also for a time at the Congregational Mission near Fort Yates. I worked as nurse and interpreter under Doctor DeVall. She was working for the Congregational Mission Society from Massachusetts. Here I met my husband. We were married in 1889. We have nine children living; they are all married now and have homes of their own. My husband, J. F. Waggoner, and myself have retired from our ranch life and we are making our home in the South Dakota State Home.

PART 2. WITH MY OWN EYES

CHAPTER THREE

Chief Lone Dog

My grandfather, Lone Dog [Šuŋka Išnala] had many strange experiences in his life. Some of these were very interesting; some of these I will relate as I heard them told. My grandfather was a great warrior, a brave man who defended his tribe. He had a friend, Black Eagle. They were together in many battles against other tribes who were their enemies. Both these men were Brulés. At that time the Brulés were mighty and numerous. They were feared. They drove all the southern tribes from the best hunting grounds in the sandhills of Nebraska. The sandhills were the ideal hunting grounds. For ages these hills were the pastures of thousands of head of buffalo, antelope, elk, and deer. This place was the contention ground of the many different southern tribes, and many were the bloody battles fought over these hunting grounds. These young warrior braves had to qualify themselves and count the coup on their enemies four times before they could be considered brave enough to think of taking unto themselves a wife and to raise a family. First, they had to learn to fight to learn to defend their tribe. It was considered a disgrace for a man to marry without doing these customs; he was considered a coward and not a true man.

At one time my grandfather, with his bosom friend Black Eagle and others, was in a great battle in the sandhills with the Pawnee in 1838. Lone Dog and Black Eagle were what was called Blotahuŋka, or war leaders. They were the ones who led in the charge. In this charge, Black Eagle was wounded. After the battle, a travois was made to carry him. A raft was made to carry him across the Missouri River. The Brulé warriors swam their horses across at the place where the Missouri River is narrow and followed Pease Creek or what the Indians call Caŋagnahaŋ [among trees]. This place is where the town of Geddes now stands; here is where the Brulé Sioux's home was. The main hunting grounds were around

Lake Andes. Here the grass was always luxurious and deep with plenty of the finest water, a paradise for the wild game.

Now, my grandmother, Ptesaŋwiŋ [Gray Buffalo Woman], was betrothed to marry Black Eagle [Waŋbli sapa]. This was to be his fourth war path, after which he was to marry my grandmother. He lived for about a week and died. He was buried right where Geddes is, on a high knoll, high on a scaffold with a red blanket wrapped around. After Black Eagle died the Brulés broke camp. They had to travel fifteen miles to recross the Missouri River on rafts. My grandmother, although she was not yet married to Black Eagle, was treated as a widow. Her hair was cut for mourning; they put mourning clothes on her. Often, as the procession went on, she could not refrain from looking back to see her lover lying high up on his scaffold in his scarlet blanket, visible for miles. Her mother sang his deeds of bravery as they slowly wound their way.

Black Eagle, on his dying bed, requested his friend Lone Dog to take his place and marry my grandmother Ptesaŋwiŋ. He said, "I know you can take care of her as I would have done." Lone Dog promised he would.

Now in those days, about every four years there would be a reunion of all the Sioux Nation about the month of June. There were the Yanktons, the Santees, the Brulés, Oglalas, and some of the northern Huŋkpapaya, Sans Arcs, and the Itazipco. At this gathering my grandmother was abducted by a Yanktonais young man in broad daylight. She had prepared some pemmican and was going across the court of the circle of tents when the young Yankton, whom she had never seen before in all this gathering, took her with the help of two friends. The two little boys she was with were sent back. My grandmother had to be taken back to Yankton. She was there a year when her husband suddenly died. After two years she was able to return to her people with her child, but her child died. Soon after her return, Lone Dog came after her to fulfill his promise to his friend Black Eagle. He brought her back to the Black Hills where the Brulés dwelt.

Lone Dog's father was a full-blood Santee, which relationship was always recognized. Lone Dog was a first cousin to Pahaśa or Red Hill, the chief of the Santees of Nebraska. Pahaśa's father was Iŋkpaduta.[1]

My grandmother had four boys and one girl. The boy Swift Bear, being the oldest, was the next heir to the chieftainship of the Red Top Tent band of the Brulés.

In the early 1830s, the Brulés were often on the war path in the south against the southern tribes. On one of these trips my grandfather captured four spotted mules; they were a wonderful sight. There were never any such a sight as spotted mules. These mules were captured from the southern Pawnees and these Pawnees rustled their mules and horses from Mexico where they were bred, so in this way the Mexican stock were gotten and passed on to the most northern tribes. All the tribes were continually capturing horses from each other. The Crows and Bloods and Piegans would come down on the Sioux and take every horse that the Sioux had in one night, leaving them afoot, so that often only dogs would be used to carry the luggage.

Lone Dog and his band often went to Minnesota to trade for hardware that the Santees got from the fur traders of Minnesota. Lone Dog died at Pine Ridge; a day school was built right over his grave in 1872.

CHAPTER FOUR

My Mother, Huŋtkalutawiŋ

My mother was the oldest child of five children. She was the only girl in the family. Her father's name was Lone Dog. He was considered a brave man, although he was not a chief. They lived in lodges that were painted red at the tops, so their band was named Tiśaoti or Red Lodges. My great-grandfather, Lone Dog's father, was a Sisseton Santee. His name was Tawapahaśa, meaning Red Warbonnet. They were intermarried into my mother's tribe, the Brulés. The Tiśaoti were very active and strong in the hunt or in battle and were respected for their integrity. It was one of their great sports to catch wild horses that ranged over the Platte River country. The taming of these wild horses took tact and strength. It was no easy matter to train them. I may stray away from my subject a little, but I will tell here how the men of our band caught wild horses.

There were a very few tamed mares owned by this band; these mares were driven out near the wild herds. It would not be long till the king of the herd, the wild stallion, would join the tame herd of mares, bringing some of the wild mares and colts with them. When the two herds were joined together pretty well, the young riders, who have been watching from hidden places, come riding fast to drive the whole herd with their long lassos of rawhide ropes. The first one they aim to catch is the leader, the stallion. After he is caught the rest are easy to manage. The mares and colts are caught. They are picketed out and handled each day till they are tamed. The Tiśaoti had plenty of horses. They were able to trade horses to the other bands for hardware, generally from the Santee in Minnesota and Wisconsin. From these trading trips they brought home guns, powder, axes, knives, hoes, awls, needles, and other useful things.

Another thing worth mentioning was the caches that this band Tiśaoti made. A slanting circle was cut in the sod. This circle was lifted, but carefully, so as not to break it. Then the ground was dug out where the circle had been cut to a depth of about seven feet deep, enlarging it as the hole was dug deeper. All the dirt dug out was placed on some skin and it was carried away by the women and children to some low place, so that the dirt could not be found very easily. This was done so that the cache could not be found.

There were dried meat and pemmican, dried fruit such as cherries, pounded and dried, dried wild grapes, buffalo berries, June berries, dried wild turnips, wild beans—all encased in parfleche. After all this food is placed in the cave, there is dried grass put over the provisions. Then a buffalo skin is placed over all. Then the circle of sod is put back at the mouth of the cave, a tepee is placed over the cave, a fire is built so as to resemble an old camping place. Then the band leaves the place to go hunting or trapping. In the spring of the year, when food is scarce, the tribes wander back to their old camps to open up their caches.

They dwelt between the Black Hills and the country lying around Laramie where the buffalo ranged. There were wild bands of horses that ranged all over the sandhills of Nebraska; my people caught them and tamed them. They were rich with horses, and many were the enemies who came at night to steal their horses. Elk were plentiful in the Black Hills. Every year there was a pilgrimage made there to get lodge poles and elk hides. The elk hide was the best hide that could be had of the deer family.

My uncles were Swift Bear, who became chief of our band;[1] then there was Iron Fire and Little Bear and one who died. These four uncles of mine were great travelers. They were joined by all the other young men of our band on war parties against other tribes to drive them away from the Powder River and Tongue River basins, which was Sioux territory. On some of these trips, great herds of horses were brought home. Some of these were captured from the Utes and Shoshones, who had been taming horses for a hundred years before the Sioux. Our young men traveled west to the Salt Lake country. They, with the Cheyenne young men, traded down in Texas. They knew of Colonel Bent's fort; Bent was married to a Cheyenne woman.[2] From this fort they traded and brought home hardware and blankets. On one of these trips they got into a battle with some Pawnees. After a hard fought battle on the Republican River, our band succeeded in capturing their horses; among the herd were four spotted mules. The Pawnees were considered wonderful horsemen. They had bred up their horses till they were of a larger size and could outrun the ordinary ponies. They were so swift they could keep up with a herd of buffalo.

My uncle Swift Bear and many others tried their best to clear the country of the invaders. They allied with the Cheyennes and Arapahos for this cause. They watched the traveled ways to make attacks to intimidate the travelers, but there seemed to be no end to the emigrants. Down in Kansas, below the Republican River, my uncle Swift Bear and some of the foremost braves were sent down to make raids and cripple as many of the emigrants as possible. They spent the whole summer up and down along the Republican River and its tributaries to head off the oncoming emigrants. They made attacks and raids; they ran off stock such as oxen, mules, and horses. At one place, my uncle said they surrounded an emigrant train and besieged them till they used up all their ammunition and, as they drew in closer on them, these white people all fell on their knees within the circle of wagons with their heads bowed without any resistance. Everyone was killed and the wagons were all burned. This was the days before they knew or heard of religion. The Indians wondered why they went down on their knees with bowed heads. They did not understand because their form of prayer was different.

When my mother came to maturity she was selected to be the banner bearer. Only those who were virgins and pure in their lives could hold this place. The banners were sacred to the tribe. It was a long stick painted red with emblems tied at the top. On ceremonial occasions it was carried around among the circle of dancers. And in the victory dances all the women that danced put sunflowers in their hair; that was when it was summer. The banners were used to remind them that all material things and favors were given to them from the Great Spirit, even the lives of the enemies.

My mother also had the honor of being entered into the Huŋka order which meant the order of the "Brotherhood of the Sioux." This order was only for the very select and it cost quite a bit, as her people were expected to give away horses and robes to the poor. Although there were many orders among the Sioux, this was the only order where women were entered, and it was only a privilege given to a very few; those who came from families that were considered worthy were allowed.[3] My mother was the virgin who was the pipe bearer in the ceremony in the worship of the white buffalo robe.

No one knew at that time that it was the fate of my mother to be a leader among her people, that her influence would swing the destiny of her band. It was her marriage with my father that led our band to be friends with the white people. Her influence was always for the good of her people.

CHAPTER FIVE

Bordeaux

My father, James Bordeaux, was born at Saint Louis in 1814.[1] His father, Paul Bordeaux, and his father's brother, Phelix Bordeaux, were boys of a large family and had the spirit of adventure. These two brothers sailed west with a ship to South America to seek their fortune. They found that hunting or trapping was impossible, on account of the torrid, tropical heat in the low swampy country with its myriads of snakes. It was not long till they found passage to North America on a sailing vessel. About the year of 1790, they landed at New Orleans. Here, the brothers worked for a while, but they found the country unsuitable. It was not long till the brothers pushed on up the Mississippi to Saint Louis, at a time when the city was starting up as an important shipping point. The brothers got interested in the fur trade. Because the winters were mild, these brothers made many trips along the streams that flowed into the Mississippi, always returning to Saint Louis with their season's catch. Trips were made further each year to the level regions lying west of the Mississippi where the buffalo, elk, and deer roamed by the millions. One day Phelix Bordeaux, the oldest brother, went on a steamboat north, up the Mississippi, to hunt and trap in Wisconsin and Minnesota. Nothing was ever heard of him for many years. Years later, his name came out in a newspaper that he was one of those who made a treaty with the Chippewa Indians to traffic in the fur trade. He probably married, for there are many Bordeauxs in Minnesota and Montana.

Paul Bordeaux took up farming land, started a plantation adjoining Saint Louis. Here he married and there were seven children born. Margaret was the oldest, then my father, James, then Joseph, John Baptiste, Charley, Mary, and Martha. Paul Bordeaux's wife died after bearing these children.[2] His second wife bore many more children, but just how many more I could not say. Only once I heard from one of my father's half sisters, from Saint Charles, Missouri, who found out where we lived and that we were related—a Mrs. Tyow, my aunt. There were many by the name of Bordeaux in Saint Louis and New Orleans. Most of these are said to be related, who came from the old city of Bordeaux, France. My grandfather's plantation was sold, as well as all the slaves who worked there and were owned by him, and the plantation became the heart of the city of Saint Louis. As this was only over a hundred years ago, the records could easily be traced if they are still in existence.

The city of Bordeaux in France is an important seaport, the home and origin of the Bordeaux. This was in the province of Gironde on the left bank of the Garonne River, about sixty miles from its mouth on the Atlantic Ocean. Small ships could easily ascend the river to the shipping docks at Bordeaux at high tide. Its harbor was broad and extensive; considerable commerce was carried on. The town of Bordeaux was old even in 735 A.D. before the Roman crusaders entered it. It was the seat of several rulers and kings. Henry of Normandy, who afterward became King Henry I of England, was a ruler there at one time. The Black Prince also ruled here. During the revolution, it was the seat of the Girondists, who suffered so from the terrorists. The Girondists were opposed to the Napoleonistic rule. Since peace had been established, Bordeaux became one of the foremost trading and exportation centers of France. Among all its articles of trade, which are too numerous to mention, were its wines. The Bordeaux wines were unexcelled and considered the best in the world; they were shipped to all parts of the world. Bordeaux was a great manufacturing center, but it also was a great educational center. Its cathedrals, monasteries, theaters, and college buildings are said to be without peer. From this place came the Bordeaux as adventurers into North America as many of the noblest of France have done.

My father, James, the second to the oldest child of Paul Bordeaux, left Saint Louis in company with his cousin LaRamee in a flatboat or, in those days, what was called a Mackinaw boat. The men who went on this expedition, about one hundred in number, were trappers. These boys were allowed to go along to help to do chores. This trip was not the first expedition of these French traders; there had been many trapping expeditions made, but this was the first trip made by Antoine LaRamee and James Bordeaux.[3] What we are writing are the recollections and dates kept by my father and told many times to his family.

The boats were awkward and hard to manage; they had to be rowed from one side of the river to the other side in order to avoid the current.

Many times, when this could not be done, there were ropes fastened to the boat and everybody had to get in line and pull with all their might— the men all on the shore—as the current changed every mile or so. The pulling of the boat was not so long, but it was hard work. It was hard on shoe leather and moccasins. When they reached their journey's end, their shoes were all gone and their pants would be frayed half way up; then it was that moccasins and buckskin pants had to be resorted to. These trappers traded and trapped along all the streams starting in the spring, as soon as the ice floe on the river cleared away. The voyage from Saint Louis to Fort Union, where there was the American Fur Company post, took all summer and fall till November 13, 1833. My father recalls this very well because while he was there the stars fell[4] and Fort Union had already been bought by Pierre Chouteau in 1830. All these men were working for the American Fur Company.[5]

The forests, streams, and plains furnished what seemed at that time an inexhaustible means of living to those who entered into it. From the streams and boundless plains came the fur treasures that fed millions with wealth and ease. The Indians found a profitable trade; they were anxious to be at peace with the traders. If Napoleon had not bartered off the Louisiana district, there would have been a different history and if the French had known of the hidden gold, perhaps they would have hesitated to sell their possessions for the paltry sum which was received in exchange.

My father's diary[6] said the French people had been trading up and down the Mississippi and the Missouri for over half a century. He knew all the trading posts up and down the Missouri River. On the Cedar Island was the Loisell's trading post which was built about thirty-five years before my father's advent into the country. There was the Trudeau house built in 1796 on the east bank of the Missouri, near where Fort Randall stood afterward; Fort Pierre at Bad River and Lisa near Grand River; the La Framboise, the Primeaux house, Fort Clark, Fort Berthold, and all the posts owned by different companies. It was not till 1806 that the upper Missouri traders built a post near the mouth of the Yellowstone River. Prior to this there were Spanish trading posts of which my father knew nothing—only to see their ruins as he traveled over the country.[7]

The American Fur Company was formed about 1808. The officers were Drouillard, Lisa, and Benoit, sometimes pronounced Benoway.[8] My grandfather had worked on his plantation at Saint Louis till he sold his farm about 1807 and retired to Louisiana, which was the home of his second wife. My father, James Bordeaux, started to work for the American Fur Company at the age of fifteen years. His cousin LaRamee was born from the sister of my grandfather. The boys were almost the same age. For a few years, my father's wages were collected by his father, until he became of age at eighteen years.

In the spring, after wintering at the mouth of the Yellowstone, the company sent its voyageurs up the Yellowstone to trap. My father said it fell to the two boys to make hoops out of diamond willows to stretch beaver hides on. As the trapping started early in the spring, all kinds of weather had to be endured. Camp was generally made by some stream where trapping seemed good, in some sheltered timber out of sight of Indians. Trap lines were set, sometimes with great difficulty on account of ice gorges, swollen streams, floods, and overflow. The weather was not always favorable, as the drizzling rains of the spring was cold and penetrating. The men had to walk several miles on each side of the stream to set their trap lines, sometimes going ten miles to hunt besides trapping. All the hides were taken off the beaver, mink, and otter, or anything that was gotten through the day, and carried to the camp where the hides had to be stretched and cured or dried. On one of these trips, my father said one of the old men kept telling the two boys, James and LaRamee, to rub in lots of sand on the fresh beaver hides. Being obedient, they did rub on a lot of sand. It was not till years later that my father caught on why this was done: the beaver castors were paid for by the pound and the sand that was rubbed on was to make it weigh up. Then he found out that there were tricks to all trades. This company traveled up the Yellowstone to its headwaters, into the Rockies. In all his dealings and thousands of beaver hides he bought from the Indians, my father said that the Indian-cured hides were the best and the cleanest. He was never afraid to buy from them; they were not tricky in the curing of their hides. In the fall the furs were all brought back to Fort Union to be sorted, packed, and shipped down to Saint Louis. These men worked to get the beaver hides along streams as they brought what was considered a very good price. Every stream that emptied into the Yellowstone on both sides of the river from Fort Union to the Rocky Mountains was combed for beaver. They had trading material in hardware, such as needles, awls, knives, hatchets, axes, and steel links that were used to strike fires.

In 1835 it fell to my father's lot to carry mail from Fort Union to Fort Laramie. At this time my father was about seventeen years old; he was a good shot and was used to the wilderness and could take care of himself. He knew the modes of traveling and camping. The country was dangerous for a white man to travel alone. He knew the directions well; the topographical features and streams were familiar to him by constant travel. There were many different tribes to be encountered between Fort Union and Laramie. It was a distance of about five hundred miles and the journey had to be made on foot. The journey had to be made through the heart of the Sioux game reserve. The different tribes were at war over this game country at that time. Whatever this message was that the head man at Fort Union, Pierre Chouteau, trusted him to carry was very important and had to reach Laramie soon. The message could not be sent by boat because it would take a year to reach that destination. Many of the other men wrote letters home, as from Laramie there was traveling to Saint Louis by fur traders all the time. The letters were more likely to reach their destination sooner.

I do not remember the last name of the man that was assigned to go with my father; he spoke of him as Pete. When the time came to start, my father was given the mail covered in an oilcloth then wrapped up good in a buckskin sack with straps to put around his shoulder and on his back. He was instructed to travel on the east side of the Black Hills, then southwesterly toward Laramie. They departed with many misgivings and ejaculations from some of the men, such as, "They will never get there! Pretty risky!" One old man said, "Boy, you watch out for the bears. If you see one, don't stop to shoot or waste your ammunition. Run as fast as you can away from him." At all this advice my father listened and weighed the matter in his mind. He knew it took more than one shot to kill a bear. Their skulls were so thick and hard, that if the shot did not hit the eye or the nose, it was apt to glance from his head.

The perilous journey was started. My father and Pete were given powder, balls, rifles, and a pistol apiece. They could not carry very much provision except a little flour which was already mixed with salt and soda. Meat they could get all the way as they went. My father had learned the sign language from the trappers in their dealings with different tribes. He could also talk English as well as French. Pete could only talk French. When they started from Fort Union, these two travelers promised each other that if one should die from any cause, the living one should fall heir to all the possessions of the other's wages, back pay and all—as part of the wages were generally held back till the end of the year. This was a very sensible way of dealing with these men, as there were many drifters seeking their fortune; they were restless roamers looking for a get-rich-quick method. The way the payments were made by the American Fur Company required steady, industrious, honest men.

It was the middle part of August, for Father could remember that wild cherries were abundant everywhere. Sometimes ten miles was made in the forenoon by starting early, followed by a long rest and a sleep at noon. Bread was baked by stirring a little dough, wadding it on the end of a green stick, and holding it over coals, turning it many times. Tea could be made from the leaves of Juneberry trees or rosebush leaves and there are many different barks that made good tea. Any kind of game the men got, which was mostly deer, was roasted on a bed of coals. Just a small portion was carried of the meat, to be cooked for supper and breakfast. A pretty good sized roast could be carried a day or two, till another animal could be killed for their use. Nearly twenty miles was made each day, unless they got into heavy rains and they had to wait and their march was delayed.

My father and his partner Pete encountered no Indians. They saw herds of buffalo, elk, deer, and bears, but no humans. They had went about two-thirds of the way; many streams had been crossed—the Little Missouri, the upper Grand River, the Cheyenne, the Belfourche—without any trouble. Bear Butte of the Black Hills was only a mile away when Indians appeared coming from the Hills.[9] My father said they started to run for a good position where they could defend themselves and ward off an attack. My father and Pete were both young and could run fast. The Indians came over a rise half a mile away, and it was not long till they started in pursuit. When my father and Pete were within a short distance from a woody ravine on the west of Bear Butte, the arrows began to sing by them. They put in more effort to reach the timber. They had been walking all day, were pretty near winded. The arrows of the Indians came faster and thicker; one of them struck Pete in the shoulder. He still ran with the arrow dangling down his back. When they reached the timber they were headed for, my father used his gun to show the Indians that they were armed. This stopped their advance and the Indians were afraid to come any nearer.

My father said he and Pete climbed clear on top of the butte. He pulled the arrow out from Pete's shoulder. It had not went in deep, as the arrow had nearly spent its speed before it struck Pete. My father could see that these Indians were Rees by the way they dressed their hair. Pete was suffering a great deal from the wound. From the top of this butte they could see for miles and miles. They spent the rest of the day waiting for the Rees to come back, but there was no sign of them anywhere. Pete began to swell all over and he realized he was going to die. "Now," he said, "I am about to die and I will write a note to Pierre Chouteau to give you my wages that is coming to me at the end of the year. You can also have my belongings, my gun, and pistol. There is only one thing I want to ask you to do for me," said Pete. "It is to get me some water. I know it is dangerous and a hard thing to do, but I must have some water." This was the same day as being wounded and the fever was killing him. The wound was only half an inch deep, but a poisoned arrow is always fatal.

My father took a cup and went in search of water and, like a miracle, there was a spring and some water way at the top of this high butte. The water relieved Pete, but it was not long till he became a raving maniac and he died in convulsions. Pete said to my father when they first got on top of the hill, "If I should die, place me under a ledge of rocks and place this arrow in my hand so it will be known what I died from. Put enough rocks over me so that the wolves nor coyotes cannot get at me and, if you ever see my folks at Saint Louis, let them know where you buried me." These were the dying wishes of Pete. My father promised faithfully. After Pete died, my father dug deep under a ledge of rocks, put poor Pete into it and carried flat rocks and covered him good.

It was sundown when my father was through with this sad burial. He laid down to rest on the top of Bear Butte, but sleep would not come. He planned through that night; he thought out the way to go so that he may reach his destination. Above him, the stars glistened and the moon sailed right along. There was life all around him. He could hear the voices all through the night, calls and cries of animals, but a loneliness gripped him for human fellowship, alone way up on top of this isolated butte and death laying beside him so still, so silent.

My father was a good Christian man. He said while danger lurked all around him he prayed to God to protect him and bring him safe to his journey's end. This prayer was answered. He reached Laramie in a very few days.[10]

It was a surprise to the men at Laramie to see this wanderer straggle into the fur trading post at Laramie with a message from Pierre Chouteau. It must have been an order to move all freight out down to Saint Louis. All the furs there were on hand. The messages brought by boat to Fort Union from the outside world told of the rise and fall of the prices in the fur trade. Trusty, reliant men that could brave the dangers of the wilderness to carry the business messages across from one post to another were the hardy men picked to do the work. As soon as he arrived, preparation of the wagons and teams took place. In a day or two, the freighters with oxen and teams were stringing out of the post laden with packs of furs for the Missouri River where the freight would be transferred to Mackinaw boats bound for Saint Louis and out on ships.

From Laramie there was a company of men going west to trap. My father joined this company. When at Laramie, my father drew his own wages and Pete's, on the presentation of the note written by him. Many years later, Pete's father came to Laramie. My father and he went to Bear Butte. They got his remains. They found him undisturbed with the arrow still in his hand. Pete's remains were taken to Saint Louis.

Long years after this happened, I talked with a Brulé Sioux by the name of Crazy Hawk. He told me that Bear Butte, in the early days, was thickly timbered. He also told me that there had been a spring on top of the butte, although now it is bare and dry. Three forest fires, at different times, had reduced it to barrenness. Crazy Hawk found this same spring, which he believed saved his life once. He was on a hunting trip near Bear Butte on a hot day in June. He became sunstruck, he believed, because he became dizzy and went out of his mind. He didn't remember how long he wandered around. When he came to, he found that he was lying on top of Bear Butte, weak and thirsty. This butte had a flat surface on top and Crazy Hawk found this same spring that my father found over thirty years before.

My father bought shares in the American Fur Company with his year's wages and his extra pay received for carrying mail from Fort Union to Laramie—besides Pete's pay and wages. He remained at Laramie; at that time it was called Fort John. That winter his cousin LaRamee, in company with some independent trappers, came back from the mountains from Fort Yellowstone at the mouth of the Bighorn River. The other trappers traveled on, but my father induced his cousin LaRamee to stay. They trapped together all winter, as the American Fur Company had bought the trading post from Robert Campbell and William Sublette in 1835.[11] When this trading post was bought, my father said, there was only a long dobie shack. After Jim Bridger and Sublette became agents of the fort, my father, LaRamee, and four or five other trappers worked and built better and more substantial houses out of logs and built a stockade around the place during the winter of 1836, besides setting trap lines. The men took turns to go hunting, as wild game was depended on mostly.

As the early spring furs are the best, a company of men was formed to go to the Rocky Mountains to make a wide circle. My father and LaRamee went with them. They traveled from the Rockies and all the small streams, then came down around Salt Lake. They traded with the Utes and Shoshones on the Wind River. The furs were brought back to Laramie in time to be to be shipped out. About November, my father and LaRamee went out to trap on the upper part of the river. They separated on each side of the stream to set their traps. LaRamee was attacked by some Arapahos and killed. When he did not come home to their camp as usual, my father went out in search of him and found him riddled with arrows. He returned to the fort and got a team and help. LaRamee was buried near the fort; he was the first man buried there. Jim Bridger and Sublette decided to call the place Fort Laramie and the river was named after him because he had lost his life on it. There was also the Laramie Plains, Laramie Peak, Laramie City, and Laramie Road.[12] My father was a medium height man, but he said his cousin was a large, tall man and very fine looking. Laramie became a very important place; it was a trading center for the Indians.

My father spent two years at Fort Yellowstone after his cousin died, where he married a Ree woman in 1837. He learned to talk their language. From this Ree woman there were two children, a boy and a girl. After he brought her back to Laramie, she was dissatisfied and wished to go back to her people. She could not understand the Sioux language; she got lonesome and homesick. There were many fur traders who had married Indian women traveling back and forth, so he sent the Ree woman back to her people with them. Taisant, who was married to a Ree woman, took her back. She refused to give up her children. Many times my father tried to get his children to send them to a Catholic school, but he was never able to do it.

Men traveled in companies in those days for protection. The different companies were antagonistic against each other and fought each other over the smallest differences. The Hudson's Bay fur traders enticed the Indians against the American fur traders and often caused trouble. Fighting and murder would happen every time they met, although these Canadians were trespassing on American soil. The fur companies were all trying to drive each other out of business. It was a hard life and a dangerous one. Most of the goods that the French people used came from France by boats. What the Indians wanted most were guns, gun powder, muskets, woolen blankets, all kinds of hardware and cloth and blankets—

mostly things that were useful to the Indians. The Hudson's Bay Company were the first to introduce liquor. When the Indians were drunk, it was an easy matter to cheat them. This was the cause of many bloody fights between the fur traders and the Indians. A trapper's life was an uncertain one. At any time, Indians who had been wronged in one part of the country were liable to take their revenge on an entirely different company who didn't know anything of the transactions with other companies.

The fur trader made big profits; the money went fast. For nearly two centuries, a million dollars a year has been estimated to have been made in the fur trade. These beaver trappers made the trails across the wilderness by following the travois trails made by the Indians. They suffered hardships, fought and died along unknown trails, making the way for the millions who followed in ox teams, mule teams, horses, then the automobiles.

CHAPTER SIX

At Laramie

Jacob Herman, a well-educated German, was the blacksmith at Laramie. He could speak several different languages—German, French, and English. He was good at anything, repairing any kind of machinery. He was a mechanic. He could fix sewing machines, clocks, or watches. Not only that, he was an excellent agriculturist. He plowed a garden spot. He raised cabbages, onions, beets, carrots, tomatoes, squash, corn; he irrigated by hauling water in barrels. He planted an acre of potatoes. Mr. Herman had root houses built for all the vegetables. He had ditches plowed right in the garden and set the cabbages into them with the heads downward. These were all covered up with soil by a team, two or three feet deep. Father said they kept good all winter and, in the spring, they came out as fresh as could be. He could preserve and pickle all kinds of vegetables; he made his own vinegar. He was the most excellent cook and could bake any kind of cake. He was so energetic he did everything in a hurry and with good will. He was about the first blacksmith sent to Laramie by the American Fur Company.[1]

He married a Ree Woman that was part Cheyenne.[2] Jacob Herman and my father became brothers-in-law, for they married sisters. Mr. Jacob Herman had four girls and three boys from his Indian wife. There was Mary, the oldest, Louisa, Theresa, Sophie, Frank, Antoine, and James.[3] These children were all like their father, unusually intelligent. There are several grandchildren living today; most of them are scattered to different places. (I heard of one, a Jake Herman, who was a wonderful rodeo actor, winning many prizes by his good horsemanship.)[4] Mr. Herman was one of the most useful men who came to Laramie; he had good habits and was well liked. He came to an untimely end. After leaving Laramie, he worked for my father when he had a military contract to put up hay at Fort Randall in 1882. He accidentally fell forward from a big load of hay.

His head struck the wagon tongue; it broke his neck. The team he was driving stood there without moving till he was found. He was buried at the Randall cemetery by the Odd Fellows. At that time this was a flourishing garrison, but since it was abandoned, the cemetery is a desolate place. Some stockman had his pasture there and I have heard that the graveyard can hardly be distinguished. The head stones are knocked over, the soldiers buried there have been removed, the cattle tramp over the place, and the only thing visible is the sage brush.

A trapper by the name of Taisant also worked at Laramie. His wife was also a Ree woman. Those of the white men that could afford it sent their children down to Marysville, Kansas. Father DeSmet founded this school about the year 1830. It was run by the Sacred Heart Sisters and Fathers. The place overlooked the Missouri River on a rising knoll.[5] Even in those early days, my father said the orchards were wonderful. Every kind of fruit tree planted seemed to take root, grow, and flourish. Fruit was shipped all up and down the river from this mission; fruit was dried, sacked, and sold. Vegetables also found their way to many different markets. This mission was first founded as an orphan asylum. Hundreds of the children of the fur buyers born of Indian mothers were brought here to be cared for by these Sisters of the Sacred Heart. These children were brought up with piety and deepest religious training, instructed in the work of agriculture, horticulture, and all the trades of masonry, carpentry, and all branches of labor that would be useful knowledge to them after leaving school. In the domestic arts taught to the girls, there was nothing neglected. The girls were taught plain and fancy cooking, preserving and canning, sewing (plain and embroidery), house keeping, and the painting of pictures on canvas, tapestry, and textiles. Most of the mixed-blood children taken to Marysville never knew any other home but the mission. Although born of poor and humble parents, at Marysville they received the highest instructions that the whole world could give. From Belgium, Germany, and France came the highest class of intellectual men and women who renounced all worldly desires to serve God and humanity, gave their lives to look after these poor little lives, to take the place of father and mother in a world of strife. Words are too meager and inadequate to describe what Father DeSmet and these Sisters of Mercy have done. The good that was done and begun then, when it was needed the most for humanity, was surely heaven sent.

My father sent his daughter from his Ree wife to Saint Louis to be educated, as he and his wife divided their children when he sent her back to her people from Laramie by Taisant, who also had a Ree woman and was going back there.[6] Mary Bordeaux, my half sister, grew to be a beautiful girl; she graduated there at Saint Louis. The Sisters gave a picnic to the children after the closing of the school. While games were being played by the children, Mary wandered away to the river. Whether she drowned or not was never known. A search was made for two or three days, but she was never seen or heard of again.

My father's brother John Bordeaux came to Laramie about 1837; he worked a while for the fort there. He too married an Indian woman of the Sioux tribe. This woman had two children. John decided to go back to Saint Louis. My father told him to take his child, John Bordeaux, to Marysville. John took this son away with him and placed him at this mission in care of the Sisters and he returned to New Orleans. He never saw his son again. This boy was trained to be a musician and grew to be a handsome young man, was christened John Baptiste Bordeaux. After he left school, war had started. He enlisted in the army from Kansas for the North. After the war he was sent west, was stationed at Laramie where my father met him. John, my cousin, married a half-breed girl and had one boy and two girls. He was crossing the river near Yankton when he fell in an air hole and drowned.

The next man to help my father when he was in charge at Laramie was Sam Smith. My father sent him back to the States to attend school in higher mathematics for a year. When he came back, he was the clerk at Laramie for several years, till Laramie was sold in 1849. He remained a clerk in my father's store at Sarpy's Point eight miles below Laramie. Sarpy's place was built by the Mexicans in 1832. The logs with which it was built were all hewn cedar; the ceilings, ridge logs, and flooring were all hewn out of the native cedar which was gotten within a mile of the place. Sarpy had an Omaha Indian woman for a wife at that time. When my father bought this place, it had been standing about fifteen or sixteen years, and the stockades in the ground were rotting. This was eight miles below Laramie. Mr. Samuel Smith had a large Indian family. He was highly educated, but was addicted to drinking heavily and was killed while in a drunken state. It fell to my father to take care of his family and bring his children up. Smith's Indian name was Nape Śica, because his left hand was crippled.[7]

Joseph Silko Robidoux was another interesting character in the early days. He built the first log house at Saint Joseph, Missouri. He was married to a Yanktonais Sioux woman; he had two sons from the widow of

John Baptiste Bordeaux. After coming up northwest to Wyoming, he ran a blacksmith shop on the Oregon Trail on a branch of Horse Creek. His place was a little southwest of Scotts Bluff. It was near the creek with quite a good deal of timber. His two sons have many descendants on the Rosebud Reservation. In the olden days, there were many Robidouxs in Saint Louis and Kansas City, where the original families came from. Joseph Silko Robidoux lived on Horse Creek for twenty years, and died there; he was still living there in 1849. Fort Mitchell had not been built yet when he died.[8]

Another interesting person was Louis Chardon.[9] He was a trader and he usually camped where Chadron is now. He was married to a Brulé woman, the daughter of Bull Tail, who was one of the principal men of the tribe.[10] (When Bull Tail died, he was left in state in his tent at Sarpy's Point near the Bordeaux ranch. It was in this tent that Grattan's interpreter took refuge—Lucien, or "Wause" as pronounced by the Indians. He was dragged out, killed, and mutilated. He was a half-breed and had an Indian woman. There was a daughter living and many grandchildren are living today at Yankton Reservation.)

Clement Lamareaux was also a fur trader and a freighter. He freighted from Saint Joseph up the river to Kearny, to Laramie, to Salt Lake, to Denver. At first, he freighted with oxen, then it was too slow a way so he hauled with mule teams. The outfit consisted of many wagons. At one time, he was living in Denver where he was mining. He found gold in the mountains in Colorado; he filed to hold possession. He was at Denver when the townsite was first laid out and owned several lots in the city of Denver. Lamareaux was from Montreal, a Canadian French. He was all over the middle west, made many freighting trips to Denver in the early fifties. Lamareaux married my sister, Louise Bordeaux, in 1856. After this, he stayed and worked for my father. My father had had three different trading places on the Oregon Trail: one on Horse Creek and one on Rawhide Creek, besides the home ranch at Sarpy's Point. Lamareaux became the overseer of my father's business places.

I can remember an instance, although I was small, when my sister was shot with a steel arrow accidentally in the leg. She was bleeding pretty bad and my folks hitched up a travois to a mule; we started pretty late toward Laramie. When we got to the bridge at Laramie, we had considerable trouble with our mule. He got balky and would not cross the bridge. We spent quite a while there trying to get the mule across; he had to be unhitched and backed over across. By the time we got him across, it was break of day. It was a provoking time, but Sam Smith and Mr. Lamareaux finally got across. My mother and I accompanied them to the garrison where my sister was treated by the surgeon. The steel arrow head was cut out from between the shin bones.

From her union with Clement Lamareaux my sister had ten children. Mr. Lamareaux built up a large ranch on the Niobrara River in Knox county. My sister and her children remained on this ranch while Mr. Lamareaux still freighted. On one of these trips, he was sleeping in the wagon and he accidentally shot himself by kicking the trigger of his gun. Some of the buckshot lodged in his forehead, just penetrating the skull. He was taken to Laramie and the shot was taken out. A silver plate was put over the wound, but a tumor developed in a few years and he died. He was a Free Mason and was buried by that order at O'Neill, Nebraska. When my sister died a few years later, she was buried beside him at O'Neill. It was the wish of Mr. Lamareaux that this should be done.[11]

The two brothers, Isaac Bettelyoun and Amos, came from Pennsylvania. They were descendants from the early Dutch settlers. The Bettelyoun family emigrated to Peoria, Illinois. From there Amos and Isaac came to Fort Laramie. They were engaged as ox drivers in freighting at Laramie for Lamareaux, my brother-in-law. On one of these freighting expeditions, the long train of freighters were attacked by Cheyenne Indians. One of the drivers, Bill Nelson, was shot and killed. When Lamareaux made it known to the Cheyennes that they were married to Indian wives, the Cheyennes withdrew.

Both the Bettelyoun brothers married Sioux wives. They settled on a ranch eight miles south of the Platte on the Laramie River. Here the brothers were engaged in raising cattle and horses. Times were dangerous: the Mormons were still always on their journey west, the Cheyennes and Sioux were on raiding expeditions. The Bettelyoun ranch on Laramie was enclosed by a stockade. The families each had log quarters and their bunk houses built so that the buildings were in an E shaped enclosure leaving an open court with a stockaded front. The family depended on a fine spring under the bank of the stream. Times got so dangerous and the Cheyennes had besieged the place twice, so that a tunnel had to be dug underground from the kitchen to the spring. When there were Indian signs around the place, the corrals and barns were padlocked and the horses were kept within the enclosure. There were always enough men in the place to repel the Cheyennes when an attack was made, and the underground passage to water was a lifesaver. About the year 1865 and

1866 were the most dangerous times for these ranchmen. Their best horses were stolen often times and lame ones left in their place.

The Bettelyoun brothers furnished beef to the garrison, sold wood and hay. Amos, the father of my husband, moved to Pine Ridge in 1878. His wife had died while they were still on the ranch on the Laramie River and was buried there. He was with his children on the Pine Ridge Reservation for ten years. Amos died in 1890, was buried in the Episcopalian cemetery. Isaac, the younger brother, stayed on at Laramie. He and his wife passed away and were buried down there. There are many descendants living today of the Bettelyoun name. My husband, Isaac Bettelyoun, was named after his uncle; we were married while he was a scout in 1891.

Bissonette was called Wapahahota, Gray Hat, on account of the gray hat he used to wear. He was married to an Indian woman; she had seven children, five boys and two girls. Mr. Bissonette was a fur trader who generally traveled to the Rockies and traded with many other tribes. His second wife, a cousin to the first wife, had fourteen children. Bissonette traded all along the Oregon Trail; he was a good business man, but he continued to do trading till he died. There are many descendants of Bissonette on the Pine Ridge Reservation. At one time, Bissonette got into trouble near Laramie. He found what he thought looked like a grave, away from the main traveled road. He thought it might be a cache of some kind. He dug up what he found. It was all fine goods, muslins, ginghams, and linens; some of the most beautiful lace and trimmings and ribbons was among them. He brought the find home, but someone reported it to the commanding officer, so he was compelled to pay for the goods. It took quite a good deal of money and Mr. Bissonette was nearly broke, so that winter he and his family stayed at my father's ranch. This was in 1868. Times were very dangerous at this time; the Indians were all on the warpath. The fur trade was at a standstill and the trade had never recovered.[12]

Enoch Wheeler Raymond was born November 26, 1824, in Sullivan County, New York State. His parents were Lewis and Betty Raymond. He came to Laramie as a soldier in 1850 when he was about 26 years of age. In 1851, he married the daughter of a Brulé chief of the Oyoupe band. Mr. Raymond died on November 19, 1909. His wife, Wiciŋcala, died two years before his death. They were married at Fort Laramie by the post chaplain. At that time this was a remarkable occurrence because there were not many marriages. The whites who came out west and took Indian wives were regardless of marriage laws. It was very seldom that there was morality enough to cause one to marry lawfully. It was all right on the part of the Indians for they knew not the laws of the white man; common consent was the custom among the Indians and this law was as good as gold.

It was in 1901 that Mr. and Mrs. Raymond celebrated their golden wedding anniversary. It was quite an affair; people came from all parts of the surrounding country to help them celebrate. The carefully kept marriage certificate was as new as the day it was signed fifty years before. It had always been kept rolled up in buckskin. The wedding ring was pure gold and was worn in two, thin as paper.

After working several different places, contracting for wood and hay for the military, Mr. Raymond settled down on a ranch in Tripp County near Turtle Butte on the Keya Paha River. He moved there in the early part of the eighties; he raised fine horses and cattle. His shipping points were to Sioux City and Omaha; sometimes he took fancy first-class cattle to Chicago. Mr. Raymond was an example of a man. He was sober and industrious, a kind husband and loving father. At this writing, he had two sons and a daughter living. The oldest was Solomon Raymond at Millsboro, South Dakota, and Garfield Raymond lives on Rosebud. These are living; two of his sons died. John died of the flu; Enoch died of heart trouble. There are many descendants living. Victoria Raymond, a daughter, is also living. These children were all well educated.[13]

Another man I can recall was John Richards, a French man who came up from New Orleans.[14] He married a woman of the Brulé band; she was a half-blood. The Indians named him Owaśakala. He had four sons and two girls: Charles and John Richards Jr., Louis Richards, and Pete, and the daughters were Mrs. Pourier and Mrs. Rose Geureu. Mrs. Pourier had twelve children; she raised them all. The reservation has many descendants of the Bissonettes, Pouriers, and Richards. The second son of Richards, Charley, was killed over the rivalry of a woman. John was sent to Saint Louis to school. The boys all were highly educated, but education did not help John, nor did his Free Masonry. He was wild and full of adventure. He got into trouble at Fort Fetterman by killing a sergeant.[15] He took a cousin to the mountains and claimed his cousin was lost. He was in all the raids against the emigrants and joined the hostile Sioux in the battles against the armies invading the country during the sixties. He left his inscriptions where ever there was a fight. His name was Lean Elk in Indian. Sam Terry, who was living then, said he was one of the most bloodthirsty men he ever saw.

At last Richards met his death when he visited his two Indian wives whom he had while he was with the hostiles. John Richards, Billy Garnett, and Shangreau had been cutting logs way up in the pine hills and were rafting them down the Platte River. The men had all been drinking when they came upon the Indian camp where Brown Eagle's camp was. He was a Brulé. His brother-in-law, Red Willow, was there and the two sisters who had been the wives of John. The chief had refused to let his sisters go back to John because he drank so much and they were afraid of him.

Richards called on them and through some pretext he killed the brother of the two women without any reason at all. No one expected that anything would happen. It was so sudden. Brown Eagle died instantly. Red Willow and Yellow Horse grabbed John on each side and stabbed him to death and threw him out. The women left their brother's body and ran away. It was evening and all the women took refuge in the darkness and escaped. The other mixed-bloods, Garnett and Shangreau, had to get away from the place as fast as they could to keep from being killed.

John Richards was married to Emily Janis at this time, Nick Janis's daughter. She was wild when she heard what had happened. She went to the camp, took an ax and mutilated the body of Brown Eagle and built a bonfire and burned him up. The ambulance from Laramie came after John Richards, who was buried by the Free Masons at Fort Laramie. He led the wild and lawless life of the plains till he died.[16]

Another old timer at Laramie was Sefroy Iott. He was an old fur trader. His first wife had one child; the second wife was a sister to the elder wife—she had four children. These all died of tuberculosis. Iott married the fourth time a relative of my uncle Swift Bear; she never had any children. There are some descendants of Iott living today.[17]

There were many of these mixed-bloods that went to school at the University of Saint Louis, which had just been started by the Jesuit Fathers. The Richards attended this school, the Primeaus, and many others.

Joseph Knight was also a man who worked at Laramie. He married an Indian woman; she was Waŋbliśuŋ, a stepdaughter of Richards.[18] Mrs. Knight died in 1865, was buried in the Laramie cemetery beside Spotted Tail's daughter. They died the same spring. When Spotted Tail's daughter died, it was the most spectacular scene of the wildest mourning. It was planned to take the body to the Laramie cemetery. Word was sent to the garrison that Spotted Tail was bringing his daughter Hiŋziwiŋ to the garrison for burial. The officers turned out in full dress in honor of the chief, and his daughter was honored with a military burial. The chaplain of the garrison read the services. She was only eighteen years old, was a very beautiful girl. An army officer was in love with her and begged many times to send her to school to be educated, but Spotted Tail would not consent to send her away.[19]

Another old trapper that I can remember well was Beauvais. He was in many of the Rocky Mountain trapping expeditions in many different companies. At times, he would guide travelers going west; there were some of these travelers who took the route toward Salt Lake, others went north toward Fort Hall to cross the Snake River. Mr. Beauvais guided the travelers over the Rocky Mountains; from there he returned. Beyond the Rockies, there was not much danger of Indian attacks and the trails all led to the coast. My father was in charge at Laramie under Jim Bridger.[20] Bridger was nearly always gone on long trips either buying furs or guiding some of the emigrants who were continually on the road. My father did nearly all the fur company's business for eight years, from 1835 to 1843. Beauvais was the cook in Laramie part of that time. He was a man of about middle age then, when I remember him last. Beauvais was married several times; he has sons and a daughter living at this time, a grandson at Belvidere and another one living on a ranch on White River. There are several of Beauvais's fifth generation on the reservation.[21]

While Beauvais was cook at Laramie, he was kept busy all day long. The armies and emigrants and travelers were constantly coming or going; a great many of these stopped at Laramie to eat. The cooking was not so fancy, but it took a lot to feed so many. The Indian hunters under my father were out all the time getting wild game. Deer, elk, buffalo, and antelope ranged only a few miles over the hills. Wild meat was all we used. My father had a herd of cows, some pigs, and quite a lot of chickens. He was always trading with the emigrants for chickens, cows, and pigs. My father got quite a lot of mares by trading horses when the teams grew jaded and thin. It was not hard to trade a fresh gelding for a mare with a colt by her side. The colt was a drag on the mare and with a suckling colt she soon lost flesh, but would pick up after a month or two of rest.

Some of the emigrants brought a great deal of unnecessary furniture that overloaded their horses and had to either trade it off or unload it, so that it was not a surprise to see some of the finest marble-topped tables, bureaus, tables, stands, and colonial carved chairs in some of the humblest of log cabins along the Oregon Trail.

Thousands of emigrants were passing every day by Laramie. Adolf Cuny ran the Beauvais place, had turned it into a mercantile and grocery store.[22] Everything was sold high, on account of the long distance freighting overland by ox teams. There was trouble every day over the high prices of things. People or emigrants expected to pay the same prices that they had been paying at home. One day some Mormon emigrants stopped to trade at Laramie. After they got what they wanted and went out, they came back in and started a fuss with my father, who was not armed. There were five or six stalwart, heavyset fellows—rough looking men. Two of them pulled out their bowie knives and started toward my father. He turned toward one of the rooms where he kept his guns in the living room, but they had stabbed him before he got very far. The second stab was near his neck; the knife was borne on downward, laying his whole back wide open to the waist. If it were not for his heavy shirt and underwear, he would have been badly wounded, but, as it was, the wound was not so bad and it soon healed in a few weeks. There were several relatives of my mother's in to trade that day. My grandfather Lone Dog with his tomahawk knocked several down and saved father, chased the Mormons away.

There were all classes of travelers who stopped at Laramie. There were rich English lords who were traveling for adventure, to kill big game in the mountains, who were guests at Laramie; rich French gentlemen and some of Spanish blood who wanted to get some of the thrill of hunting that the west furnished those days. The only accommodations were buffalo robes, which were plentiful at that time. When a man asked to stay all night at Laramie he had to pay in advance. Supper was dished out in a pie plate. Meat and bread was the bill of fare. Sorghum molasses was a luxury, but it was served once in a while and a big tin cup of coffee. Buffalo robes were thrown on the floor to stretch out on. No one received much courtesy or attention. One gentleman asked where he could find the lavatory. Beauvais, the cook, told him, "I don't know what you mean by that my friend, being a French man. But, if you mean you want to wash, there is the water," he said, pointing to a tub of water at the well. The long table was always full, coffee was always piping hot, with hot biscuits and meat, which was sometimes jerked meat. The coffee and biscuits went fast, but the travelers suspiciously avoided the dried meat. One Irishman wanted to be genial one day at dinner. He said, "Begorra, I would rather drink my black coffee off a board than a carpeted table any time." Upon which remark the rest laughed, but Beauvais never knew if this was meant for a compliment or not. Lord Blennerhasset's party passed through Laramie on a big hunt, but these higher classes of gentlemen understood the conditions of the country and accepted things as they came. Father DeSmet, when journeying west, stopped here. He sat on the bench or on the floor with the Indians and ate with the rest of the hired hands at the same table. He was used to all kinds of modes of traveling and could rough it. He adapted himself to all circumstances in order to reach the people's hearts.[23]

Another man I can recall was a Scotch nobleman, Lord Metcalf, who came to Fort Laramie. He was traveling through the country for adventure in 1846. He was said to be a very handsome man. He was out hunting buffalo several times with Indians. He met a beautiful Indian girl; he fell in love with her. She was a Brulé, part Cheyenne. Lord Metcalf bought this girl and lived with her in the lodge; he slept between buffalo robes, ate dried meat. He came in June and left for California in the fall. That following spring, this Brulé girl had a boy. This boy was enrolled at the agency by the name of Metcalf. When he grew older he married and raised a large family—he was the father of eight. There are three of his boys living and one girl living. This third generation of boys are all married with large families and all these men's families are going by the name of Metcalf. The descendants are very industrious and intelligent.[24]

During those early days there were the devastating, ravaging diseases of cholera and smallpox that took hundreds of the immigrants, who were buried by the roadside wherever they died. The scourge swept the country. The Indians left their sick and dying and fled to the remotest parts of the mountains. They threw away all their robes and tents. Hundreds fell by the scourge. The traders were blamed, but not altogether. The emigrants were bringing the cholera right along into the country, spreading it as they went. From 1837 up to 1852 the country was in a terrible shape; trade was ruined for years to come. The few surviving Indians were afraid to come near. From 1838, when the steamboats carried the smallpox up to the Berthold Indians, thousands had died from it, and since then these unknown diseases have been communicated to the Indians by boats or by traveling emigrants. Some years it was smallpox, other years it was measles of the worst kind. There was no known remedy. In a few years, it was the cholera.

The diseases spread not only among the Sioux. It was among all the tribes in the remotest part of the Rocky Mountains. Thousands of the Blackfeet were reported to have died from it; the Snake Indians, the

Crows, were greatly reduced in numbers. Some of these, it was told, killed their dying, then killed themselves. People fled from each other as the disease made its appearance. No one stopped to bury the dead. In Fort Berthold, when the Rees, Mandans, and Gros Ventres took the small pox in 1837, it was winter time, and no one had the strength to bury the dead. Holes were cut in the ice and the dead were thrown into these. It was reported that many suicides were committed here. Those that lost loved ones jumped right into these holes, preferring a watery grave.

Not only disease took lives, but there was famine in the land from which many perished. In every village the death rate was by the fifties and hundreds. It was said that whole nations became extinct. From the Mandan Nation, of which there had been three thousand, there were only thirty adults left; half the Rees and Gros Ventres had died. The scourge passed on into Canada as the refugees that got up there from the south carried it. All up and down the Yellowstone and the Missouri there were thousands of Cheyennes and Assiniboines lying unburied. In all parts of the west there was no one spared; no matter what tribe they belonged to, they were being swept off the face of the earth. It was the most heart-rending circumstance; very few overcame it. They were marked for life. It was a common thing for a long time for a hunter to find skeletons any place, a few years after, lying where the sick had been dragged away and left, the bones bleached as white as driven snow. Along some of the streams, the Tongue River, Powder River, and some places along the Laramie even, the lodges were deserted. The terrible fear of the scourge made people even desert their homes. When the measles was brought into the Indians camps, very few children survived; some were saved by drinking hot cedar tea as it is told in the Sioux winter calendars.

During the time of the cholera, which had reached Laramie by 1848, it was a very dry year. There had been no rainfall all spring and summer. The disease seemed to be in the air and even in the dust. The cholera broke out in places all over so suddenly and without warning that no one knew what to do; even running water brought on the disease. People were afraid to drink water. My father had went down to Saint Louis with a load of furs. His family had been living then at Sarpy's Point where the Bordeaux ranch was—the Laramie post had been occupied by the army then for some time. When the cholera broke out, my mother locked up the place and went with all the children and her household of relatives that were staying with her while Father was gone and went to Robidoux's place on Horse Creek. He had a blacksmith shop right on the Oregon

Trail. Robidoux was pretty well-to-do; he had five or six hired white men. Some of these looked after his stock, some of these helped in the shop. Some Indians rode up from the Laramie River, which was four or five miles west of the Robidoux ranch, and told us the Indians were traveling and breaking up camp everywhere, that there were some of the dead laid near the Platte River who had been dressed and painted.[25] Among the dead laying on the ground there were some living ones who had the disease and were deserted and left with the dead. So far the disease had not reached Robidoux's ranch. It was noon and while the men were eating dinner they heard an Indian singing a death song. A rider came to the door and said, "Be on the lookout. This man coming, singing, is White Roundhead. He is coming armed to kill every white man that he sees." My uncle Swift Bear took his gun and stepped outside, firing above the man who was coming along the edge of the creek bank. Every once in a while, White Roundhead was doubled up with the cramp. He kept on coming with his gun in his hand and bow and arrows strapped to his back, although he was warned not to come any further. By this time, the white men were out with their guns and, as he did not heed the warning, he was shot as he stopped with a cramp again. He tumbled out of sight over the bank. Men took spades and caved the bank over him so the disease would not spread. White Roundhead had lost his whole camp of four or five tents. Blaming the white people for bringing such a scourge into the country, he was out for revenge. Wherever there was a healthy camp, no visitors were allowed. Anyone coming to the camp sick was shot right on the spot; mothers deserted their babies, when they got it, in several cases.

Within a few days, my father returned from Saint Louis in a light buggy. He found my mother, the children, and all her relatives at Robidoux's place. He brought home a gallon of medicine, a prescription put up for him by a physician. My brother Louis, who was then ten months old, had the cholera, so the medicine came just in time. A few teaspoonfuls of the medicine cured him. Under this physician's instructions given to my father, all drinking water was boiled, all food was thoroughly cooked, also the milk. In August cholera was at its worst. Messages were sent out by young Indian riders to different camps to boil all the water that was used. Horse mint, wild peppermint, and wild mustard was used, made into a tea, which allayed the scourge till it died down.

In whatever direction one might travel, there were scenes of the most heartrending desolation, mute evidences of the struggle for life, and death the victor. In one case, it was most pitiful to learn of a boy, nine years old, who was deserted by his mother and aunts. It was a smallpox case. The tribe had traveled all day with the travois and camped near a timbered creek in Wyoming. That evening, the boy had recovered enough and had followed the trails the travois left; he reached his relatives' camp. The mother and aunts cried to see him, but could not keep him in the same tent with them so they put up a pup tent for him outside. He was well enough to drink the soup that was handed to him, but the smallpox had left his throat so raw that he could only whisper. Next morning, camp was broke up. When they looked in the pup tent, the boy was gone. On examining the grounds, they found the tracks of a mountain cat and saw where he had been drug toward the timber. Having lost his voice, he could not holler when he was attacked by the wild beast.

These diseases were the forerunners; spreading over the country, one thing after another came to rob the Indians of their possessions and lives. The wealth of furs did not enrich them; it brought nothing but disease, misery, and crime. In nearly every fur post, whiskey was used to entice the Indians to trade. In the drunken brawls men killed each other without reason or cause. In a few years the grasshopper plague came and devastated every green thing; all vegetation, trees, fields, and even clothes hung out were devoured. Then came the early blizzards and dust storms. But the trains of emigrants never ceased. The prairie fires that swept the country for miles were blamed on the Indians, but most of it was done by the carelessness of the emigrants.

My grandmother, who was born in 1797, who had lived to be 90 years when she died in 1887—Ptesaŋwiŋ was her name—was the sole survivor of her band. She was as straight, as active, as ever in her last years, only that she was blind in her last years. When the cholera struck the Sioux they fled north in different directions. The band grandmother belonged to started northeast. Each night's camp there were less and less in number, as the people were buried all along the way. Some of them were in the throes of death who were to die anyway so were left behind. By the time they reached the Niobrara River, the whole band had passed away but my grandmother and one of her brothers. They each lived in separate tents in the timber on the south side of the Niobrara River. Winter had come on early with a great deal of snow deepening and making it impossible for traveling. My uncle was busy trailing deer every day in the snow and brought home the deer. He said to my grandmother, "You dry all this meat and make pemmican; it may be hard to find deer when this snow leaves. It is not very far from here to where some of our people are on White River—it is straight north of here. You could not lose your way even if you were to travel alone." So my grandmother worked hard drying the meat as fast as my uncle, Brave Eagle, brought it in. One day, she heard a shot as she was cooking breakfast. When she went into my uncle's tent he had dressed himself in his best clothes, had painted himself for death, and the gun with which he had shot himself was still smoking. My grandmother was left alone. She dressed herself warm and left the place. She started north while yet it was still midwinter, because she knew if a sudden thaw should come she would not be able to cross the many streams that would be filled with rushing water from bank to bank.

These are only a few instances of the terrible happenings during the days of cholera. It broke out for two or three years, but certain remedies were found which helped to control the disease after half the Indians had died. My grandmother reached White River near Rosebud where she found the Brulés. Among them was my grandfather Lone Dog, whom she had never expected to see alive. My grandfather Lone Dog died at Pine Ridge before there was any settlement there, near where the first schoolhouse was built. He was not a chief, but he was a noted man in his day. He died in 1871. He was a few years older than my grandmother. They had many horses and spotted mules. They were of the Red Top Tent band. He was part Sisseton.

CHAPTER SEVEN

Crow Butte

In 1849, when my father returned from Saint Louis, he brought home medicine that cured the cholera.[1] It cured my brother, and all around the neighborhood, whoever was sick was given the remedy which brought them right out of it. The following year, my father went to Saint Louis with his cargo of furs; when he got back he had fever and ague. There were times when my mother and others would have to hold him to keep him from shaking all to pieces. It was something strange and new; no one seemed to know what to do for it. He had the fever for three months and it was not long till his whole family got it, one by one. In the hopes of curing the fever, my mother made all kinds of wild tea: wild peppermint, horse mint, calamus, and everything that was recommended. All winter someone of the family had it, till my elder sister Julia died with it from complications that set in. Some of our neighbors had it. My mother lost a brother, a young man of about eighteen years, with the cholera in 1848. He died below Scotts Bluff. He was taken away and laid near the Laramie River below a high bluff. Where my uncle was buried, a Cheyenne young man was buried in a scaffold. My father discovered that the Cheyenne's skeleton was petrified; some scientists took the petrified body with them to Saint Louis. Afterward, my father saw the petrified skeleton in the Saint Louis Museum. My father knew this Cheyenne when he was living; he had died of cholera.

My father had bought a hundred head of horses from some fur traders who were returning from the Rocky Mountains; they had traded for these horses from the Flathead tribe of Indians. My father was going with goods to trade to the Indians near a place that is now called Chadron and he had a place on White River. He had three two-wheeled Red River carts full of goods for trade. My father had camped two nights out from Fort Laramie when Crow Indians, who had been hunting, ran the buffalo

49

right into our camp. There were four hired men; these were French men. Three of them each drove a cart, and one of them was on horseback helping my father to herd the horses. There were about 68 head in the herd. This was the fall of the year; the leaves had all fallen off the trees. The buffaloes ran right through our herd. The horses were so frightened they ran right back toward Laramie. The men got on their saddle horses and three of the hired hands were sent back after them. It was quite late when they brought the horses back, so they camped near where Crawford is now on the Little White River. My father, with his powerful telescope with which he could see miles away, saw that there were Crow Indians in the country. He saw them plainly at times, butchering buffaloes. The Crows were very cautious. They had scouts watching on the hills while they worked. My father generally traded horses for furs from the Brulés and Oglalas—that's what these horses were being taken to Crawford for. There was no town there, but a very large camp of Indians.

During the after part of the day, the Crows had come while the men were eating and drove away my father's horses. Near where we were camping there were rough, barren bluffs and hills. In one of the thick timbered draws my father placed my mother and the three children that was with them. My brother Louis Bordeaux was about two years old then and was still nursing. My father had a gun; it was loaded with only one bullet. I don't know why he did not carry any more ammunition nor bullets; at that time I think he overlooked doing so. He told my mother, "Now, we are going after the Crows to get our horses back. You stay here till we get back. In case we have a fight and we are defeated and I am wounded, I will fire my gun to let you know they got me. It is not far from here to the village; you can get there in half a day's traveling. So, when you hear my gun fire, you start right away for the village of the Brulés," said my father.

While the men were gone, it began to snow thick and fast. She covered the children up and waited, listening for a gun fire. The night was dark except for the white snow on the ground. The leaves lay thick and heavy on the ground. As the rabbits or gray squirrels ran over the ground, they made such a loud sound as if they were horses' hoofbeats coming or going. About midnight, my mother heard human footsteps coming up the timbered coolie. She kept very quiet till she heard my father's call. They started on foot for the Brulé camp, as all the horses were taken, and traveled toward the camp. It was daylight when they were going over the hill into camp. My mother began to sing the death song that was made for my uncle Swift Bear when he was wounded by the Crows. It caused the excitement to run high in camp. The Indians knew something had happened or Huŋtkalutawiŋ would not sing like that. Quickly, men ran to meet her. She told that the Crows had come upon them and had captured all their horses. It was not long till there was a gathering of warriors, equipped with guns, bows, and arrows prepared to start after the Crows.

On that very day of the pursuit, the Sioux found the camping place. They went fast to catch up to the Crows. It was not long till the trail was struck. The Sioux knew they were only half a day behind the Crows. The Crows saw the Sioux coming. They saw that the Sioux outnumbered them. Crow Butte, Nebraska, which is situated near the Little White River, was within sight. On one side of this butte was a gradual slope; there was quite a tableland on top of it. About two-thirds around the butte it was very steep and impassable. The Crows drove the whole herd up there and kept guard of the entrance. As the Sioux circled around the butte, the Crows rolled down rocks so that it was dangerous to go very near the perpendicular walls of the cliff. One Crow appeared to take aim and lost his life; he was knocked backward and instantly killed. Another was wounded. As the Crows had a better position, they wounded and killed several of the Sioux. They could see the Crows up there shouting and singing defiantly.

Toward the end of the second day, the Crows still tried to hold the horses up there, but the horses were milling around because they were thirsty. These Crows even had boys with them—boys of about twelve and thirteen years old. The Sioux could see them playing and jumping rope. The horses made a dash and finally broke away from the Crows; they ran for the creek so fast no one could catch them. Still the Crow boys were seen jumping rope. In the evening a fire was built; the Sioux could smell the sage brush burning. Next morning, a Sioux circled the butte and found tracks leading away from the butte. The Crows outwitted the Sioux; they had been braiding ropes out of rawhide and let themselves down on the steep side of the bluffs and even their horses had been let down. They had escaped down a hundred-foot cliff while the Sioux were guarding the passageway to the top of the butte. All that was on top of the butte was a dead dog the Sioux had killed. The Sioux took up the trail and followed the Crows. They found where the wounded Crow had died and was left behind; his scalp came into Sioux possession. The snow began to deepen as they came to the mountains and the food began to give out. The Sioux did not follow them into the fastness of the mountains, as long as they regained their horses. But to my father the strangest thing happened. The Brulés who had captured the horses were the possessors. So, it was a total loss for him except in cases where he bought some back, and that was not very many.

This incident went into the annals of Sioux history and the butte on which the Crows retreated was called Crow Butte in the state of Nebraska. In the winter count of the Brulés it is called *Paha akan najiŋ wica api.*[2] The Indians do not always get the exact date right, and I am not so very sure either, but the nearest I can get the date is by my brother Louis Bordeaux who was two years old when this happened, so I have always contended it was the year 1851.[3]

CHAPTER EIGHT

Three Stories of the Battle of the Blue Water

I

At the Grattan Massacre over the killing of a castoff cow, the Indians were willing to settle for this deed that was done by Ituhuwaŋka's son, a Minniconjou who was visiting the Brulés.[1] The chief, Mato Oyuhi or Scattering Bear, went right up to Grattan—Lucien was the interpreter—and explained that this man was a visitor from another band who did not mean any harm, that Scattering Bear himself would give a mule, while the crier of the village went around and collected more horses to pay for the lame cow.[2] Now, this camp was right at my father's trading post, within sight from my father's store. The Oglalas camped a little to the west of our house; the Brulés were camping nearer.

Grattan and the company of thirty soldiers and the scout went by the Oglala camp and by my father's store. Grattan and his soldiers were coming in an army wagon hitched to mules; the only one riding on horseback was Lucien, the interpreter.[3] He was an Iowa half-breed married to a Sioux woman. He was not a good interpreter—he spoke broken Sioux. But interpreters got good wages, so, as long as they could talk English, they were hired. Grattan and his soldiers stopped at my father's house to inquire his way. My father told Grattan that he was doing a foolish thing. "Why don't you let the old cow go," he said. "It was laying there without food or water and would soon die. It was too lame to walk—its feet was worn through to the flesh. It was shot by some boys who wanted a piece of skin." But Grattan replied that he was on his way to get the man who killed the cow. So my father said no more. Trouble was sure to come. The ten white men who were within my father's stockade hid in the warehouse under buffalo robes. After all soldiers were killed, one wounded man got away in the turmoil. He got away by running under the hill near the spring where we got our water; he hid in among the rose bushes. My uncle Swift Bear found the wounded man and brought him in. He and my father hitched up the light wagon and hauled him to Laramie in the night. He was shot not very deep across the stomach. His bowels protruded but were not perforated. I never heard of him dying, so I have always believed that he got well.

The Indians had collected here at our place. There was some trading, but they were waiting for the agent to come to Laramie so the annuity issue could be made. All the treaty annuities were already hauled and were stored at the Beauvais place five miles this side of Laramie. The Indians had waited nearly all spring; the agent took his time in coming. As soon as the annuities were received, there was to be a Sun Dance right there on the Laramie flats. I may be off my subject a little, but this Grattan trouble with the Sioux is what brought General Harney out to punish the Sioux—although Grattan was the aggressor and the Indians were only defending themselves. Scattering Bear had lost his life while trying to negotiate a payment for the lame cow. After the soldiers were killed, the Indians knew their issue would be withheld, so the consequence was that the Indians got into the warehouse at Beauvais' and divided all the annuities among themselves. My father's store was not molested nor a thing taken; the Indians only took what was coming to them at Beauvais' place. Grattan's body was taken back to Laramie at night. The commanding officer in charge, Lieutenant Fleming, sent a note to my father to bury the soldiers, as there were only two or three companies of soldiers in the garrison and he could not spare any of the men. Laramie gates were closed and no one could get in without a countersign.

All these happenings were glamorously published in the eastern states. My father was blamed a great deal and called a liar and a renegade because he expressed his opinion that the Indians were forced to fight. Scattering Bear was always friendly to the whites. He did many acts of kindness to the whites, admonishing his warriors to keep the peace treaty and to keep away from the raids being made on the emigrants. The eastern newspapers said that Grattan and his small company of soldiers were led into an ambuscade and massacred, but, to his last moments, Scattering Bear requested his warriors to not molest my father nor take anything belonging to him, but protect him.[4]

Although reports of this affair was sent into Washington, nevertheless, General W. S. Harney's army was sent out to punish the Indians. The expedition came up from Fort Leavenworth, up the Platte, the summer of 1855. Near the forks of the Platte, Harney found the Indians camping on the Little Blue River.[5] Now, at this time, the Brulés had been on a big buffalo hunt down on the Republican River where they had a very successful hunt. The summer hides are thin, easy to tan. They were lighter, were generally made into tents, while those killed late in the fall had thick fur and were more suitable to be made into robes. On the Little Blue is where the Brulés intended to camp a while to dry their meat and to tan their hides—an ideal place to camp close to water and plenty of grass. These people were not anticipating trouble; they were busy preparing and providing for their future needs.

On the morning of September third, General Harney marched up to this sleeping village. He sent his cavalry around on the opposite side to cut off the retreat, while he marched up the Little Blue. Tesson, the old trapper who was married to an Indian woman, was the interpreter for the cavalry.[6] The camps were strung out along the river. It was about sunup when the Indians discovered that the soldiers were coming upon them. Horses were hastily run in, camps were pulled down, travois that were always ready were thrown on and some of the people were getting away. It was a surprise attack and no one was ready.

Now, the chiefs wanted to make peace and give themselves up. My father, hearing that the Brulés had got back from a big hunt on the Republican, sent Sam Smith, his clerk, to buy and transact for the hides that were to be sold. Chief Little Thunder, Iron Shell, and another went up to meet Harney with a white flag, but no attention was paid to the flag.[7] Sam Smith, who was staying at Iron Shell's tent, was asked to go along and tell Harney that the Indians did not want to fight and were willing to arbitrate, but the army officers would not listen to it. Now, my father, at this time, had to go up to Laramie a few days before the trouble. News came by wire that Harney was marching up on his way. My father sent word twice that Harney was on his way to Iron Shell, for him to move his camp out of the way, but the chiefs did not want to move away, thinking they could make peace.

The Indians were encamped where the army would be passing on their way to Laramie. General Harney met the chiefs who said they did not want to fight and asked for peace. Harney told them there would be no peace unless they gave the ones who killed Grattan and his command. Now, this was impossible as some of those who had a hand in that killing went west to join the hostiles. Little Thunder, Iron Shell, and another chief were threatened. The only thing the Indians could do was to get away while the chiefs were talking. The people were hastily packing to

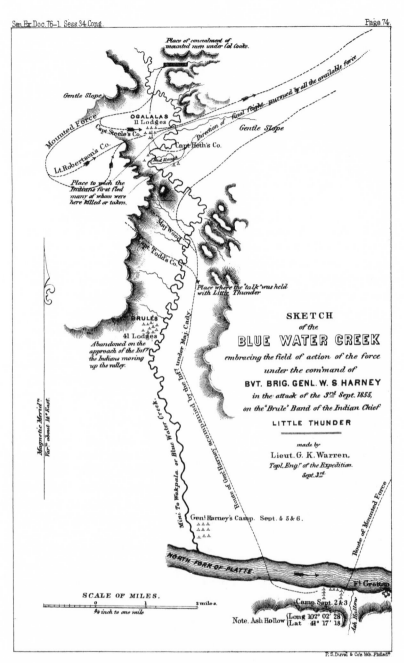

"Sketch of the Blue Water Creek," map by Lieutenant G. K. Warren

56

leave and were leaving as fast as they could, but they met the cavalry. The Indians were unarmed and were shot down as they fled. Of those killed, over half were women and children who were on foot. It was a case where everybody was for himself. In this fight, Spotted Tail gave his horse to his wife; he told her to get away. Instead, she stood on the brow of the hill and watched on while her husband fought. Spotted Tail was not quite dressed; he was barefooted. He ran right toward the soldiers. The first soldiers that came up tried to use the sword on him. He wrenched the sword out of the soldier's hand and knocked him off his horse with his own sword and he got on this horse. Being a powerful man of six foot two inches tall, he was a man to meet any foe lone-handed. In this fight, it is said he unhorsed thirteen soldiers—knocked them right off. Some of these were killed. Each time he unhorsed a man, his wife gave a war trill; she refused to go until he joined her. Nearly all the Brulés were in this massacre. It was for many years after this that the western people called Harney "Squaw Killer Harney." [8]

Iron Shell also fought bravely. In this battle, his mother and three wives were captured and his mother-in-law was wounded. She ran as fast as she could; a soldier on horseback was chasing her. Just as she turned to look back, he had stopped to fire his gun. She felt a burning sensation on her stomach and she fell. The soldier, thinking he had killed her, went on in pursuit of others. There was quite a deal of smoke and dust, so she drug herself along slowly and carefully. There was no place where she could find refuge, but a little ahead, down a slanting hill, she saw a buffalo wallow into which she crawled. There is always, more or less, tumbleweeds, so she covered herself with these. Thundering hoofbeats passed her by many times. This was Iron Shell's mother-in-law. She told me this story herself, long afterward. Late toward evening, the noise had ceased and everybody was gone; she arose from the place where she hid. There was not a living soul around. She looked around for tracks; she found a great trail going west, which she followed. The sun was nearly setting— she had no breakfast nor no water all day. The loss of blood made her weak. There was no food of any kind. She ran across a little skunk wandering around. With a club, she killed this. From her belt there hung a scabbard with a skinning knife. She butchered the little animal, started a fire with a steel link and flint. She roasted the meat. She ate for the first time in twenty-four hours. With the skin from the skunk cut in strips, she bound up her wound. Luckily, her bowels were not perforated, but they protruded. So, with the bandages, she walked along the great trail all night, resting often. Toward morning, she heard a bugle blow. She walked toward it and found the great camp. The prisoners were in the center with guards surrounding them. Outside the camp, the sentries were walking post. On meeting one of these, she lifted both hands with palms forward—the Sioux sign of peace. The sentry let her pass by. She joined the prisoners. She was carried in an ambulance from here to Laramie with those that were wounded.

All along the Blue, there are long grasses overhanging the banks; there were women and children hiding under these. These were afterward gathered together and taken prisoners. General Harney, with great difficulty, stopped the soldiers from making a complete slaughter as told by some of the women prisoners who were saved just as they were about to be shot. These prisoners were within the garrison.

The friendly bands came in and, from these, Harney demanded the murderers of Grattan. But most of these, as I have been told before, withdrew west into the mountain country of the Powder River. As a hostage was demanded, Spotted Tail, Red Leaf, Long Chin (two brothers of Scattering Bear), Red Plume, and Spotted Elk came forward. They were all dressed in their buckskin war suits, in all their war regalia, ready to die—coming to the garrison singing their death song. These men surrendered. These men, with their families, were sent to Leavenworth. They were kept prisoners for two years.

To my memory, these men were taken to Leavenworth in 1857, the year I was born, so it was not Harney that sent these Indians to Leavenworth. After the Ash Hollow fight there were raids made even on the mail, where money was taken. Two years after this battle, Spotted Tail came in to Laramie and gave himself up. There were twelve men who went as hostages. Most of these had their wives, but not all of them. This is the record among the Sioux.[9]

2

The Indian who came down to hunt and visit the Brulés the summer of 1854 was a Minniconjou; he did not belong in the Brulé band. Ituhuwaŋka's family and two or three other families had come down from the Missouri River near Pierre to hunt with the Brulés down south in Kansas. While waiting around staying with the Brulés, Ituhuwaŋka's sons, who were out with their bows and arrows, shot a lame cow abandoned on the emigrant trail. Now, it was a custom of the Indians when anything was abandoned to not claim it anymore, so, supposing that the poor skinny cow which had been traveling hundreds of miles had been thrown away, the Minniconjou boys shot it for its hide.

The Indians—about two thousand were camping about a mile northeast of my father's place—were very much surprised to see a troop of soldiers march into the center of the arena of camps with two howitzers. No one knew what it was about, not even the boys who killed the lame cow nor their father. The chiefs started to tell their young men not to make any disturbance, that everything would be settled in peace. Scattering Bear went right up to the soldiers and began to talk to the interpreter to see what was wanted. Lieutenant Grattan spoke very cross and severe to Scattering Bear's offers. He demanded immediate surrender of the man who killed the cow, which they refused to do, but offers for a settlement was being negotiated by the Indians. A collection of horses was being taken up around the camp by the crier of the village. When the shooting was started, my father has said it was hardly twenty minutes till every soldier was dead. Only one wounded soldier got away to the river and my uncle Swift Bear found him. My father hid him and took him to the garrison in his buckboard at night. It was reported that right after this fight my father was robbed, but it was not so. This was another false report. My uncle Swift Bear was right at my father's ranch with his band to protect my father's property. There were many Indians came to our place to buy ammunition and guns while they hastily struck down their tents to get away from the place of the troubles, fast as they could the same day. By three o'clock every tent was gone—not even a dog was left behind. They struck out north and west because they did not want any more trouble.

This blow was a bad influence on the Indians; bad for the nice promises that had been made just four years ago in the treaty with the United States in 1851. After the Battle of Ash Hollow, General Harney moved to Laramie and, not satisfied with all the lives he took and the captives he had in the garrison, he demanded the murderers of Lieutenant Grattan. Now, when the shooting started, the soldiers began first and the Indians who did the shooting all ran away. Only the friendly Indians who had always lived at Laramie, like Swift Bear and Spotted Tail—good men who were trying to live up to the treaty stipulations—remained. From these friendly Indians Harney demanded a hostage. These hardly knew what to do; they could not go all over the country to look for these—no one knew where they had gone. These might have fled to Canada. In fact, by the Indian records made afterward, these that fled wintered near the border of Canada near the Rocky Mountains. They had many encounters with their enemies the Crows that year. This was the winter that was on record in the winter count as *Hetopa waŋ ktepi*—"when a war bonnet with four horns was pulled off of a Crow by the Sioux."[10] It was a hard winter and part of the Brulés and Oglalas wintered with the Huŋkpapaya. It would have been impossible for the friendly Indians to have gone up there to bring in the murderers of Grattan. If they had reached up there to ask for those who shot Grattan to come to Laramie to be held as hostages for peace, they would have been laughed to scorn, for the Indians knew they were attacked by the soldiers. These soldiers shot first and killed their chief when the battle began. They felt justified in doing what they did. So the friendly Indians decided to furnish the seven hostages that Harney wanted.

Spotted Tail was the first to give himself up to the military to be punished for the Grattan massacre. Others joined him: the two brothers of Scattering Bear came up—Red Leaf, a brave young man, and Long Chin—also Red Plume and Spotted Elk. These five men came up to the garrison singing their death song all dressed in their buckskin suits and war bonnets to present themselves as the hostages for the rest of the tribe. Harney accepted them. The military coach was being prepared while the Indians invited the prisoners to a last feast. Spotted Tail at that time had four wives with many children, so the younger sister of the wives was given to him to take along. She was just about eighteen years old and very good looking. All the men were allowed to take their wives with them; some of them took their smaller children. They started early next morning in a government coach and a freight wagon carrying their camping equipage. The warriors sang a brave-heart song as they left Laramie going east to the Leavenworth prison to be punished for two years. These prisoners did this to exonerate all blame for the rest of the tribe. It was a very noble and a brave deed to do, as they did not know if their lives would be demanded or not—they did not know if they were ever to return again or not.

Red Leaf was a chief. He was the next heir to the dynasty of hereditary chiefs; he was the oldest brother of Scattering Bear. He also had three wives and many children and descendants that are living today. He died at Rosebud and was buried out in the pine hills. Spotted Tail had thirty-six children. The youngest wife, who went with him to prison, was Mniakuwiŋ or Brings Water. She bore nine girls for Spotted Tail. One of the other women, next to the youngest, bore nine boys. The oldest wife had thirteen children, while the other two had only one or two children. (No one can remember when the custom of having plural wives and concubinage originated. It must have started in the dark ages and, as time advanced, it was practiced more to increase the tribe.)

In 1857, these prisoners were returned from Leavenworth to their bands. Harney had been at Pierre and made a treaty with some of the Sioux, but, somehow, the promises he made to the Indians were never carried out.[11] There was a bitter feeling among them because of this, which brought on more troubles a few years later. The Sioux joined with the Cheyennes and Arapahos in carrying on raids to retard the invasion of the white men. Red Cloud grew into prominence by taking a part in this defense that started because of the treatment of the Indians in the Battle of Ash Hollow.

3

In the year of 1854, my father was living on his ranch on the Platte River eight miles east of Laramie. This ranch had been built by Sarpy who belonged to the Saint Louis Fur Company (this was mentioned in another chapter [6]). After the killing of the lame cow on the Oregon Trail by the sons of Ituhuwaŋka (who had no use for the cow the Mormons left on the trail as the cow had been driven many miles and was in a very poor condition, besides being lame), my father knew there was trouble brewing. Being an interpreter, he had many dealings at Fort Laramie at the garrison. Although the matter was kept quiet, he heard by good authority that General Harney was coming out the following year to punish the Indians for the Lieutenant Grattan massacre. My father secretly sent word by my uncle Goose, a brother of my mother. He carried the message to Chief Iron Shell to move away from the main-traveled road as there was an army coming under Harney to kill all the Indians they could find. Part of the Brulés had been down on the Republican River hunting buffalo as buffalo was very plentiful down there at that time. There was wonderful grass; the buffalo grazed in Kansas where the forage was up to their bodies. The country was well watered by streams and springs everyplace. This was the ideal hunting grounds where millions of wild game grew fat on the land.

With all their dried meat, the Brulés were traveling north toward the Platte River country, then the home of the southern bands of the Sioux. The camp had been pitched at Ash Hollow on the headwaters of the Little Blue; buffalo hides and deer hides had to be tanned where there was plenty of water. Here, the travois were unhitched for a few days' rest. The Indians had not brought their hides to my father's ranch. Now, my father was greatly worried about Harney coming; at the garrison he had heard he was on his way. There must have been some mixed-bloods who could read and write with the Brulé bands because my father wrote a note to Iron Shell to warn him again and told him to move away as hastily as he could. When Iron Shell received the note, he told my father's clerk Samuel Smith, who bore the message, to tell my father not to worry as he was not going to fight the soldiers if they came. He was going to surrender to save trouble as the Indians were not prepared for battle and would not do so. This message reached Iron Shell a day before the battle. Iron Shell told the Indians that they must not fight as he would put up a white flag and have a talk with the officers for peace. So the Indians were confident of peace.

When Harney reached the camp of the Brulés and partly surrounded them, Iron Shell put up the white flag. Spotted Tail, Little Thunder, and a few of the principal men went to meet the officers to try to make peace, but the soldiers started to form a skirmish line. Now, I have heard Iron Shell and Spotted Tail and others tell that there was no mercy shown — the firing of the guns started right away as the chiefs started toward the army carrying the white flag. Sam Smith, who brought the message from my father, was caught by the soldiers and another mixed-blood was nearly killed. Little Thunder, a chief, was shot right down and badly wounded. Men, women, and children were shot right down and lay strewn on the prairies everywhere, trampled under the feet of the sharp-shod cavalry horses. The wounded ones were trying to crawl away to places out of the way. Some succeeded in falling into the cutbanks of the Little Blue River. Some of the women crawled under the overhanging weeds and grasses along the banks. Some were wounded and were bleeding; children's cries had to be subdued. They had no time to bind up their wounds. Groans from the dying could be heard. The hoofbeats of the soldiers sounded right above them.

Iron Shell's mother-in-law, a fine-looking, stately Indian woman, years later showed her scars to me. Cokawiŋ said things were happening so fast and sudden she was bewildered. The men threw away the white flag of truce and began to fight. Spotted Tail and Iron Shell fought side by side. When she saw that there was to be no peace, she started to run without a thing, not even her blanket. But, as luck would have it, she was girded with a wide leather belt. On her belt was a scabbard with a knife in it. The smoke of the battle blinded her. As she looked all around, she could see the soldiers galloping after groups of old men, women, and children who were running for their lives. Some were running across the valley only to be met by soldiers and shot right down. It seemed as though there was no place to go. There were wounded horses everyplace. Some of these were trying to get up but couldn't. If Cokawiŋ could only run onto a wounded horse that could travel, she said she would have gotten on one to get away on.

Only the bravest men were fighting, while those not able to fight or that had no guns had to retreat. Finally, as Cokawiŋ ran she looked back to see if anyone was following her. Sure enough, there was a soldier just taking an aim to shoot her down. If she had not turned around that instant, he would have shot her right in the middle of the back, but, by turning, the shot tore her stomach wide open just below her belt. She was a large, fleshy woman of about forty-six years of age. The bullet ripped her open for about six inches, a glancing shot. She was disemboweled, a gaping wound, and her bowels protruded from the wound as she fell. The soldier thought he had gotten her and went on after the shot to look for others to kill. Cokawiŋ saw a washout nearby and she crawled toward this place. Finally, she reached it in an exhausted condition. It was a deep buffalo wallow; she layed down in this and covered herself with the tumble weeds that had collected in it. She tore off the wide calico sleeve of her dress and stuffed it in her wound to stop the bleeding. There she lay all day listening to guns roar and to the hoofbeats of the horses, the shouting and yelling of the soldiers who came so near at times that she thought she would be discovered. Once in a while she could hear a Sioux war cry. At these times, Cokawiŋ said she felt like singing and giving the trill. It was a desperate time with her people; in her anxiety she almost forgot her wound.

Day was almost at an end. Most of the fighting Indians retreated because Harney's army had captured a great many of the women and children and old men. If they kept up the fighting, these would all be slaughtered, they feared. The army started to drive the captives before them; as the sun was sinking in the west there was not a soul on the bloody battleground. Cokawiŋ thought she had better follow along on the trail if possible. If there were others in hiding, she did not see them. All over the valley were dead horses and dead bodies.

It is generally evening when the wild animals come out to search for food. Cokawiŋ found a little skunk wandering around, sniffing this way and that way, unconscious of the terrible tragedy that had taken place. Cokawiŋ said she pitied the little animal, but it was the only food in sight so she killed it, skinned it, and she struck a fire with her flint and steel, as a bag of this was also attached to her belt. Part of the skin of the skunk she tied around on her wound. With a stick for a cane she kept walking all night where the trail led.

Toward morning, she heard a bugle blow. Now, her wound tore her stomach open, but luckily her bowels were not perforated. She had walked four or five miles west, resting many times, as it would have been sure death if she attempted to remain behind. Morning was coming on when she reached the soldiers' camp, which was just visible. Way to the north, beyond the Platte, were signal fires along the hills. The reflections flamed in the gray dawn. These fires were built by the warriors who were retreating north to show the way for those stragglers who might be lost or who did not know the direction of the retreat. As Cokawiŋ, the mother-in-law of Iron Shell, nearly reached the camp, she could dimly see the sentries walking their beat back and forth by the camp. Cokawiŋ said it took a lot of courage; it was like facing death. She began to sing a death chant. In Indian life there are songs for everything, but to sing your own death chant is an awful thing—it takes a brave person to do it. The sentry who met her presented arms and spoke. As she could not understand what he said, all she could do was to raise her arms. She was allowed to go where the Indians were in the center of camp. Most of the prisoners were old men, women, and children.

When breakfast of hardtack and coffee was over, the journey began for Fort Laramie. The wounded ones were allowed to travel in the wagons; there were wounded soldiers as well as Indians. There were some ponies with travois which bore the children and luggage. When Laramie was reached, the sick were looked after. Cokawiŋ walked to the place where a doctor was doing surgical work. She was laid on a table or platform where seven stitches were taken in her side without any anesthetics. Anesthetics were scarce and were saved for those with broken bones. Here the wounded were taken care of and fed by the military. Among the prisoners were many young, nice-looking women who became the property of their captors.[12] Iron Shell's wife's younger sister was taken back east by an officer and was never again heard of. None of her relatives ever heard what was her fate; the poor girl might have soon died of grief and lonesomeness or might have taken her own life. In about the month of October, after the Battle of Ash Hollow, Harney's army moved away toward

Old Fort Pierre. The prisoners could not be taken along so they were allowed to go back to their bands.

This was the beginning of the Sioux battles with the U.S. soldiers. For twenty years after this, there was a continual fight one place or another. In the beginning, the trouble began with the killing of a lame cow belonging to a Mormon. The Indians wanted to pay for the cow. Scattering Bear, a Brulé chief who was trying to negotiate for the payment of the cow, was shot down by Grattan. He lived a short while and finally died of his wounds. As soon as the firing was opened up by the soldiers, the Indians started. The chiefs had instructed their warriors not to shoot unless the soldiers shot first. This unfortunate affair should never have happened. The Mormon should have been made to take the payment of horses as long as his cow was too worn out to travel. The ponies would have taken him as far as he wanted to go. As it was, this trouble cost the government thousands or millions of dollars. The peace that had been made by the government with the Indians four years before was broken by the U.S. soldiers. It cost many lives on both sides, it threw the whole country in a turmoil, put fear into the hearts of the emigrants.

The whole country was unsafe. The soldiers would go out on scouting expeditions in the surrounding localities from the posts, Laramie and other places. If they ran into Indian hunters, they would kill them and take their scalps as trophies to take back east. On the other hand, the Indians began to raid the emigrants, the settlers, and run off the horses and cattle of the travelers, and war was declared against all invaders. The soldiers were hated more than anything. They brought immorality among the young Indians. The burning of garrisons was carried on. Many times, Laramie would have been burned to the ground if it were not for Spotted Tail and Swift Bear, my uncle. They, with their bands, stood by this post. Through their influence, the hostiles kept from doing any great damage, but, within two or three miles from the post, herders were killed and beeves taken, or a lone herder would be killed and horses taken. Many a surprise attack was made and it was dangerous for a man to go alone on any errand beyond sight of the post. It was nothing to find a lone Indian dead and scalped, or a soldier dead and also minus his scalp. The Sans Arc or the Brulés would come down from the north to the Platte on forays. My father had to keep his herd of horses well guarded, for the northern Indians came down in large numbers looking for emigrants' herds and my father, being a white man with plenty of good horses, was no better to them than the Mormons who were on a constant string along on the Oregon Trail westward. (Some of the eastern people who knew nothing of the tribes and different bands of the Sioux probably thought these tribes dwelt in one large village together. I have talked with many and read many books and even in military reports where the soldiers fought against all the Sioux and conquered them in one battle. Now, this was very far from the fact; they were not all together. This made the matter so hard to reach them all at one time when the government wished to negotiate with them.)

My father's ranch was on the south side of the Platte. We could see the Minniconjou on the war path along the Cottonwood Creek north of the Platte. They had an eye on my father's horses. When the warriors go out that way, they generally take a young lad along of about thirteen or fourteen years old to carry the provisions and rope or to stay at the camp. Such a camp was made on Cottonwood Creek by the Minniconjou; a boy was left behind to guard the camp. When some soldiers who were out scouting found the camp and the lone Indian boy sleeping, they killed the boy, took his scalp and, on coming back, stopped at my father's ranch. Sgt. Gerry Shaw was with the soldiers. He had the Indian boy's scalp dangling down tied to his bridle. The sight horrified my mother and the relatives who were staying at the ranch. When the Minniconjou came back and found the boy dead and scalped, there was a great mourning among them. They rolled him in robes and gave him a tree burial, which place was a great landmark for many years.

Red Horse and his brother had been in the battle of Ash Hollow. They were great warriors and were with the war party as the captives were taken to Laramie. Red Horse's brother, Kills Eagle, had a very good-looking woman of about twenty-five years old. Sgt. Gerry Shaw took her for his woman. She had two small children, a small child that was still nursing and a boy of about five years. When Mrs. Kills Eagle found out that she was to be taken inside the garrison, she left the older boy with relatives, sending word to her husband to come and get her son. Into the garrison she went carrying her smallest child. They were prisoners and they thought they had to do as they were told. It was not long till Kills Eagle came. He hung around the post trying to get a glimpse of his wife and baby, but he failed to see them. He took his little boy with him. The child missed his mother and would not be comforted. It was not long till the poor child died. Kills Eagle wandered over the hills mourning and crying for his wife and baby till he also failed, took sick, and died. It was not hardly a year till Sgt. Gerry Shaw tired of Kills Eagle's wife. He put her out and married a younger woman. When she returned to her people and found that her baby and husband were dead, almost any night one could hear her crying and wailing. Red Horse, when he heard her crying, used to laugh. He said he was glad to hear her cry. He said she could have run away from the white man and come back to her husband and child if she had wanted to, or, even if she had tried to do so, it would have been good news to her husband, Kills Eagle, who languished and died of grief. Red Horse accused his sister-in-law of being satisfied where she was because she was well-fed and wore fancy clothes of the white man. It was not many years after this, when the agencies were formed, that this Gerry Shaw was made an instructor among the Indians and was carried on as a government carpenter for many years.[13]

One of the last survivors of the Battle of Ash Hollow died at Rosebud, Chief Iron Shell. He was buried near Wanblee where all his relatives were buried. It is a beautiful location on a high plateau overlooking a wide expanse of valley and hills dotted with trees here and there. A very kind gentleman, Dr. R. A. Burnside, is planning to erect a monument above Iron Shell's grave in the spring of 1936.

CHAPTER NINE

Conditions from 1854 till 1868

After the Ash Hollow fight, there was restlessness and discontentment. The Sioux sent a pipe of peace to the Cheyennes, who were ranging down from the South Platte and along the Republican, by Red Cloud; the same pipe was sent to the Arapahos in 1857. Red Cloud was then a man of about thirty-five years of age, a dashing warrior with courage and bravery, a born general and fighter that could equal a Napoleon if he had had his advantages and numbers. The Oglala tribe was gathering forces to protect their country and game grounds. Methods of attack was being discussed in all the councils. The soldiers who were coming in, great armies, were hard to battle with what arms the Indians had. It was thought best to go out in small groups and to strike and retreat; to cripple the armies by running off their horses and beef herds. This method was practiced from that time on.

The Mormons were still emigrating west by the thousands and they were not in a friendly mood. They were antagonistic to both the Indians and Americans, as afterward shown by the Mountain Meadows Massacre.[1] It was known that many of the raids made on the way to California on emigrant trains, who were poor and ill-armed in the search for fortune, were made by the Mormons dressed and painted up like Indians. As was intended, the Indians got all the blame. The country was overrun by highwaymen, called by the Indians "Gray White Men." They were holding up returning wagons from the west laden with gold, stealing the choicest horses they could find. These were as much to be feared as a soldier; it was sure death to meet one of these who had strayed away from the so-called civilization.

The Indians felt uneasy—no matter where they camped they were not safe; it seemed as though the white people wanted to fight them. Many of their relatives were shot down, wounded, or hanged. They were angered by these ruthless injuries. Nearly every day, runners came in from all parts of the country—north, east, south, and west—telling of the movements of the armies marching through their country. The crier of the village, as every village generally had a crier, was kept busy haranguing the camp, telling of what had happened in some remote part of the country. The Indians met in groups and at council lodges talking a great deal about these difficulties. There was a feeling of enmity and hostility and an antagonistic feeling of resentment and a disposition to fight. Most of the Indians were armed with bows and arrows; there were not very many guns. Guns were scarce and very costly. There were only a very few Spencer rifles—most of their guns were the old-fashioned flintlock smoothbores and muzzleloaders.

There were many Sioux with the Cheyennes during the Sumner campaign of 1857 which cost so many lives and great sums of money.[2] It was never any great thing that started these wars. The Cheyennes found some stray horses and had them in their herd. Some traveler saw these horses and reported it to the commanding officer. The Cheyennes were ordered to return them, which they did. But there was one of these horses that was not a military horse; the owner had had him for a long time. A group of soldiers went out after this horse, but the owner had left with the horse in question. He and a few of his relatives went into the Black Hills. The troop that went out killed one Indian, caught one of them and brought him in as prisoner. He was held at Fort Kearny for a long time.

Trappers could not go out after this, for they were white men and, when found, they were immediately dispatched. Trapper Garnier, who had trapped up and down the Platte for many years, was killed by the Cheyennes and scalped.[3] He had often stayed at my father's place. Charles DeSersa was a trapper, but after it got dangerous he was cook at my father's ranch.[4] In the fall and spring when the greatest catches took place, my father had to keep the trappers when they were in. He dealt for their furs and kept the trappers while they were idle. I can remember them as they came in with their furs in great Red River carts drawn by ponies. Most of these trappers married Indian women and had large families. They went out in the wildest places where the animals were to be caught along timbered creeks. These white men lived in tents and adapted themselves to Indian ways. A winter camp was generally made in the timber some place; a few families would go in together for protection.

Now, the Indian wives of these men were good, faithful souls who did the best they could. As civilized goods did not last very long for clothing, they would set to work to tan hides. They made their men buckskin shirts and pants, fringed them along the seams so they would not rip easily. Their caps were of fur. As marten, beaver, and mink were furs that could be sold for a good price, their caps were generally made from cheaper grades of fur such as skunk, badger, and muskrat. These were lined and worn with fur out. The moccasins were of tough buffalo hide, smoked so they were preserved in their shape. In the wintertime the fur was worn next to the skin; in the summer the hides were tanned with the fur off so that they could keep cool. I have often seen these trappers come in after a long winter hunt wearing long hair and beards that grew way down to their chest. On looking close, as we children used to do, they did not look like human beings. They looked more like animals with bushy heads, for there was no part of their faces that could be seen but their blue staring eyes. If they stared at us too hard, we generally made a hasty retreat.

These trappers' camps were like an Indian camp, but the one remnant of civilization that clung to them, although living in the savage wilds, was their love of music. When one approached one of these camps, you could hear the sweetest strains of violin music. Sometimes, a deep voice would break out in some foreign song and a chorus would start, to end with shouts and laughter. Some of these men came from fine families, perhaps from far away France, England, Germany, or Spain. They adapted themselves to the ways of the wild: hardships, danger, hunger, cold, and the inclement weather; the rocks, the mountains, and the torrents were things to overcome. These things only added to the very spice of life to them.

My father had formed a partnership with Elbridge Gerry in 1855 to do business with the Indians at his ranch. Someone had to stay on the place while Father went east to market the furs and buy goods of such things the Indians needed. My father's long experience with the Indian trade taught him the things that were used by them. He was always on the road to Saint Louis or Saint Joseph with a string of freight wagons. Some of the wagons were trailed behind other wagons and a herder, generally my young brothers, were taken along to herd the horses with two or three hired men. A great deal of provisions were gotten at Saint Joseph; this was nearer and made the hauling easier than from Saint Louis. At this time, the Mormon trade had grown to a prodigious size. These Mormons were not used to traveling. They brought things that they could easily have gotten along without: tables, rocking chairs, cupboards,

Josephine Waggoner (seated center), 1870s, perhaps taken upon her arrival at Hampton. (Other girls are, standing: Topala and Wakaŋ Mani, seated: Takiseay and Noŋge Wanica.) Courtesy, South Dakota State Historical Society—State Archives.

Josephine Waggoner, 1912. Courtesy, Nebraska State Historical Society.

Susan Bordeaux Bettelyoun. Courtesy, NSHS.

Susan Bordeaux Bettelyoun, Old Soldiers Home, Hot Springs, South Dakota, 1930s. Courtesy, NSHS.

Huŋtkalutawiŋ, Red Cormorant
Woman. Courtesy, NSHS.

James Bordeaux, 1860s.
Courtesy, NSHS.

White Thunder, Wakiŋyaŋska.
Courtesy, NSHS.

Brulé delegation to Carlisle
Indian School, May 1880. Back row
left to right: Interpreters Louis
Robidoux and Charles Tackett, Susan
Bettelyoun's first husband; front row:
Black Crow, Two Strikes, White
Thunder, Spotted Tail, and Iron
Wing. Courtesy, Cumberland
County Historical Society, Carlisle,
Pennsylvania.

Isaac Bettelyoun, 1902. Courtesy,
NSHS.

Louis Bordeaux. Courtesy, NSHS.

Oglala camp on the North Platte River, 1859. Courtesy, NSHS.

Fort Laramie, 1858. Possibly the earliest photograph of the fort.
Courtesy, Lee-Palfrey Family Papers, Manuscript Division,
Library of Congress.

Enoch Wheeler Raymond and family, Rosebud Reservation, 1902.
Courtesy, NSHS.

Crow Butte, Paha Kaŋgi, Dawes County, Nebraska. Courtesy, NSHS.

Swift Bear, Mato Luzahaŋ. Courtesy, NSHS.

Iron Shell, Tukimaza. Courtesy, NSHS.

Spotted Tail, Siŋte Gleśka. Courtesy, NSHS.

Burial scaffold of Hiŋziwiŋ, daughter of Spotted Tail, Fort Laramie.
Courtesy, Wyoming Division of Cultural Resources.

Lakotas and whites at Fort Laramie, 1868. Standing left to right:
unidentified, John Finn, Amos Bettelyoun, Old Man Afraid of His
Horses, Red Bear, and James Bordeaux; seated: Packs His Drum, W. G.
Bullock, and Benjamin Mills. Courtesy, NSHS.

James Bordeaux in front of 1868 treaty council lodges of Man
Afraid of His Horses. Courtesy, Edward E. Ayer Collection,
The Newberry Library.

wardrobes, and bulky things that should have been left at home. Some of these things were unloaded all along the way. My father said during the days of the cholera, when whole outfits nearly of the emigrants passed away along the Oregon Trail, there was every kind of a board used for a marker. The side of a cupboard, the bottom of a rocking chair, the head of a bedstead were hastily torn out, names and dates were inscribed and placed at the head of the new-made graves. But, as most of the way along the Oregon Trail was without fuel, and when buffalo chips were wet, these head boards were used. The charred ends could be seen at the camping places.

Elbridge Gerry, who was of Scotch descent, was a very good business partner. Father said Indians were generally waiting when he was back from a freighting expedition—Gerry had nearly everything sold before it was unloaded. Being a good Indian talker, he was very popular with the Indians. He managed to keep the business in a flourishing state. He was named Iśtaska or White Eye. He was so very well liked that two very prominent Indians gave their daughters to him. He had had two wives before, which he put aside in order to take these two younger ones when he was named and adopted into the tribe.

Gerry was in favor of trading with the Cheyennes as, at that time, the Cheyennes claimed the country lying along the South Platte, the headwaters of the Republican River, the headwaters of the Smoky Hill River, up to the mountains and east of Denver and all of Laramie River and south of it to the mountains. They held this wide scope of country for many years—all the South Platte country. The South Platte River was Waśin Wakpa or the Dakota word for Fat Meat River. The buffalo in this part of the country always grew fat first. While the buffalo in the north were just shedding their winter coats, the South Platte buffaloes were sleek and fat; they were a month ahead. To this Fat Meat River country Eldridge Gerry went. He set up a horse ranch after two years of partnership with my father. His ranch was built on the south side of the South Platte, right west of where Crow Creek empties into the South Platte. His place was about a hundred miles, more or less, from Denver and about the same distance west from Julesburg and Fort Rankin. His ranch was the stopping place for all travelers that came up from the south. It was a regularly traveled trail called the Bozeman Trail.

The Bozeman Trail took in a wide territory. It was a trail that had roadhouses or way stations where travelers could stop for feed for their stock and be protected every ten or fifteen miles. There was just as much traveling on the Bozeman Trail as there was on the Oregon Trail at this time. People coming from the southern states took the Santa Fe Trail till they came to the Bozeman Trail, which led from Texas north into Montana and into Canada. A branch of this road also led to the eastern markets to the principal cities like Chicago, Saint Louis, Independence, and Saint Joseph.[5]

At the Gerry ranch, travelers stopped to trade horses or get their supplies. It was not long till Gerry became very wealthy in stock and horses. It was safer for a ranchman along the South Platte at this time from 1857 on, as the Sioux uprising was taking place all along the Oregon Trail and northwest of there. My father spoke well of Gerry. He said he made money fast and grew to be very wealthy. But several times, just as he seemed to be doing fine, he lost all his stock. Horses and cattle were just stolen and swept away during the Cheyenne and Sioux uprising, so that he had to start all over again.

When the fur trading was at an end at this time, most of these old trappers whom my father brought into the country were employed as scouts and guides. Gerry did a great deal of this kind of work for the government. Understanding the Sioux and the Cheyennes, he did a great deal of service for the government. At one time he saved an attack on Denver when it was just a camp. Nick Janis became a scout. Sefroy Iott, at one time, was appointed Indian agent. Indian agents were appointed often as, for some reason, they would not stay. Sometimes they were civilians. I knew Eldridge Gerry's wives personally. There were many children born to him. There are many descendants living today of Indian blood.[6] It may seem strange to a white person to think a man should have so many wives, but when a white man took an Indian woman for a wife, and was considered one of the tribe, he was expected to follow the custom of having plural wives. Generally, the oldest woman would be the wife and her younger sisters or cousins would be concubines to her. It was always considered the best plan to marry sisters or cousins so the children would be closely related. Another custom which was very closely guarded against was intermarriage; no persons who were anyways related were allowed to be married. The relationship of the children was closely guarded and impressed on young minds. There is no greater disgrace among the Indians than for a man to marry anyone who was a kindred— even if distant.

One by one the trappers who had been with my father got married and left to start homes of their own. Some of these I remember to be

Valandra, Du Bray, La Deau, Charbonay, Morale, Moran, Pratt.[7] Nick
Janis was always an interpreter and guide for emigrants or soldiers who
were passing through the country, but his family were residents at Laramie.[8] Beauvais was a well educated man when he first came out from
Saint Louis. He was also a member at my father's ranch until he saw that
he could make his own start at the saloon business. He built up a place
four miles east of Laramie and lived there till the military bought it a
few years later. Steve Estes was agent at Laramie in 1868.[9] Joseph Prue,
Charles DeSersa, and a great many more of these trappers settled down
on ranches and succeeded a great deal better than trapping, which was a
dangerous life.[10] Their Indian wives, who were patient, kind, and true,
made good homes for them. There was not many cases of desertion
among them; most of these men, though rough in their way, were kind
and loved their children. Some of them, at great sacrifice, sent their children away to schools to be educated. Their descendants are numerous on
every reservation.

In the year 1858, gold was discovered in Colorado. When it was heard
by the outside world, there was a gold rush, as it was nearer and more
convenient [than California]. People came flocking with ox teams, mule
teams, on horseback, by pack burros, and on foot. It was not strange to
see emigrants going west with such pushcarts or wheelbarrows. No one
could ever tell the hardships that were endured, unless it was those who
were among them to know the facts. There were whole days that were
traveled without water. My father did many good deeds for people who
were down-and-out. He had a charitable heart and it did not make any
difference what nationalities they were; if they were worthy people he
helped them out. There were many who stayed at my father's trading
post all winter, and if there was a way, he sent them on where they wanted
to go. I remember one fall there was a colored couple among the emigrants who came to Laramie. They came in a one-horse buckboard; their
horse died, so they could not go any further. If I remember right, this
was in 1861; I was then about four years old.[11] How frightened I was! It
was the first time I ever saw colored people. As my father engaged this
couple to cook, I left home. I would not be induced to stay. I went to
my married sister's and stayed all winter. Any time I didn't behave just
right, all they had to say was that Uncle Ben was coming and I would
straighten up immediately.

My father dealt in many different trades, whatever he thought would
bring an advancement.[12] My father had Indian hunters who went out and

always brought in game of all kinds. There was always buffalo meat, elk meat, deer, and antelope fresh from the hills. There was a German family came to Laramie. They were stranded there for some reason. My father, being strictly religious, a man who was honest, hard working, earnest, and truthful—I never knew him to turn away even strangers who were in distress; he always managed a way for those who looked to him for assistance. The Indians that my father hired were just as honestly dealt with as the white men who served under him.

Ford was the name of a German family who came to Laramie in 1864. I can't remember which direction they had been traveling (some of the Mormons were always coming back, while others were going west). This family was stranded; their horses had either died or strayed away. In these days, horses were continually being rustled by highwaymen as well as Indians. My father built a little eating place of a couple of large rooms at Laramie, outside the garrison near the bridge. He hired Ford and his family to run the place. We had plenty of fresh meat that would spoil if it was not used up. Ford and his wife were excellent cooks; the place was always filled with officers who wanted change from their usual diet. Travelers and emigrants kept the place busy. My father kept this place for a year or until we moved away and Mr. Ford and his family moved to Denver where there was a boom. Gold had been discovered and Denver was the center of attraction. People who had no aim in life and were without homes, who were footloose, all flocked into Denver.

There was a curious thing that I recall happened at this time. The Fords had a girl about twelve years called Una. Now, there was no school building at Laramie, but a class was taught by a scholarly soldier. There were many officers' children and many of the laundresses' children attended. My brother John attended also. It was my first knowledge of how white people whipped their children. Every day, as regular as clockwork, Una was whipped by her high-tempered German mother—a great many times without cause or for trifling reasons, sometimes just for walking too slow. I believe she was whipped every day of her life. The girl was too young to have responsibilities. I expect she had to take care of the younger children and help with the work. When she lagged in the work, she was whipped. One day she was punished unusually hard. Una took a gray army blanket from the back room and ran away. It was dark when the parents noticed the absence of the girl. After a search was made and the girl could not be found, the commanding officer was told that Una had disappeared. The soldiers were called out; the scouts with lanterns went out on the grounds searching everywhere. The father, Mr. Ford, thought the Indians had captured her. At midnight the scouts reached my father's house. My brother and father dressed and joined in the search. It was an all-night search, but the girl was not found. The coming and going of people had obliterated her tracks so that no one could find them. The commanding officer would have had her followed if someone knew where she went. Next morning, Una came out from under the Laramie Bridge. She had had a good night's sleep hiding under the bridge and kept the garrison awake searching for her. The poor girl always had welts across her back from the unmerciful whippings she got.

My father kept about twenty head of cows and supplied the garrison with milk. He did not have to deliver it, as every day a wagon came out with ice in it to pack the cans of milk in. The eating place was also supplied with milk from my father's ranch. The Fords moved after a year to Denver and we never heard of them again. Soon after this, we moved away from Laramie to the new agency at Whetstone, South Dakota. Since then, I was never in Laramie again.

My neighbor at the State Home, Mrs. Jencene C. Casey, who was an emigrant from Denmark, came over the Atlantic in 1859 when she was nine years old from Herring, Denmark. There came what were called Brighamites, preaching the gospel among the Danes. These preachers called on the people to leave their crowded old homes and come to America where there was so much room, where there was more freedom in God's country, where a man could raise all manner of fruit and vegetables and stock. These Brighamites did not tell about the practice of polygamy. Mrs. Casey says they came across the Atlantic in a sailing vessel and landed in Philadelphia. From there the Brighamites took them to Iowa, where they stayed at Council Bluffs for the winter, and in the spring of 1860, when the emigrant train was formed, they went across the Missouri River in a scow drawn by hand on a cable. Mrs. Casey said they were a week getting across the Missouri with the 400 wagons; there was a thousand head of oxen or more. These wagons and oxen were there to meet them to escort them to Salt Lake City. As the emigrant procession moved along, slowly the children walked along behind the wagons they belonged to, barefooted and happy. There was always a guide with them to let them know the best camping places. Soon after starting on the way, Mrs. Casey saw thousands of wigwams as far as the eye could reach. The emigrants were of different nationalities, so that they camped in groups so that those who understood each other would be together. The Casey family did not stay very long at Salt Lake City. Most of them could not understand the religion of the Mormons; plural wives did not appeal to them. The tithing was also very strict; no matter what was raised, one tenth would have to be given to the church. So there was always a whole string of disaffected Mormons to be met returning from Salt Lake City in all kinds of rigs. This emigrant train that the Caseys were in were lucky. They went straight through without any trouble. Indians were raiding along the Platte and the Republican Rivers, but at that time the Indians were in groups in Wyoming and Montana, trying to put a stop to the traveling across the hunting grounds.

In Bancroft's history of Colorado, he reports the travel westward was the largest in 1859 and 1860.[13] There were one hundred and fifty thousand people came up the Kansas and the Smoky Hill Rivers and up the Platte. In a very short time, nearly all these travelers came trooping back discouraged and dissatisfied, most of these being foreigners and, not knowing that there was a controversy between the government and the Indians, wandered over the best hunting ground, scaring the game and frightening them away. Many were killed and the horses confiscated; women and children were captured. On his freighting expeditions, my father had passed as many as five thousand wagons, all going to the Colorado mountains to seek for gold. At Denver at that time, there was a large village of Arapahos. My father dealt with these people there till the gold rush came—these Indians left there.

In the earlier days, when my father had to go to Saint Louis to do his trading, men were scarce and he jerk-necked some of his oxen, that is, he led them behind. On reaching Saint Louis he generally looked around to see if there were any young men adventurously inclined and who could handle ox teams. This is how he had brought out young men with him to drive his yokes of oxen. Up to 1845 the buffalo pelts were pressed into packets of about a dozen hides in a press that was fixed with a lever. This way they were easy to handle. Through the winter, timbers were cut in the mountains, rafted down the Laramie, and whipsawed into lumber. This was before sawmills were established. Then the great flat boats, or Mackinaw boats, were built. My father said when the spring rise would come on the Platte, these boats were put into the river and he had shipped as many as eight hundred to a thousand of these packets on three or four boats for the American Fur Company in one season. Business was better from 1833 till 1845. My father was in charge of the American Fur

Company post when it was sold to the military; he knew the fur trade from A to Z. He dealt with nearly all the western tribes, lived in tents with them, hunted buffalo and other big game in the mountains. He knew when Fort Fetterman was to be burned; he advised Spotted Tail, Swift Bear, American Horse, and the other chiefs against the attack on Fort Phil Kearny. It was his business to buy what furs the Indians brought in and he had to sell them what they wanted. Most of their wants were powder and ammunition and guns.

All the Cheyenne country was overrun by emigrants and buffalo hunters. The buffalo was nearly all killed off by 1860, but the Indians did not believe it. They were just being killed by the thousands just for their hides. It was not long till it was a hard matter to find the wild herds. It was dangerous for the Indians to go hunting; they began to be hungry and in want. Their game being gone, they made raids on ranches and travelers to subsist.

From 1857 and for twenty years there was a continual battle. The Sumner campaign against the Cheyennes included the Sioux, for some of the Oglalas were always with the Cheyennes. In 1857, a number of Cheyennes and Sioux were attacked by soldiers. The troops were commanded by Col. E. V. Sumner on the Arkansas River and later in the summer he attacked them again, on the Smoky Hill River. While the fighting was going on the Sioux and Cheyennes—now tentless, as the soldiers destroyed everything—were fleeing from place to place. This does not mean all the Sioux and Cheyenne Nation, but a few bands that were living along the Smoky Hill and Republican Rivers. They came up from the Solomon Fork of the Arkansas, but were met again by the soldiers who had been trailing them up. The cavalry were in advance while the infantry marched behind and the train of wagons coming steadily in the rear. This sabre attack was considered very lucky because although the fighting was close, the Indians say it did not last very long as the cavalry horses were jaded and it was easy to get away from them. After this battle, the train of wagons pulled in at Laramie where there were a large train of Mormon emigrants to be escorted across the country. I can remember myself the great camp of the Mormons who were waiting for an escort. My father at this time was on his ranch a few miles east of Laramie. He traded and sold to the Mormons every day. Horses, cows, sheep, pigs, chickens—anything they had was valued and bought by my father. He never let a chance to trade go by. The cavalry horses that came in from the battlefields were lean, poor, and tired. The mules were also jaded and poor, many of them with sore shoulders from jogging over rough ground. That summer there was a great city of tents; the Mormons would not go any further than Laramie. In this battle of Colonel Sumner's expedition against the Sioux was Two Moon (his father, Carries the Otter, was killed) the Cheyenne chief. Of the Oglala, there were Man Afraid of His Horses and young Crazy Horse and others who had went south with Cheyennes on a hunting trip. A few days after the Mormons were escorted away, the Sioux that were in the battles with Cheyennes came in back to their bands and related their adventures in my uncle Swift Bear's lodge. Most of those that were killed were Cheyennes.[14]

In 1862, messengers brought the news of the troubles of the Santees in Minnesota. In 1863, Sibley and Sulley's campaign was reported: the attack on the Yanktonais at White Stone Hill and all the battles fought all the way from Minnesota to the Missouri River; Sully's attack on the Huŋkpapayas at Killdeer in 1864. Red Cloud began in earnest to stand in the way of the white man. All the summer of 1865 was one short battle after another in the Powder River country; Connor's expedition against the Sioux, and Cole's march through the country, which was made difficult by the death of his horses and starvation of his men. I need not dwell on these battles as others have given a thorough history and account on the white man's side.[15] I only know that my father did all he could by using his influence among the Indians to bring about peace.

About the Piney Creek battle there were misleading things written by many authors that was mentioned in the book written by Townsend Brady whose version was quoted in *The Boy's Book of Scouts* by Sabin.[16] My nephew, William J. Bordeaux, made a thorough inquiry in regard to this battle. After reading Brady's book, he interviewed living survivors and got their true story. He saw Ring Bull, Little Hawk, Little Bull—Brulé Sioux who took part in this fight in 1867. The story is told in *Conquering the Mighty Sioux*. I had a talk with Ring Bull this very summer, as he is still living at Saint Francis, South Dakota, on the Rosebud Reservation.

The Brulés were returning from a buffalo hunt near the Bighorn Mountains when they run into some woodchoppers, about thirty-two in number. Ring Bull said they made an attack on these woodchoppers cutting logs. These Indians knew and realized what was going on. With these logs posts would be built, the armies of the United States would entrench themselves in their country without their consent and against the agreement and stipulations of the treaty solemnly entered into by the

United States. In the treaty of 1851, it was agreed that no white man should live on their land without their consent. They saw that the treaties were being broken. These Brulés made the attack, but the woodchoppers could not be routed out of the wagon box corral they had made. They could not be brought out in the open for a fight and, as they were on their way home with meat, the Brulés gave up the fight and went on home. Besides, Red Cloud was never wounded as Brady thought he was.[17] A year before this, Fort Phil Kearny was attacked and eighty-one soldiers and civilians were killed where Lieutenant Fetterman lost his life on December 21, 1866.

In the spring of 1867 a council was called at Laramie to try to make terms with the Indians, but there was no treaty till 1868. Terms were agreed to thus: "The United States hereby agrees and stipulates that the country north of the Platte River and east of the summits of the Big Horn Mountains shall be held and considered to be unceded Indian Territory and also stipulates and agrees that no white person or persons shall be permitted to settle upon or occupy any portion of the same, or without the consent of the Indians first had and obtained to pass through the same. And it is further agreed by the United States that within ninety days after this conclusion of peace with all the bands of the Sioux Nation the military posts now established in the territory in this article named shall be abandoned, and that the road leading to them and by them to the settlements in the territory of Montana shall be closed.

"The United States agrees that the following district of country commencing on the east bank of the Missouri River where the forty-sixth parallel of north latitude crosses the same, then along low water mark down said east bank to a point opposite where the northern line of the State of Nebraska strikes the river thence west across said river and along the northern line of Nebraska to the one hundred and fourth degree longitude west of Greenwich thence north on said meridian to a point where the forty-sixth parallel of north latitude intercepts the same, thence due east along said parallel to the place of beginning; and in addition thereto, all existing reservations on the east bank of said river shall be, and the same is, set apart for the absolute and undisturbed use and occupation of the Indians herein named and for such other tribes or individual Indians as from time to time they may be willing, with the consent of the United States to admit amongst them and the United States now solemnly agrees that no persons except those herein designated and authorized so to do, and except such officers, agents and employees of the government as may be authorized to enter upon Indian reservations in discharge of duties enjoined by law, shall ever be permitted to pass over, settle upon or reside in the territory described in this article or in such territory as may be added to this reservation for the use of said Indians, and hence forth they will and do hereby relinquish all claims or right in and to any portion of the United States or Territories, except such as is embraced within the limits aforesaid, and except as herein after provided." [18]

The treaty did not include other tribes who were at war with the Sioux and to this treaty all the Sioux of the western tribes willingly agreed to and signed. Everything went along peaceful and fine with the white people and Indians. I have often wondered and regretted why, as long as the government was making a treaty, they did not make the Indians be at peace with the other tribes. The peace treaty should have included all tribes and nations dwelling in the United States; as long as the Indians were in a mood to sign a treaty, I believe this could have been accomplished as there were some terrible combats with the Pawnees, Crows, Shoshones, Rees, and Mandans after the treaty.

After the treaty of 1868, the Brulés and Oglalas and some Cheyennes made a big buffalo hunt down in Kansas. The western plains of Kansas still held some large herds of buffalo. Many of the white men married into the tribe went along. Steve Estes was then the Indian agent. My brother, Antoine Bordeaux, was the interpreter. There was no trouble during this hunt; plenty of buffalo were found and everybody had enough.

After this big hunt, my father was interested in farming and we moved to Wheeler, South Dakota. It was supposed by many that there would be a garrison at Rosebud and my father went there to put up hay and to cut wood that would have to be used by the military, and was engaged in this work when he contracted pneumonia and died at Rosebud in 1878 in October.[19] Many of the old-time trappers and Indian traders lived and died on the reservations or near there in the surrounding country. They died and were buried where they had spent their lives.

There was another buffalo hunt again in 1873, after Father had moved away. The Brulés and Oglalas started south; my brother Antoine and Agent Steve Estes was with them. These Indians found some Pawnees north of the Republican River. Steve Estes and my brother tried to restrain the Sioux from an attack, but my brother said you might as well stop an avalanche. As soon as the Sioux saw their enemies, they made an attack. It was in the middle of the day and most of the Pawnees were gone on a hunt; there were only a few men left in charge of the women and children. The Sioux killed all the men and captured the women and children. These were brought home at Laramie. After the return, Mr. Steve Estes gave the Indians a good talking-to and ordered the Pawnees to be taken home, which was done. My brother Antoine did the interpreting at that time.[20]

CHAPTER TEN

Two Stories of Horse Creek

I

The treaty of 1851, prepared during President Zachary Taylor's administration, designated the Great Sioux Reserve. On the south the Platte River was the border line, the Bighorn Mountains on the west, the Yellowstone on the north, from the mouth of the Yellowstone straight to the Missouri and on down to a certain point in Nebraska till the line reached the Platte. The United States obtained permission to build roads and forts. An agreement was made on annual annuities commencing on September 17, 1851. Nearly all the Sioux tribes were represented there at Laramie to sign the treaty. The majority of the Indians did not understand the treaty in the full sense of the word. They knew they agreed on the Oregon Trail to go through, but for roads to be built anywhere the white people wished to build in their country was not understood. There were trappers who overran the country and buffalo hunters who came in and killed buffalo by the thousands. The treaty was consummated while President Franklin Pierce was in office.[1]

It was not long till the stipulations of the treaties were broken. Grattan's massacre was blamed on the Indians for taking a castoff lame cow. This animal was not worth so much, and as long as the Indians wanted to pay for it in horses, the payment should have been taken, the whole affair settled peaceably, and the Mormon owner told to go on his way. But young Lieutenant Grattan, who had just come from West Point, hotheaded and spoiling for a fight, took his small band of thirty volunteer soldiers out to the great Sioux camp of about five thousand people, and, while Scattering Bear was trying to negotiate a payment for the cow, Grattan ordered his men to fire on the Indians. The chief was shot in the breast by Lieutenant Grattan. Scattering Bear died the next morning right near my father's place. It was his dying request that the Indians must not bother my father. Grattan fired the first shot; as a natural result the soldiers were all massacred. Lucien, the interpreter, took refuge in Bull Tail's death tent, but was killed.

The raiding of the emigrants, the raiding of the settlers, began as the roads began to be built right through the Sioux reserve. Garrisons were being built to protect the emigrants and miners against the Indians on their own land. All the Indians were rebellious. They saw that they were being robbed and that there was no protection for an Indian. It began to be dangerous even for the fur traders who had been allowed to hunt and trap along all the streams wherever they wished without any molestations in their going or coming. Since the troubles were started, times began to be dangerous for the travelers. Fur traders had to form companies and travel together.

In 1864 more raids were made by the Brulé, Oglala, and Cheyenne—who had united together to fight off the settlers and emigrants—than ever had been done before. In the spring of 1864, just when plowing corn was taking place, a raid was made along the Little Blue and the upper part of the Republican River. For three hundred miles, homes were burned, horses, cattle, and even women and children were captured.

During this time, a band of Indians came up to Laramie and had quite a talk with the commanding officer at the garrison. Two Face and Black Foot were the principal men of this band.[2] They told Lieutenant Fleming they were good Indians and had come from the north and had never fought a white man. They told that they were hard up and wanted some tobacco, ammunition to hunt with, and some rations. All these requests were granted. Two Face wanted a recommendation written on paper so he could show it if he should meet some soldiers on the hunt. This was also done for him. With this "Good Paper" in his possession, his band left Laramie, following the river east.

My father had sent after freight; my brother-in-law, Lamareaux, had charge of the twenty wagons. My brother Antoine Bordeaux was helping with two other men. There was also two other fur traders who had ox teams: Ward was married to an Indian woman and Bullock was also a man married to a half-breed woman.[3] In all, there were about fifty wagons and two hundred oxen. There were a few saddle horses among the men. Most of the wagons were being trailed, so the party consisted of about ten men in all.

When the freight teams were nearing the forks of the Platte, while supper was being cooked and the cattle were driven out a little way to graze, a band of Indian riders galloped up and drove the whole herd of oxen away. They seemed to have plenty of ammunition, for they fired toward the camp as they left.

My brother Antoine Bordeaux had a good horse picketed near. He got on this horse and rode to a fort above the mouth of the South Platte where soldiers encamped. The place was only about twenty miles away and he made good time. He brought a company of cavalry with him.

When my brother was coming back from the fort, he saw a great smoke way in the distance and he was anxious because he thought there might have been a battle and wagons were being burned, which was a thing that was often done after a raid. But it proved to be further away north to the sandhills. The Indians had killed a fat steer, had built a fire, and were roasting meat. We heard a few years afterward that there was a dispute over the kidneys. One of the Indians, who, it seems, was a simple person, pouted and went up the hill. He saw an army of soldiers following on their trail; he hollered and told them, "The soldiers are right here, almost upon us!" They had no time to pick up any of their belongings; they barely had time to get on their horses and flee. The oxen were recovered. The packages left by the Indians in their haste to get away were opened up, and there was the commanding officer's recommendation written by him and signed, date and all, only three or four days ago for Two Face and Black Foot. The soldier, whoever was in charge, took it back to the commanding officer—the recommendation. This was in the year 1864.

The following year, Two Face bought a white woman that was a captive among the Cheyennes with the idea of returning her to the garrison in exchange for more powder, balls, and rations, not knowing that his "Good Paper" had been recovered in the camp he left in such haste. I have heard my brother tell of this experience many times. In the spring, Two Face brought the white woman in. He and Black Foot and ten others were arrested and thrown in the guardhouse. There was a Cheyenne hanged already, accused of stealing horses from emigrants. Near where the Cheyenne hanged, another scaffold was built—west of Laramie on a sloping hill. A short conference or court martial was held; the Indians were sentenced to be hanged. They all died singing their death songs.

No one dared to go near the place; a sentry was always walking near there with a gun on his shoulder. All the travelers going west could see these bodies hanging there from the scaffold. The Cheyenne was hanged with the ball and chain with which he was manacled, and it was not long till the body was decayed and the ball, from its weight, pulled the limb off. So, he hung there for two months after with one limb.[4]

The sight of this incensed the Indians to an attitude of revolt. There was a division of opinion, or stand, among them. Some were for the signing of a new treaty then being talked of. Others said the treaty of 1851 was the only treaty they wanted to live up to. The treaty signers hung around the agencies living on rations, while those who wanted to retain their land as it was pulled out on their travois to live by hunting as they always had done. Red Cloud, the Oglala, and Spotted Tail had been to Washington. They had seen the multitude of the white people and were in favor of making another treaty.[5] Crazy Horse had been appointed chief by the Oglalas out in Wyoming. He was young, brave, and full of fire; he had been in many battles and was affiliated with the Cheyennes and Arapahos for a number of years.

According to the pictograph records of different tribes of Sioux, this was one of the most strenuous years for them. Battles had to be fought all over their country and endless trains of emigrants were still passing through Laramie every day. Some mornings we awoke to find a city of white tents. They were armies sent out to explore the country; some were going west. Telegraph lines had already been established from coast to coast. A big battle had been fought at Killdeer Mountain by the Sioux against Sully in 1864. That fall, the Crows had stolen nearly all their horses. The Santees had trouble in Minnesota, which drove them into Dakota with the soldiers after them. There had been a battle at White Stone Hill. At Laramie there were a thousand white tents and cavalry horses ready to push into the Indian country. Red Cloud and his Cheyenne allies had been burning out settlers and raiding below Laramie in 1864, which brought out more people under the escort of armies, although peace had been negotiated with the Cheyennes and Arapahos. But the Assiniboines came against the Sioux, and in the battle ten were killed. The Red River half-breeds were coming more and more into the Sioux territory as game grew more scarce. At Tongue River they dug entrenchments when the Sioux besieged them; only a few of these got away by climbing a steep hill. While in the eastern part of the country peace was being preached to the Indians, way out in the Powder River country soldiers were making war on the Indians: Cole and Walker against the Sioux, while Connor was punishing the Cheyennes.

The Indians knew as well as anyone that if peace was accepted it would mean extinction, it would mean peace at a terrible cost, it would mean death and destruction and the end of the race. Their land was coveted and would sooner or later be taken. The wild game over a thousand hills that meant life to an Indian would be all a thing of the past. The wild life of roaming in fresh fields free from diseases, camping on the perfume of new-grown flowers, the pure air of the prairie, the breath of the pines and sparkling streams—what God had given the children of the prairies—would have to be exchanged for goods that they were not used to, foods that did not satisfy, foods robbed of the natural vitamins, minerals, and proteins.

The healthiest meat that humans could subsist on was the dried meat cured the way the Indians cured it. The meat cut in thin sheets and hung on poles was dry in an hour. That is, the surface got hard within an hour in the wind so that no flies or germs could penetrate it. Meat cured this way would never be the cause of sickness nor scurvy. It made as good a soup as anyone would want. In those days, when the Indians lived near to nature, sickness was scarce. There were no such a thing as obese persons, only in very rare cases.

Their diet was not always meat. There were many kinds of wild fruit gathered and dried through the summer which made a variety in the menu. Every kind of wild fruit was dried, such as cherries, plums, grapes, Juneberries, wild apples, buffalo berries, that was cooked in the winter in several ways. There were also wild vegetables: wild turnips, wild rice, sweet corn, dried squash. Everything was kept dried, which seems the healthiest way. There was no such a thing known as death from ptomaine poisoning by eating these simple foods.[6]

Since the Sioux came into the possession of the western country, which was ceded to them by the treaty of 1851, there had been a constant battle—sometimes three or four times a year—to keep possession. It was a battle with all the other tribes that surrounded the great Tongue and Powder River basin, the richest game country in the whole world.

And east as far as the Missouri, orders came to Fort Laramie to move what Indians were living around Laramie to the Missouri River at a point where the treaty annuities and rations could be brought up in boats and issued. The hanging of Two Face and Black Foot was not so easily forgotten by the Indians. They were in an ugly mood. Perhaps, if they had been allowed to bury their dead, it might have been different. But fifteen days after the hanging, the Indians were ordered to move on to the Missouri River.

The commanding officer appointed my father Assistant Indian Agent.

My father left a hired man in charge of his place and was taking his family along in his own team and wagon. All the half-breeds and white men having Indian families were included in this issue of annuities. They were all in the procession under the escort of only one troop of cavalry. There was never any thought that these Indians would revolt. The Oglalas and Brulés were a western prairie people; they never wanted to live along the Missouri River. They were made to go there against their will. It was believed by them that this was another scheme to get them out of their own country, a scheme to draw them to the desolate barren breaks of the Missouri River country.

On Sunday, June 11, 1865, the journey to the Missouri River was started from Laramie with two thousand Indians consisting of many lodges of Sioux. These were mixed remnants of the Oglala and Brulé, the most friendly of all Sioux, who were called Agency Indians by the wild bands who were living in Wyoming and Montana. The first camp was made at my father's place, called the Bordeaux Ranch. Next day, a fifteen-mile march was made to Cold Springs; everything seem to run smooth. I was then about eight years old, going on nine, and could remember everything very plainly. Next day, on June 13, camp was pitched on Horse Creek. It was a beautiful day, and as the camp was pitched early we children got out and played all along the shores of Horse Creek. At this time of the year the stream was swollen and deep and hard to cross unless one knew just where the rocky crossing was. There were Indians out there on horseback driving sharpened saplings into the ground along where the rocky crossing was. The poles were driven in the water in a slanting way across the river; the water was so high it came over the horses' backs even on the rocky crossing. We children didn't know why this was done till long after the trouble was over. These saplings put across in the water was to guide the Indians across. The soldiers didn't know why the poles were there or what significance they bore in regard to crossing the river.

Captain Fouts was a man who did not understand the nature of Indians, who were wild and suspicious, even of those who would befriend them. It was a hard matter to keep them at peace. Spotted Tail, Red Leaf, Iron Shell, Swift Bear, White Thunder, and other friendly chiefs were in this party. The annuities from the treaty were to be brought up near the Platte or the Missouri River, where the Indians were to be taken to receive it. Captain Fouts was harsh and severe with the Indians. He rode around the camps with his orderly and ordered them to make haste and gave sharp commands. He rode around two or three times talking in loud and impatient tones, swearing at them for taking their time. And Charley Elston wasn't a bit slow in repeating what the captain had to say. The captain was a red-faced, bald, gruff, heavyset man and was a heavy drinker. I knew this because he came to my father's ranch several times when my father had to put him to bed to get him sobered up and we children had to play away from the house to not awaken him.[7]

The Indians were feeling pretty sore over the hanging of Two Face and Black Foot anyway. While the captain was riding back, someone from the camp shot him off his horse. Then confusion started, rifle fires spat in sharp reports everyplace; it was a regular running and scurrying battle. My father and all the mixed-blood families were placed behind where the soldiers' wagons stood. Our wagon had already been hitched up as well as the other mixed-blood families'. They all drove to the military wagons. The Indian men were on horseback making short rushes against the soldiers. The bullets were whizzing over our heads. My father was trying to restrain the soldiers, saying it would be over with. My brother Louis ran to the wagon and pulled out a rifle and ran to the front in defense of the wagons. He fired away and, as White Thunder turned, he shot him in the foot. My father saw what Louis had done and came and took the gun away from him.

Just as it was planned, the families of Indians all got across the Platte, guided by the saplings stuck in the river. As the families were safe, the Indians quit fighting the soldiers and went across the Platte, pulling up the guide poles after them. The soldiers started after them, but they tried to go straight across the stream and, getting into washouts and whirlpools, they nearly drowned one or two of their horses and men, so they turned back.

It seems as though this was plotted when the trip was started. Some of the Indians wanted to wipe out the entire troop after they got far enough away from Laramie, but the chiefs held them back. They waited till they got to where it was difficult to cross before they started the fight. Those that planned the trouble did it for revenge. After the trouble, the Indians scattered by the bands in all directions.

The soldiers had eight prisoners who were still being held after so many months in custody, who had been in the same band as Two Face and Black Foot.[8] The Indians captured seven of these; they put them on horses so they got away with ball and chain fastened to their legs. Except Osape. He was lame from the ball and chain; his leg was all swollen so that he was allowed to lay in the military wagon, still manacled. The soldiers were so infuriated when they found out they could not cross the river in pursuit of the fleeing Indians that when they came back from the crossing, when they saw Osape lying there in the wagon, they shot him full of holes.

Osape was one of the prisoners held who was of the Two Face band.[9] His feet were manacled in irons. After the soldiers retreated they came back to the wagons which were already corralled by the teamsters (Beauvais, Pallardy, Iott, Robinson, Bordeaux, La Deau, Moran, Schmit, Du Bray, La Beau, Bridgman) and there were ten or twelve wagons of the soldiers. Some of these white men married to Indians had ox teams, mule teams, and horses that were all driven away by the Indians. A deep, round trench was dug where all the families were placed. When the soldiers came back after they retreated for about two miles back to the corralled wagons, old Osape was led out. Two soldiers shot him, but did not kill him, so Osape sat up. Now, a sergeant who had an arrow in his thigh and one sticking in his head came up and said, "Why didn't you do your job right?" He lifted his revolver and shot Osape through the head. The sergeant tried to take his scalp but couldn't with his pocketknife. Pallardy cut the scalp and jerked it off.

Mrs. Fouts and her two daughters who were on this trip screamed and cried over the captain, but whoever shot him had a good aim, got him through the heart. My brother told me there were four killed— the captain and three privates—and five wounded. Mrs. Fouts begged the soldiers to kill every full-blood Indian in sight. Now, among the mixed-bloods, there was Green Plum. He was a widower; he had lost his daughter-in-law and son. There were four small children he was taking care of. Another daughter was married to a French man by the name of Iott, who was along on this trip.[10] Green Plum made his home with his daughter. He took his four grandchildren by the hand and moved up in front of the soldiers. He pointed at Mrs. Fouts and said, "I am a full-blooded Sioux. I am alone in this world with these little orphans who have neither father nor mother. If it is your wish to see us killed, now is your chance. We don't fare the best in this world anyway. We might as well be out of the way." But Mrs. Fouts relented and would not allow it. If Green Plum had been killed, there would have been a battle right there with the mixed-bloods and the soldiers.

As the Platte River rose higher and crossing was impossible at Horse Creek, the army went as far as Fort Mitchell and returned to Laramie. It became dangerous for the fur traders to stay on their ranches. The Indian warriors traveled in small bunches all over the country rustling horses and cattle in retaliation for all the buffaloes that were slaughtered and the carcasses left on the prairies to decay. All the fur traders and their mixed-blood families moved to Fort Laramie for protection. There was Bissonette, Herman the blacksmith, some women whose husbands were out in the mountains west working: Mrs. Ostroder, Mrs. Robinson, Mrs. Bigler, Mrs. Julia Burnett—these are all I can remember. There were several other families I cannot recall. The American Fur Company occupied the Beauvais ranch after they sold the Laramie post to the United States.

That winter, my father went back to his place at Sarpy's Point and nearly all the mixed-blood families moved there with us. My father had many warehouses and storerooms that were empty, so they moved right into these places. The stockade was still in good condition.

The winter of 1865 and 1866 was passed without much trouble. My uncle Swift Bear had joined the Santee relatives of the Sissetons who were then wintering at Crow Creek, South Dakota. Red Cloud moved up to Crawford, Nebraska, and Spotted Tail went on to Beaver Creek, Nebraska, at Camp Robinson.[11] Red Cloud was out in Wyoming and was not in the Horse Creek battle. The Oglala and Brulé who had joined the hostiles were still raiding; they raided all along the Platte and down on the Republican River for a radius of two or three hundred miles. My father lost all his horses and cattle; two hundred head were taken at the time of the Horse Creek battle. My father stayed on his ranch at Sarpy's Point till the treaty of 1868. After this, as subagent, he took what Brulés there were under Big Mouth to Whetstone Agency on the Missouri, while Spotted Tail was hunting out west during the winter. Spotted Tail killed Big Mouth in 1869. Here at Whetstone, whiskey was smuggled in to the Indians; there was murders and fights.

Along the Platte, grass was scarce. At Horse Creek, Father lost all the cattle, and horses were scattered all over. Among some straying back, there were ten head of our milk cows. One was limping along with an arrow sticking in its side. My mother and Mrs. Robidoux got them back. He sold the wounded cow to the soldiers. About thirty head of mares and colts came back to my father's range. These had sneaked away from the place they were driven to. All the French men with Indian families, of which there were about three hundred living up and down the Platte, suffered from these raids. The Janis horse ranch up on White River, Robidoux on Horse Creek, Ward on the Platte, Peter La Grant, Beauvais—all lost some stock.

Ward's place was ten miles above Laramie on the Platte. He married a beautiful woman of the Wajaja band. Her name was Wasna. I can't help but mention the sad story of her life. She was sold to Mr. Ward; she had four children by him. She had loved a young brave, but being a woman she had no choice but to be sold to benefit her brothers. Whenever Ward went with his furs to Nebraska City, which was the trading point in later years, he stayed so long, sometimes six months as all the traders used to do. She met her sweetheart of old and ran away with him, leaving the children with her mother. When Ward got back, he was furious to think Wasna would desert her children. He swore he would get her back and his mother-in-law sided with him. He hired a family to go up to the Powder River country to go after her and bring her back. Wasna's mother put in several messages to her. In a month she was brought back. She never tried to run away anymore but she grew thinner and droopy and just pined away. When she died, my mother and some other women went to Ward's to bathe her and dress her for her burial. When they undressed her they found the otter fur that her lover had worn on his hair, bound next to her body. She had died of love. There were many tragedies at Laramie in those old days.[12]

The winter of 1865 and '66, when all the mixed-blood families camped at Laramie, it was not always gloomy. We got rations regularly. The soldiers would all chip in and get up a dance. There were many fiddlers among the half-breeds and soldiers. There were quite a number of half-breed girls, all dressed up in bright calico with ribbons in their hair and on their waists, that could fly around in a quadrille as well as anybody, stepping to the music in their moccasined feet. There were many little girls my size that were right in the swing as well as myself. Stick candy and ginger snaps were passed around. We were just as happy and enjoyed it as much as if we were dancing in marble halls with chandeliers with their brilliant rays, as the candles' lights we loved.

Among the fur traders there were many who were artists with the violin; pretty near every Frenchman could play. These people seem to be born for gaiety and music; it is life with them and they are never as happy as when the music was on the air and a crowd of people were moving to its rhythm. There was a dance every week and we half-breed girls were always there to get in on the candy and ginger snaps. Sometimes the emigrant women and men would join in, play the music and dance. I have heard many different calls from all the different states; they all had different calls for the same dances. It was the only sport that the old-timers enjoyed. Many times some of the older men were called out to the center to step off a jig to fast music and they sure could do it to perfection.

One of the saddest things at Laramie, there was a young half-breed girl left with some girls to go up to the store in the garrison. While they were up there, some of the soldier boys invited them to dinner. They spent more time up there than was necessary, so when the girls returned, this certain girl, Olewiŋ [Looks for Woman], was scolded by her mother. She told her she could not go up to the garrison again, that it was no place for her, and I guess the mother was a little too offensive. The girl resented what her mother said; she picked up a rope and went away toward the woods. The mother didn't think anything of it as Olewiŋ often brought wood home with a rope. Some children were playing near the river and saw a scarlet object in the trees above the water further up river. When they got there, it was Olewiŋ. She had hanged herself. She was cut down, rolled in a scarlet blanket and put on a tree grave. This tree was a lone cedar tree that grew out of the gray bluffs near Laramie high above the bottom timber. The scarlet blanket could be seen a long distance by every traveler that passed. It was not long till the skeleton fell to the earth.

In 1865, when Father DeSmet came to Laramie, it was the first part of August. I remember we children had been picking cherries in the timber; this was after we came back to Laramie from Fort Mitchell. Father DeSmet was the guest of the commanding officer. As soon as the good Father arrived and took a survey of the surroundings, he could see the Indian bodies hanging from the scaffold, dangling in midair. Every hard wind that blew just swayed them back and forth. The Cheyenne young man had a large silver Mexican medallion tied up in his black handkerchief around his neck. As he swung in the wind it shone bright and glistening like a looking glass against the sun. Father DeSmet got permission to give a Christian burial.

When the Father put on his scapular, with two boys to hold the incense and holy water to perform the requiem mass at the burial, all of us children followed in the rear of the procession to the burial. The grave was dug and the skeletons were drug into it. They were covered with new blankets and the earth was piled over them. This act was reported among all the different tribes of Sioux and they were grateful to the Father for this act of respect and kindness. During Father DeSmet's stay at Laramie, there were many baptized. Many were white children of the garrison, as there were many soldiers who had wives who did laundry work for the soldiers. And many of the French half-breed and Indian children were baptized.

Before 1854, when the Grattan Massacre happened, there had been perfect peace among the Indians and the fur traders who had mingled with them in the hunting grounds. There were vast herds which roamed the prairies and furnished all the needs of the Indians. The Laramie Plains were the richest region in the world for the sustenance of the Indian. The country was dear to them. The waving grass, the sparkling streams, the wooded hills were filled with life-giving foods that the red man appreciated more than gold. But the arrival of the gold-crazed emigrants and the discoveries in California and the gold coast came like a living avalanche sweeping before it all that the Indian prized. They followed the streams up the South Platte to Salt Lake and up the North Platte over to Sweetwater and beyond the continental divide and up Green River. The devastation of the game! Many of these emigrants knew they were on Indian soil. They were armed to the teeth. A great many started shooting before they were attacked, which caused the Indians to attack, to scalp and mutilate, resolving to stay the tide of the encroachment at any cost.

Agent Twiss, who was the military agent at Laramie, was very much pleased with the friendly and peaceful conditions of the Indians at Laramie while he was agent.[13] He knew that Spotted Tail, Swift Bear, and their bands remained faithful to the government. It is always those who are in charge that have poor judgment and are incompetent to carry the work with the Indians entrusted to them.

After the Grattan Massacre, my father was ordered by the commanding officer to bury the soldiers who were killed, as the Indians were in an ugly mood. My father, being a trader and married into the tribe, was never molested. He took his ox team and plowed out two long trenches about five or six feet deep. Into these trenches the soldiers were laid. My father took a large, dry buffalo hide hitched to the neck yoke of the oxen. The dead bodies were rolled on the robe. He hauled three or four at a time, laying them carefully in their last resting place with the help of his hired men. When all the bodies were placed in the grave side by side, my father bladed the dirt over them, then hauled large, flat sandstones from a distance and covered the graves. While the work was going on, we children from several families edged up to see the sight, gruesome as it was.[14] Lieutenant Grattan's body had many arrows in it; the others also had many.

My father also helped to bury the soldiers killed on Horse Creek. These lay in separate graves rolled in their blankets without any coffins. Flat rocks were also placed over these so wolves nor coyotes would not dig the bodies up. For many years travelers could see these graves as they passed by them. No one ever disturbed the soldiers' graves.[15]

Fort Fetterman had been attacked and burned down. Then Connor's whole command camped at Laramie. Major Powell's command had went on up the Platte. Colonel Sawyer's command, with the surveying engineer corps, camped at Laramie. The Indians around the agency did not know why all these thousands of emigrants and soldiers were daily passing here. It was reported that Spotted Tail visited the camp of soldiers to inquire where they were going. He was told the expedition was going up to Powder River to build forts. He listened to all that had to be said and at length said, "You tell them that Red Cloud is up there. He has sworn to stand in the way when you soldiers get there. Tell them they will have to watch out for their hair."

That fall was the most dangerous time for travelers. Connor, Cole, Walker, Reynolds, and Sawyers expeditions were fighting.[16] The Indians could not understand why the soldiers were out against them. In the Grattan and Harney massacre it was self-defense; the Indians were forced to fight. It couldn't be considered revenge that [the soldiers] wanted. Messages were coming in every day at Laramie of how the battles were fought and who was killed.

George Stead, a half-breed boy, was enlisted at Laramie for a mule skinner; he was with the Carrington command. So was Jim Bridger. Both were frontiersmen capable and brave. Lieutenant Fetterman was fresh from West Point and was full of enthusiasm for Indian battles; he was going to get Red Cloud's scalp to show his friends back east. He had often expressed utter contempt for the Indians with their bows and arrows. Jim Bridger answered him one time, so Jack Steel told us, "Lieutenant," said he, "you are a pretty young man and it seems too bad, but let me tell you when you go out and fight Injuns, I reckon it will be your first one and your last one."

Lieutenant Fetterman was so mad at Bridger that when he went out to the hills where the woodchoppers were fighting Indians, he would not take Jim Bridger along. But Jim Bridger, George Stead, and the other mule driver had to go after the bodies after the Indians had killed them.

The men found the bodies all stiff and frozen and, as there were only four wagons with high wagon boxes, the bodies had to be all stood upright, all packed as tight as they could get them. When they drove into the fort in this manner, George said there was a terrible commotion, but such was the fate of most of the soldiers who fought in the Indian country.[17]

2

The year of 1865 was perhaps one of the most dangerous years. There was fighting everywhere along the Platte and Powder Rivers. There were about two thousand Indians under the military at Laramie. These Indians got some rations from the commanding officer; it was hard to give so much to them. To bring provisions overland five or six hundred miles was a tremendous undertaking as dangerous as it was on the roads, but it was an order from the Department to feed all the Indians who surrendered and remained peaceable at the fort. The military could not haul food fast enough.

There was never any winter freighting done as the weather was too uncertain and the distance too far. There were never any travelers on the Oregon Trail after November. The country from Laramie to the Missouri River was one vast field of endless snow, forever drifting. There was no range open for stock to feed. There were no animals living that could break their way through the drifts across the country to Laramie. Even mail was not brought in through the winter—the military did all their communication by wire. The emigrants never attempted to travel till the last part of May, when grass was fairly high enough for stock to graze. Even after the way stations were built, which the Indians continually burned out, the winter mail did not reach its destination for two or three months at times. All travel in and freighting was done through the summer months when grazing was good and the animals could stand it. At Washington, the War Department did not seem to understand this great difficulty. Fort Laramie was not equipped with the facilities to feed two thousand Indians. And some of these would come in to visit their relatives, and as soon as rations were received, they went right back out to the wilds of Powder River again.

Some of these Indians, the Brulés and Oglalas, had been out attacking the telegraph parties from the garrison. Some had been taking a part in the Platte Bridge attack by the Cheyennes west of Laramie. There were many of these Indians among the friendlies who had been raiding emigrants since May, when the emigration started, with the Cheyennes—

both on the North Platte and the South Platte. At the Platte Bridge fight, Chief Young Man Afraid of His Horses and his band were the principal leaders with the Cheyennes. The chiefs of the Cheyennes being Little Wound, Wild Hog, White Shield, Tangle Hair, and others. These bands of Sioux and Cheyennes had been at the fight at Sand Creek.[18]

Four Antelope had been hanging at Laramie all spring. Then, about the last part of May, Two Face and Black Foot were hanging right beside him.

At Laramie the complaint was strong about feeding so many Indians. The complaint reached the War Department, it seems, for one day my father came home from the garrison saying all the Indians had to be removed to the Missouri River, where transportation of annuities and provisions would be made as promised by the treaty. The Indians were sullen and unwilling. They thought it was a scheme to get them away from their own country, the country they had been promised to hold unmolested by the government—a scheme to gradually transport them to some hot country where they would all die off like some of the tribes who were taken to Oklahoma and Florida.

The Indians who had been hanging on around the garrison were accused of being stupid, accused of saying yes to everything proposed by the government, of being foolish and bewildered by the soft, sweet food fed to them by the military. The hostiles were more alert and suspicious of the good intentions of the government. They knew the government wanted control of them so they could take away their hunting grounds. They were not used to the white man's food. They saw only extinction in the future.

The night before the Indians were prepared to start on their way to the Missouri, there was a meeting among the very select warriors. The friendlies were not notified of this meeting. It was said that the plans were made that night. There could be no revolt at this garrison; they planned on being willing to go till they were far enough away so the handful of soldiers who accompanied them could be easily whipped. These Indians, as friendly as they were, did not want to give up the wonderful Powder River basin, nor the Black Hills which held enough game so that the Indians could live independently for years and years to come if the white men could be kept out of it.

Right at the time when the Indians were to be taken away, there were three thousand emigrants camping on the Laramie Plains waiting for a military escort. On account of the two spare companies going with the

Indians, the emigrants had to wait. Reports were coming every day of the Cheyennes and Sioux raiding up and down the Platte. There was no grazing at all at Laramie for a radius of two or three miles surrounding the post; cattle and horses were herded out to the south with heavy guards and all stock was brought in at night, corralled with guards. The majority of the hostiles were out along the Yellowstone, and the agency Indians were at their respective agencies.

The road that led east from Laramie was on the south side of the Platte. The military led in the procession, the Seventh Iowa Cavalry with Captain Fouts in charge. There were over 120 men on horses; there were about ten army wagons with drivers and extra men who helped in the work of pitching tents and cooking. Right behind the army wagons were the fur traders who had Indian families. Each of these had two or three wagons, a driving team and ox teams with heavy wagons carrying all their possessions. There were about fifteen of these half-breed families. These half-breed families had large herds of horses; each of these men had different breeds of horses they were specializing in. Iott had a beautiful stallion; the horse was a pinto, a blue spotted, darker spots all over. One might compare him to a spotted bean. There were many young half-breed boys on horseback driving the horses and cattle. My father had a nice bunch of milk cows in the herd. The Indians had many horses too, being driven in among the herd, so there were over a thousand head of horses and about five hundred head of cattle. Beauvais was a man who had a nice team—very rich. My father also had much stock.

The camps were made at short distances. When Horse Creek was reached, the soldiers went on across half a mile beyond the creek. Then the half-breed families also went on across about a mile east of the creek. The Indians did not cross Horse Creek. They camped in a wide circle on the west side of the creek, but right near the Platte River. Now, as it was a June raise, the Platte River was wide and turbulent. The Indians knew where the rocky bottom crossings were, and saplings had been driven above this place so the Indians would know just where to cross triangularly across the Platte. When the time came to start after a night's camp, the commanding officer came with Elston, the interpreter. Being impatient with the Indians in their reluctancy, he spoke loud and severe as the Indians understood it. The interpreter, who was a white man married to a Sioux woman, was not backward in telling the Indians.

As the captain was giving orders in an irritable way, someone shot him with an arrow right through the heart. As he fell off his horse, several jumped on their horses and started in pursuit of the escort, who were killed in a running fight. Elston was also shot at, but not killed. Then, the young men were instructed to run the horse herd home to the Indian camp. The cavalry had already marched on ahead; also, the military wagons had already started. My father took the lead; the rest followed. These were a quarter of a mile across the creek. Quickly, the wagons were formed in a corral, the half-breeds' wagons facing the west so they would shield the military. Some half-breed [men] were in the camp—and a half-breed young woman. All these started running for the wagons with Indians chasing them. The woman was last. She had on a red calico dress and a red shawl. The arrows sent after her blew up the dust all around her, but none struck her. She reached the corral of wagons safe.

The men at the wagons were working fast on a round ditch about sixteen feet across. The warriors, all mounted, attacked the wagons. They made short rushes and in the meantime the cavalry were running their horses to the corral. Now, most of the half-breeds, who had camped directly south of the camp of Indians, who were already hitched up, also started for the wagon corral in a helter-skelter manner. Beauvais was in a light buckboard, driving and urging the ox teams using his long blacksnake whip, driving from one ox team to another, and the oxen were galloping. His loaded gun was between his knees.

The warriors came to head off the soldiers from the hastily put up wagon corral, but they were too late; the soldiers had got into the enclosure. They came stringing in and attacking them. The warriors would make rushes on the wagons; I think this was done to hold them there till the travois got across the Platte. There were many of the Indians who missed the marked crossing and nearly drowned in the deeper part. Swift Bear, my uncle, was looking after the crossing of the people. One of his own boys was in a whirlpool; he had to rush in to help him and nearly lost his life himself, but no one drowned. They all got across safe while the warriors held the soldiers in the corral. It appears as though the soldiers had not been issued any ammunition. The Indians had already took possession of the herd of horses and cattle. One of the warriors in the rushing attacks was riding Sefroy Iott's prize spotted stallion. When he saw his beautiful stallion he began to point at it and cry like a whipped baby.

Captain Wilcox, who had just got in and found out what the trouble was about, mustered out his men and started after the Indians with many rounds of ammunition just taken out of the wagons. But the Indians were hurrying north and the soldiers did not know just where to cross. Some got into the water and nearly drowned their horses.[19]

From Camp Mitchell, a wire was sent to Laramie. Colonel Moonlight, who was in command there, got out a strong force of cavalry to follow the Indians. The chiefs had no control of their warriors at all. About twenty head of my father's cows broke away and were straying back when they were found. It might have been that my uncle Swift Bear, knowing our milk cows, cut them out and shoved them back so that we could find them. When my father and my folks got home to Sarpy's Point, we found some of our old mares with their colts back on their range south of the Platte. All the mixed-bloods and white men who lost stock on this trip put in their depredation claim for their stock and were paid by the government later.

My uncle Swift Bear said they were making for the sandhills of Nebraska when the signal riders came in and said the soldiers were following their trail. Preparations were made to go back and meet these soldiers. The Indians watched the soldiers from behind bunches of grass, the travois being sent on ahead with the older men. When the military horses were turned out to graze, while the men were eating dinner, the rush was made. The Indians were lying low on their horses, the military horses being driven away. A few horses were picketed and were saved, about a dozen. Some of the horses were dragging picket lines. Some of the Indians followed the soldiers for a day and a night trying to steal the rest of the horses, but there was no attack made. The friendly chiefs restrained them from doing so. As the Indians outnumbered the soldiers, they could have succeeded in making a night attack, if it were not for the older chiefs.[20]

After the horses were divided, part of the Indians went west to join the Cheyennes, while most of the friendlies went to Fort Thompson, where the Santees and Cuthead Yanktonais were placed on that agency. Some horses were traded to the Yanktons and Santees for sugar, coffee, and other provisions and powder and ammunition. After the trading was done, the Brulés and Oglalas came back west, north of the Black Hills, and wintered there.

This was the beginning of the time when the government wished to place the Indians along the Missouri River for the purpose of reaching them with the annuities. It was only a year or two after this that the railroad was built into Nebraska as far as Sidney. This moving the Indians from place to place was a useless expense for the government.

After the battle, the soldiers that were killed were buried in a row, wrapped in blankets, along the banks of the Platte River east of Horse Creek. There were never any markers on their graves as far as I knew. These were later sent to Iowa. Captain Fouts's body was washed clean. All the arrows were taken out and he was taken to Fort Mitchell for burial.

All the white men with Indian families and the half-breeds were escorted to Fort Mitchell by the military. The soldiers went back to Laramie, but we stayed on at Mitchell, waiting for the Indian agent to arrive, not knowing if we should go on to the river or not. The Indian agent finally arrived in ten days, advising us to go back to Laramie. We went back and camped at Laramie all winter.

A few days after the battle, some Pawnee scouts were sent with a message to Laramie. On their way they had to pass Horse Creek. These Pawnees saw a person walking toward the river. Thinking it was a Sioux, they whipped their horses to see who would count the first coup. This person went down to the river. The Pawnees hunted everywhere, but all they could find was the person's tracks. They were the strangest tracks; there were only stubs. Whoever it was had to walk on stubs. Whoever it was must have crawled into a beaver hole. Many years later, Chief Big Mouth was inquiring for his mother, who had stub feet. They were frozen off in her younger days. In the excitement, she somehow was forgotten, her son being at the battle front. She was never seen again. Her tracks made there at the mouth of Horse Creek was the only thing ever heard of.

In regard to Captain Wilcox taking after the Indians, there was no such a thing.

Now, what prevented the Indians from killing all the soldiers that day was the mixed-blood families. They were related to the Indians like my uncle Swift Bear, my mother's brother, who were on the opposing forces. When the soldiers came after their dead, the Indians chased them again back to the wagon corrals. No one dared to get out of the corral as at any time an attack was feared. So there was no more attempts made. We were in that corral all night. Next day we went to Fort Mitchell.

That night, Haŋskerca, a brother-in-law of my uncle Swift Bear, who was mourning for his wife and was hunting at the head of Horse Creek, came to our tent over the wagon and asked my father what was the matter. He told him of the trouble and directed him which way to go, all in whispers.

Good Voice [Ho waśte] and Coarse Voice were Indian hunters kept at Fort Mitchell with their families. These were taken to Omaha.[21] All single women were to be taken. Mrs. Robidoux was a widow and would have been taken, but she told that she was Beauvais's wife, although such was not the case. So she also went back with us.[22]

The following spring, Tom Dorian, an interpreter, and Green Plum, with some others, were sent out to bring Swift Bear, Spotted Tail, and the Brulé bands in to Laramie.[23] On the way back Spotted Tail's daughter died. All the men rode in to Laramie. My father had to give several of them clothing. The camp was at Cottonwood Creek. My father escorted the chiefs and principal men into the garrison. At this time I saw Pehiŋziwiŋ given a military burial. I was with my mother. All the Indians were given rations and clothing.

CHAPTER ELEVEN

My Early Days

I went to school at Hamburg, Fremont County, at my father's expense.[1] My father bought a large residence in that little town. My mother was with us, with her four children. We were the only Indians among about one hundred white children. My father paid for our tuition to go to summer school. We went to school here from 1864 till 1871. My mother stayed only one year with us; she returned to Laramie. She was there when the treaty was made in 1868. My older sister conducted our home after this. Our home was one of the most beautiful places built by a southern gentleman. It was surrounded by magnificent trees and shrubbery bearing blossoms. The grounds were plotted out with perennial flowers; the lawns were always green.

After I came back from the school of Hamburg, Iowa, we came back to Whetstone Agency. Major Poole was then the Indian agent; he appointed two of his daughters and I to teach the agency school. It was a very hard matter to get the Indian children interested. I was the interpreter in the school. The school was very irregular. Sometimes all the children enrolled would come; other days they would not attend unless they felt like it, so our pupils ranged in number from a dozen some days to two or three at other times. The pupils did just what they pleased in the classroom; it was nothing for them to get up and get out whenever they wanted to. Some of the mothers brought their children to school and waited patiently outside of the schoolhouse till school was out. This was the first school to be taught to the Brulés; it was the beginning of school among them.

The school would have continued on, but the agency was moved from here to Nebraska, near Chadron. Then, from there it was moved to Beaver Creek at Camp Sheridan; from here the Brulés were moved to Ponca Agency, and only a year after this they were moved to Rosebud.

There, the Episcopalians came on the reservation as missionaries who built schools at Camp Sheridan, and these missionaries were Mr. W. J. Cleveland, one of the finest men I ever knew, and the two ladies, Miss Sophie Pendleton and Miss Leigh.[2] They went right along with the Indians. There were many camps made during this trip. It took about two months to reach Ponca Agency, but everyone enjoyed it.[3] These missionaries held services and taught school every day. As the camps were made every ten miles, there was a great deal of time to do the instructing.

My father made his home at Wheeler, Charles Mix County, South Dakota. After my father stopped ranching, he took up farming and raised wonderful gardens and grains of wheat, corn, and oats on his homestead, where he stayed for seven years on the north of the Missouri River. During the summer seasons he took contracts to cut hay for the military posts at Fort Randall and Lower Brulé. In the winter months he took contracts to cut cordwood for the fort. He had hired men to do all this work. He was a splendid manager. At one time there was a man who outbid my father in the hay contract. This man fell short in his contract and the military was out of hay early in the winter. My father had to supply the fort with hay after all. My father took the hay and wood contract at Rosebud Agency.

In 1878, he caught cold as the weather was cold and damp. He took pneumonia and died toward the last part of October at sixty-four. My mother continued to live at Rosebud Agency, where she made her home. Six years after my father's death, my mother passed away in June 1884, at sixty-three years old.[4]

Nearly all the French fur traders who had mixed-blood families moved up on the reservations at Rosebud and Pine Ridge where their families had rights from the Laramie country, where, in the earlier years, they had lived and grown.[5] They left behind only memories and graves.

CHAPTER TWELVE

Crazy Horse, Tašuŋka Witco

In 1851, in September, annuities were issued to the Indians. All these articles for issue were hauled in ox teams from the Missouri River, where the goods had been unloaded from steamboats. In 1854, all the annuities to be issued were stored at the Beauvais post, four miles east of Laramie. The American Fur Company owned this place at that time. The things were not issued because the different bands that were entitled had not come in to receive them. These goods are the ones that are said to have been taken after the Grattan Massacre. In 1863, another issue of annuities was made at the Bordeaux Ranch, at Father's place. All the Sioux were there to receive it. In 1864, another issue was made at Ward's place. This place was ten miles above Laramie. These were all the issues that were made that I can remember at Laramie.

In 1868, the treaty had been signed by the agency Indians; the hostiles never signed it. The removal of the Indians was started. The hostiles refused to acknowledge the treaty General Harney made with the Oohenuŋpas at Pierre in 1856. (Most of the hostiles were fighting to keep the soldiers out of the hunting grounds out in Wyoming at that very time.) For the signing of this treaty of the Oohenuŋpa, chief Bear Ribs was killed.[1] The principal chiefs of the Oglalas and Brulés had been taken to see the Oklahoma country to see if they would have their agency down there. The chiefs went down there and came home disgusted; there was no other land that would equal the land that had been theirs for so many years.[2]

At this time, the army held jurisdiction over the Sioux, and there was a dispute about who should hold the rulings of the Indians' affairs.[3] There had been war between the soldiers and Indians, and the War Department were still holding the Indians under its subjection. As no treaty had been made and the military were holding the Sioux under war basis, it was a question whether the civilians should come into the country to make peace with the Indians without military authority or not. However, on September 25, 1865, the Peace Commission arrived at the Missouri River, but this was too late in the fall to get the Indians together.[4] The hostiles would not come in; the treaty was postponed.

After the massacre of Lieutenant Fetterman, Red Cloud would not come in; he was out with most of the Oglalas during the Fort Phil Kearny massacre. These hostiles objected to forts being built on their hunting grounds. In 1870, about forty-two of the head chiefs were taken to Washington on a trip to see the Great Father. All these chiefs were from the different agencies. Red Cloud had come in from Wyoming and was with these chiefs. This was called the Sheridan Treaty. The Upper Brulés moved to where Fort Lookout once stood; the Miniconjous, the Itazipcos and Oohenuŋpas were at Cheyenne River Agency; while the Huŋkpapaya were at Standing Rock—all along on the Missouri River. Spotted Tail and all his chiefs still dwelt in Nebraska, claiming the strip of land north of the Platte to the South Dakota line. The chiefs had been given this opportunity to lay their desires and wishes before the Great Father. The chiefs of the different agencies were accompanied by their agents and interpreters. All Sioux were represented at this time but the Yanktons. Among the agents who went were Major Joseph R. Hanson, who represented the Upper Missouri Sioux, also Fort Thompson and Crow Creek Agency; Major James M. Stone, agent of the Santees of Niobrara; Major Patrick H. Conger, the Yankton agent. The Honorable P. Dole was commissioner of Indian Affairs at that time. There were interpreters of all the different bands of Sioux, some of which were Narcisse Narcel, Alex Recontre, Thomas Flood, Basil Claymore, Louis Agaard, Charles Galpin, Nick Janis, Billy Garnett, Alex Piercson, and some others I cannot recall.[5]

From 1875 to 1878, the government had not been insistent to remove the Indians to points along the Missouri River. Although the treaty of 1868 (which provided that the agencies be removed to the Missouri) had been negotiated by the agency Indians, Spotted Tail was occupying the agency at Beaver Creek, and Red Cloud was only a few miles away near Crawford. They were satisfied to remain there; in fact, they were greatly opposed to moving to the Missouri. In 1876, the Black Hills treaty was concluded, containing a removal agreement.

When the delegates of the Sioux went to Washington in September 1877, they met President Hayes. In his speech to the Indians, he promised Red Cloud and Spotted Tail to hold their agencies where they preferred them out at Pine Ridge and Fort Robinson. And still Spotted Tail refused to move to the Missouri River, as it was too late in the season to make a move—by the time he got back the tribes would be in winter quarters. The Secretary [of the Interior] told Spotted Tail they would have to move, as the boats would reach the Missouri River by October with food and annuities for the winter. It must have been quite an argument, but, finally, the Indians consented to move to the Missouri River agencies for the year then passing—after being assured that they could have their agencies located in the interior of the country the following year.[6]

Rain in the Face [Iteomagaju] was not the Huŋkpapaya chief who belonged to the Huŋkpapaya band, but, perhaps, he was just as much a warrior as the northern man. Rain in the Face was the oldest son of Mniwozaŋ [Drizzle, Mist], an Oglala of the Ite śica band who was married into the Brulé band and lived among them. There were three brothers who were never idle; they were up to something all the time. They did more individual killings than anybody; a white man was not safe out of sight of the agency. We were, at that time, living at Fort Robinson—this was also called Red Cloud Agency. The Custer massacre had taken place and there was danger of war everyplace. The Indians were coming in and going out all the time.

Fort Robinson and the agency got all their freight from Sidney. The mail also was brought to Fort Sheridan and on to Fort Robinson. One day, the mail wagon did not come in when it was expected, nor did it come in next day. An escort was sent out on the mail road. It was discovered that the mail carrier, DeCalb, had been killed, scalped, and robbed of his horses. The freighters on their way also came upon the scene as the soldiers reached there on the Running Water. DeCalb was buried right there on the mail route. DeCalb was not a married man. He had been in the west quite a while, a brave and fearless man who lost his life serving the people in the new country. The Indians around the agency knew DeCalb well. They called him White Beaver [Capaska]. It was known by the Indians that Rain in the Face and his three brothers had killed DeCalb.[7] Such was the country in those perilous times.

The early part of the winter of 1877, Spotted Tail and two hundred men of mixed Brulés and Oglalas went out as peace envoys to bring Crazy Horse in. Boucher, a French interpreter, was taken along in case they met white people or soldiers who might take them to be a war party. Most of these men took their families along; Boucher was married to a Brulé woman who was also among these.[8] Now, at this time, General Jessie M. Lee was the agent at Spotted Tail Agency at Beaver Creek. He was a likable man, large and tall physically, a fine personality. He had told the chief to talk to Crazy Horse and tell him that war was over, that peace had been declared, that most of the tribes were in agencies, that Sitting Bull was still in Canada with about ten chiefs, that he and his three hundred followers were the only ones that were still holding out, that it was useless for him to hold out any longer, that if they didn't come in the soldiers would come out against him, as many of the Sioux had enlisted as scouts in the army. There would have to be a battle again. That he, Spotted Tail, would hate to see this, as he knew that with such a small army as he [Crazy Horse] had to fight against an army of soldiers, it would mean annihilation. Being a brave man, Spotted Tail told him [Crazy Horse] that General Lee would enlist him as a scout to go out against the Nez Percés, as they were rebellious out on the warpath. Spotted Tail succeeded in persuading Crazy Horse to come in. A great many of the chiefs had grown jealous of Crazy Horse's notoriety; among these were Spotted Tail himself and Red Cloud. It was alleged that they were afraid he would be honored higher than they were; he was a much younger man than they were. The terrible tragedy of Crazy Horse's death threw the hostiles in a confusion and a dissatisfaction among them.

I was living at Fort Robinson in 1876 when several chiefs and their bands, about two hundred in number, were to be sent out to get Crazy Horse. They were ordered to make a peace treaty and to get his consent to come to surrender. White Thunder, Spotted Tail, Swift Bear and other chiefs, Black Crow, High Bear, Touch the Cloud, Good Voice, Horned Antelope, and many others were in this peace envoy.[9] When they started out in December 1876, winter had already set in severe. The snow was bad. Spotted Tail and Swift Bear turned into the Black Hills to hunt with their bands, so they were left behind and never did reach Crazy Horse's camp to talk to him. White Thunder, Touch the Cloud, Good Voice, High Bear, Black Crow, and others went on with the interpreters— Boucher, Tom Dorian, Charles Tackett. Now, Touch the Cloud and Crazy Horse were great friends; after the pipe of peace was accepted by Crazy Horse, it settled the matter. He, by smoking with the envoy, was at peace for once and for ever. The peace pipe was considered such a sacred pact that no one ever broke its laws. If they did, they came to grief brought on by their own untruthfulness, for breaking the law of truth. All that was unclean was never practiced with the peace pipe. The white people, little understanding the power of the pipe as something sacred and holy, doubted the veracity of the peace made with the peace pipe. It is often laughed and jested about by them. The peace pipe, like the white man's sacrament, was a symbol of truth and inward grace; its laws were spiritual and not to be desecrated.

When Crazy Horse listened to the promises and words of peace, he set aside all animosity; he gave up fighting as all the rest of his people had done. He knew he and his little handful of followers would not win out. It was not because they lacked courage and bravery; they also knew they were in the right and had a just cause. He knew he was outnumbered by the millions. These people were intelligent human beings who had the mind to think and to act according to their own interests. They did not want to supinely lay down and be trampled over by another race. For years, they had been fighting for this territory and won it from other tribes who were in possession during the days when bows and arrows were used. Now it was guns and gunpowder, and these had to be gotten from the white men.

Swift Bear and Spotted Tail's band came back from the Black Hills in the spring when the snow went away. They had been living good in the Hills on elk, bear, and deer meat, for, in those days, there was plenty. The peace envoy returned the first part of May, and two weeks later Crazy Horse came in with his band consisting of about five hundred souls. They were poor and destitute from having to give up their lodges and camp equipage so many times to the soldiers. I have been told many times about how they had to maneuver to escape contact with the pursuing army. At times, they had to follow the streams to hide their trails, other times they put their lodge poles across two horses' backs so as to not leave any trail—for it was the camp they wanted to capture.

All through the summer Crazy Horse's camp was perfectly contented and satisfied. They were well treated and received rations from Agent Saville, who was there at that time. Wooden Knife's band had been with Crazy Horse; his camp was below at Camp Sheridan not very far.

My husband, Charles Tackett, was a scout, but when he was not on duty he clerked in Jewett's store and had waited on Crazy Horse.[10] My mother-in-law and I drove up to the store one day when Crazy Horse was there. She pointed him out to me. He was a very handsome young man of about thirty-six years or so. He was not so dark. He had hazel eyes, nice long light brown hair; his scalp lock was ornamented with beads and hung clear to his waist; his braids were wrapped in fur. He was partly wrapped in a broadcloth blanket. His leggings were also navy blue broadcloth; his moccasins were beaded. He was above medium height and was slender. He had two wives. His oldest wife, that he had lived with for maybe ten or twelve years, was the sister of Red Feather, who was a very noted man at that time. The last wife, a concubine to the elder wife, was a half-breed woman, her last name being Laravie. It was this last woman who took sick and had to be taken to Spotted Tail Agency—which caused all the trouble and finally led to Crazy Horse's death. At Spotted Tail there lived a medicine man who could cure ailments. To this place Crazy Horse went, not thinking there would be any trouble.[11]

When scout Frank Grouard knew that Crazy Horse had come in, he left Fort Robinson and went to Camp Sheridan to take refuge there under Major Lee.[12] He knew he had done treachery and he feared for his life, though no one had said anything. He gave false interpretations and was lying to the officers who questioned him in regard to Crazy Horse. He wanted to see Crazy Horse put out of the way so he could be free from the fear of losing his life. He succeeded, and it was found out too late. When Lieutenant Clark asked Crazy Horse if he would fight the white people any longer, he replied that he would not, that he was through. Frank told Major Clark and the staff of officers just the opposite. Touch the Cloud reprimanded Frank Grouard about this and called him a liar. Everyone knew that Spotted Tail and Red Cloud were jealous of Crazy Horse and wished him out of the way.

When Crazy Horse was taken to the garrison to make a speech, he did not have much to say, only he told the people that if they were going to smoke the peace pipe, not to break the laws, but carry them out according to the sacred traditions. Spotted Tail then made a speech. After these came to pass, Crazy Horse was led to the guardhouse. Turning Bear stopped to tell Crazy Horse that it was a guardhouse to which they were leading him. The guard with his bayonet stabbed him through the side in a downward glance through his left kidney, downward to the right groin. Little Big Man, a scout, struggled with Crazy Horse, which made matters worse.

The body was given back to the old parents. They sat on the hill opposite the garrison for two or three days. When the orders came from the Department to move the Indians to the Ponca Agency so annuities could be issued to them, the journey was started. The soldier escort went first and the Indians in their travois and the half-breed families in their wagons followed. The stops were made about every ten miles; it took about a month to reach Ponca Agency. It was getting cold then. Crazy Horse's body was carried in a travois till a certain butte was reached. Crazy Horse's niece, Mrs. DeNoyer, told me he was laid on the cliffs under the ledges of Eagle Nest Butte.[13] The old father and mother came with the rest of our people back to Rosebud in the spring. They lived with the Salt Users who camped two miles northwest from the agency. Here, the old mother died two years after Crazy Horse's death and Old Man Crazy Horse died three years after his son's death. They were both buried there along the banks of the Rosebud. It has been said the bones of Crazy Horse were brought back and buried beside his parents.

After Crazy Horse was wounded, he lived till after midnight. My brother Louis Bordeaux stayed with him all night and made hourly reports to Major Jessie Lee. The old parents were also allowed to stay with him till he died in the morning when the roosters were crowing at 1 o'clock.[14]

Crazy Horse was resigned to his fate; he was a warrior and had expected to die in battle sooner or later. He saw the littleness, the jealousy and the aspirations of personal aggrandizement of the chiefs, especially Spotted Tail and Red Cloud, who he thought were easily bought and from whom he had expected more. Many of Crazy Horse's friends and relatives swore vengeance on Spotted Tail, who they considered a traitor to their race in turning Crazy Horse to the army; this vengeance was brought about by Crow Dog, one of Crazy Horse's relatives, four years later.

Crow Dog caught Spotted Tail out alone and shot him. Spotted Tail had just attended a meeting to go to Washington as one of the delegates and was returning. Crow Dog had hauled cordwood to the agency and was returning on the running gears of his wagon when they met about one mile and a half west of the agency. All this trouble was brewing for a long time. Spotted Tail had been breaking tribal laws unlawfully. He had four wives, but, like David of old, when he saw another woman that pleased him, he took the woman. The woman would leave her husband and go. He did this several times, but he had a high standing with the army. About ten days before this meeting, Spotted Tail had taken Mrs. Medicine Bear and went away with her. Medicine Bear was a crippled man, he had a broken hip and was helpless; he depended on this woman, his only help. This last act could not be forgiven. When Spotted Tail's body was brought in and laid out in his beautiful beaded buckskin suit, the insignia of his rank worked on in porcupine, his face was painted red. A piece of suet was placed in his mouth so that his spirit would have plenty. He was buried at the Episcopalian church by Reverend C. B. Clark. Ten years later, the Indians and even the white people took up a collection and a large white marble monument was placed on his grave. He was taken within the enclosure of the cemetery.[15]

The large two-story dwelling house which was built for him by the government was a building of eight rooms and a large veranda extending across the building. The four widows stayed there till they moved and lived in little log cabins along the Rosebud River. The building stood a long time empty—the windows were all broken and the doors—till William Spotted Tail, a foolish, degenerated person, sold the place for three hundred dollars to a white man by the name of Caseneau who bought the buildings and built an oil station. But the place took fire and burned down.

Nearly all of Spotted Tail's blood relatives died of tuberculosis. One by one, the Spotted Tail wives died of old age. There are about three grandchildren living. From these there are about thirteen great-grand-children living. They are scattered at different places on the Rosebud Reservation. Spotted Tail's house stood where the cholera first came to the Brulés, and so many died right on that same flat where his house stood. Years later, many a time, skeletons were dug up as cellars were dug. There is nothing there on the old places where life was so vigorous and young.

CHAPTER THIRTEEN

On the Reservation

Soon after the death of Crazy Horse, the military started to move the Sioux. Of the two tribes, the Oglalas and the Brulés, there were over twelve thousand people. The agency for Red Cloud was to be at the mouth of Medicine Creek about a few miles below Pierre, fifteen miles below Crow Creek Agency (it was to be called Medicine Agency), while the Brulés were installed at the Ponca Agency, Nebraska (the Poncas having been moved to Oklahoma to give their place to the Lakotas). The journey of Red Cloud's people from Pine Ridge was a terrible trip across the country. There were so many women and children and their camp luggage made it difficult. When they were halfway to the Missouri River, the Indians almost revolted again. They stopped and wanted to stay where they were. They wanted the agent at Medicine Agency to send their supplies to them—they were exhausted and could go no further. Their waiting camps were scattered all along White River for a distance of sixty miles, but the Indian agent refused to send any provisions. They were stubborn, but winter began to make its appearance, as it was November, and no more food was in the camps, so, after a few days' rest, the journey was continued. The Oglalas reached Medicine Agency in a freezing northwest storm. The annuities that had been shipped up by boats were there at the agency, to be given out as soon as the Indians arrived. It was only a year or so after the railroad had reached Nebraska, and, had the Indians been left alone, they could have had all their annuities shipped out on the train.

Commissioner E. A. Hayt of Indian Affairs visited the Brulés at Ponca Agency and ordered the Indians not to do any more beadwork, nor to paint themselves, nor to take the ceremonial sweat baths, because, he said, these things did not belong to civilization, that it was foolish and useless. It was not long till Spotted Tail had these new rulings annulled.

Many of the women did beautiful beadwork and got good prices for their work. Their different kinds of work was in demand by the tourists. Spotted Tail thought that if the Indians wanted to paint, they should not be prohibited to do so as all nations had this privilege. He said the white people used white paint; he thought the red people could use red paint if they wanted to.[1]

The Indians lived good in the woods all winter, but, when spring came, the spring fever came right with it. When the year of 1878 came, they talked a lot about what President Hayes had promised them. In the meantime, the authorities at Washington had reconsidered the move of the Indians back to the interior as a bad move and a great expense to the government in hauling the annuities in wagons to the Indians, and it was conceded that the Indians would remain along the river. Both agencies had been built up with warehouses and dwelling houses, but the Indians were determined to go back to their old hunting grounds. They refused to release the President from his promise. Commissioner Hayt had come out to make a last appeal to the Indians to stay where they were.

The Red Cloud Agency was at first to be called Medicine Agency, but this did not go through. The Oglalas drew rations at Lower Brulé Agency; this was about sixty miles above Fort Randall. The trip was something terrible. November had set in cold and stormy and the Oglalas made their winter camp up and down the Big White River. They rode up clear to Lower Brulé Agency to draw their rations and come back the sixty miles to their camp every two weeks. There was a terrible mortality among them. I saw the hundreds of tree graves up and down the river years afterward. The longhorn cattle who ranged in there shoved down most of the bodies to the ground.

Commissioners were sent out to make arrangements for the agencies. Commissioner Carl Schurz came out, then the Stanley Commission, consisting of Major J. M. Haworth and Rev. A. L. Riggs, came, in 1878, to Spotted Tail Agency at the mouth of the Niobrara River. But the Indians were obdurate in returning. So, the plan was agreed on the Rosebud Agency on a branch of the White River. Mr. Pollock became agent in the same year Red Cloud Agency was established at White Clay Creek, which was now called Pine Ridge Agency.[2]

When the day came to put in bids for the transporting of material to build the agencies, the bids were considered too high by Major Pollock. As there had to be wagons and harnesses issued anyway, he ordered these things to be issued at once so the Indians could do their own hauling so as to save a lot of expense and be earning money besides. This was pretty hard at first: the ponies were small, some of them balky, some were runaways; harnesses had to be fixed and adjusted. This took a few days, but it was accomplished. For many years the Indians did their own hauling. This was one of the most influential acts toward civilizing the Indians. They learned to earn money and enjoyed the work. It was not many years till the hauling of the freight came nearer as the railroads came closer. It was all a lot of worry and trouble for nothing.

Until it was finally settled, the country was all in a mix-up. The half-breeds did not want to give up the Laramie country; they were helping to keep the border in a wild state of uproar. In the year of 1868, there was more killing and murder between soldiers, half-breeds, and outlaws that were in a constant turmoil, than ever was caused by the Indians. Peter LaDeau, a young half-breed boy who was herding cattle, was waylaid and killed out of jealousy, right out within sight of Laramie. He was buried in the Laramie Plains in 1868. He was killed by Cy William, Swallow, and Goodwin. The half-breeds of Laramie took it up and went out against the three outlaws that killed LaDeau. Charley Richards was killed and Joe Bissonette was wounded in this battle. Bissonette died from his wound a short time after he killed Cy William and was buried at Beauvais's ranch. LaDeau's body was spoiled before anyone knew what had been done, and he was buried within eight miles of Laramie on the prairie. Charley Richards was killed at the Beauvais ranch, but was buried at Laramie. Charley Richards was the one to kill Cy William.[3] In 1869, Jim McClosky got into trouble with a Mexican.[4] The Mexican shot him. His brother, Toussaint, took it up and killed the Mexican, for which he was hung at Cheyenne. Baptiste Jewett brought the message of the shooting of the Janis boys, for which he was killed by Nick Janis. The brothers were killed by an Indian called Big Head. They were both buried at Laramie.[5] Bill Tucker, who got into trouble with his brother-in-law, was shot and killed. Billy Robinson was shot through jealousy by his cousin. Harsey was also killed. These last three were killed by an Indian who was drunk; all three were buried at Laramie. Afterward, Jim McClosky said, before he died, that he would rather be buried in the land that he loved than to give it up. Some of these boys had fought with and killed the soldiers whom they hated. They were attached to this part of the country.

Red Cloud's agency was moved to White Clay Creek in 1878. Here, substantial buildings were erected and all the seven thousand Oglalas were moved to it, where they were more satisfied. Only half of the Brulés were moved to Rosebud; the other half, called Lower Brulés, stayed at Brulé Agency, or sometimes called Fort Thompson, under a subagent. White Clay Creek is a tributary to White River. Their agency was within fifty miles of the Black Hills. There, the grazing was good with plenty of building material from the groves of pine trees that were scattered on the draws and hillsides. At Rosebud, a beautiful dwelling house was built for Spotted Tail. As head government chief of all the Dakota Sioux he received a salary, as through his influence and example he brought the Indians in from the wilds under the subjection of the U.S. Government and encouraged them to make gardens and to work. The chief's residence was a two-story building with eight rooms and a large council room where the Indians met to have council. Spotted Tail was said to have four wives. Three of these were sisters and concubines to the oldest wife. It was through Spotted Tail's influence that non-reservation schools were put into effect. The children attending day schools did not do so well— it was too near home. There was no interest in learning to read or write nor to talk the English language. Large boarding schools were built. A gristmill was brought to Rosebud. The Indians were hauling freight from the Missouri River, from Whetstone, getting a dollar a hundred pounds. Some of the Indians even worked on the new buildings. Seed was issued and there were wonderful results from the gardens raised. But the Indians had always understood making gardens; it was not new to them. It was an age-old, prehistoric custom for them to plant corn, squash, and beans. Through the winter months, the women did a great deal of beadwork, which brought prices.

It was all a slow, uphill work, this civilizing of the Indians; it could not be done in one generation. It took so much money to bring this Indian question to an orderly running basis for things such as buildings of agencies, dispensaries, warehouses, issue houses, dwellings for employees and farmers. Besides, the transportation of issue goods and annuities and the bringing of hundreds of head of cattle for beef for the tribes clear from Texas amounted to enormous sums of money that ran into the millions. But the peace policy was carried out; raiding, the killing of emigrants, soldiers, and miners was stopped. Thousands of lives were sacrificed. And the money spent for munitions, arms, and armies sent out to annihilate the Indians were used in the peace policy to advance and educate the Indians in a more humane way. Moving the Indians back and forth from one agency to another was the most discouraging. The authorities would move the Indians and, if they were not satisfied, they would hitch the travois and be stringing right out for their old stomping grounds. In this matter, the chiefs had a gigantic work to do to humor the recalcitrant ones, to coax and try to reason with them. Finally, Indian police were made of some of the bravest men in the tribe to control those who were inclined to be hostile. After several were put in the guardhouse for breaking the rules without permission, they began to understand that their roaming days were over, that the reservation life had begun, and, on the non-reservation schools, all the children of the different enemies to our tribes were thrown together to learn to speak to each other. We had to learn the English language.

Lakota Pronunciation and Phonological Key

There are two major orthographies currently in use for writing the oral Lakota language. The older, developed by Eugene Buechel, S.J., at the beginning of this century, was based on the earlier work of Stephen R. Riggs. It has been popularized by the publication, in 1970, of Buechel's Lakota-English Dictionary (*A Dictionary-Oie Wowapi Wan of Teton Sioux*, ed. Paul Manhart, S.J., Pine Ridge SD: Red Cloud Indian School, 1970). More recently, the University of Colorado has developed a written system for Lakota that many feel is superior (see Allan R. Taylor, "The Colorado University System for Writing the Lakhóta Language," in *American Indian Culture and Research Journal* 1 [1975]: 3–12).

For the Lakota words in this text I have employed a simplified version of Buechel's orthography. Three factors led to this choice: (1) the Buechel system is more widely known and used on Lakota reservations, (2) Buechel's dictionary enables interested readers to investigate translations and obtain a more complete and accurate pronunciation, and (3) Buechel was a contemporary of and known to Bettelyoun at Saint Francis on the Rosebud reservation; many of her friends and family members assisted him with translations.

I have taken from Buechel phonetic symbols that significantly affect pronunciation in a way the lay reader, not familiar with more complex linguistic conventions, might find useful. I have not employed diacritical marks that signify differences regarding voiced, aspirated, or glottalized pronunciation in consonants, or those indicating phonetic differences in vowels. Readers desiring this information should refer to Buechel's dictionary.

The following may be useful in the pronunciation of Lakota words:

c is pronounced like "ch"
ś is pronounced like "sh"
ŋ following a vowel, indicates that the preceding vowel is nasalized; the ŋ itself is not pronounced

Lakota Social Organization

The Bettelyoun-Waggoner manuscript makes reference to numerous Lakota bands and subbands, as well as to bands of the Yankton and Santee nations. The accompanying chart is provided to give the reader a simple reference to all these groups, known collectively as the Oceti Śakowiŋ or Seven Council Fires.

For a complete discussion of Lakota/Dakota social organization, see William K. Powers, *Oglala Religion* (Lincoln: University of Nebraska Press, 1975), and James R. Walker, *Lakota Society*, ed. Raymond J. DeMallie (Lincoln: University of Nebraska Press, 1982). Sources contemporary to Bettelyoun add insight to the changing bands among the Lakotas; see especially Stephen R. Riggs, *Dakota Grammar, Texts, and Ethnography*, Contributions to North American Ethnology, vol. 9, ed. James Owen Dorsey (Washington DC: GPO, 1893), and F. V. Hayden, *Contributions to the Ethnography and Philology of the Indian Tribes of the Missouri Valley* (Philadelphia: C. Sherman and Son, 1862). In addition, various annual reports of the Commissioner of Indian Affairs contain lists of Lakota bands, their leaders, and demographics. For information concerning the northern Lakota bands, not detailed here, see Harry Anderson, "An Investigation of the Early Bands of the Saone Group of Teton Sioux," *Journal of the Washington Academy of Sciences* 46 (1956): 87–94.

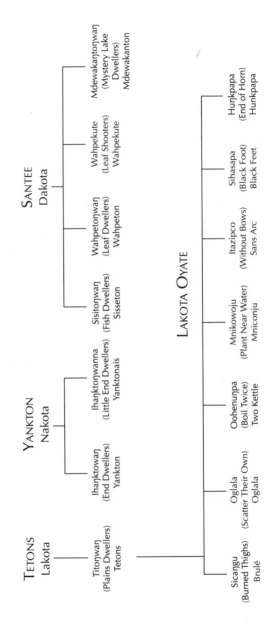

Lakota Social Organization
OCETI ŚAKOWIN
Seven Council Fires

TETONS
Lakota

Titoŋwaŋ
(Plains Dwellers)
Tetons

YANKTON
Nakota

Ihaŋktowaŋ
(End Dwellers)
Yankton

Ihaŋktoŋwanna
(Little End Dwellers)
Yanktonais

SANTEE
Dakota

Sisitoŋwaŋ
(Fish Dwellers)
Sisseton

Wahpetoŋwaŋ
(Leaf Dwellers)
Wahpeton

Wahpekute
(Leaf Shooters)
Wahpekute

Mdewakaŋtoŋwaŋ
(Mystery Lake
Dwellers)
Mdewakanton

LAKOTA OYATE

Sicaŋgu
(Burned Thighs)
Brulé

Oglala
(Scatter Their Own)
Oglala

Oohenuŋpa
(Boil Twice)
Two Kettle

Mnikowoju
(Plant Near Water)
Mniconju

Itazipco
(Without Bows)
Sans Arc

Sihasapa
(Black Foot)
Black Feet

Huŋkpapa
(End of Horn)
Hunkpapa

119

Movement of the Brulé and Oglala Agencies

Throughout her manuscript, Bettelyoun traces the movements of the Brulé and Oglala agencies. She consistently decries the uprooting of her people for the convenience of civil and military authorities. The accompanying map shows the numerous locations of these agencies during the ten-year period from 1868 to 1878.

The best source for information concerning the Brulé agencies is Richmond L. Clow, "The Brule Indian Agencies: 1868–1878," *South Dakota Historical Collections* 36; I have relied on this work for the precise locations of these agencies. For the history and location of the Oglala agencies, the reader is directed to George E. Hyde, *Red Cloud's Folk: A History of the Oglala Sioux Indians* (Norman: University of Oklahoma Press, 1975). See also Ray H. Mattison, "The Indian Reservation System on the Upper Missouri, 1865–1890," *Nebraska History* 36, no. 3 (Sept. 1955).

The various Brulé and Oglala agencies fit into a much larger complex of agencies and superintendencies. The ever-changing labyrinthine structure of the Office of Indian Affairs can be traced in Edward E. Hill, *The Office of Indian Affairs, 1824–1880: Historical Sketches* (New York: Clearwater Publishing, n.d.).

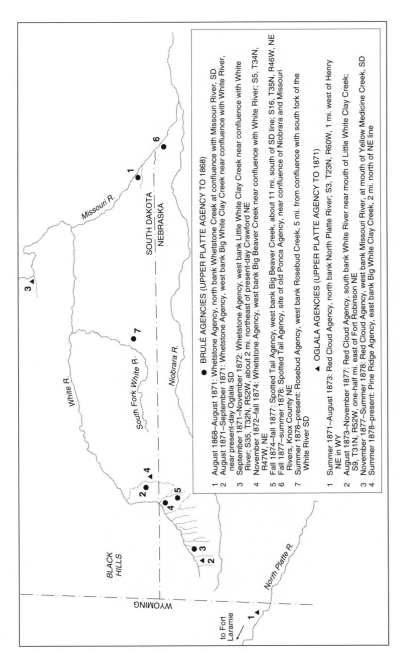

Movement of Brulé and Oglala Agencies, 1868–1878

Appendix 4

Susan Bordeaux Bettelyoun Family Tree

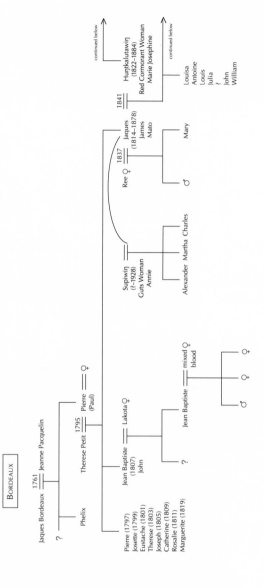

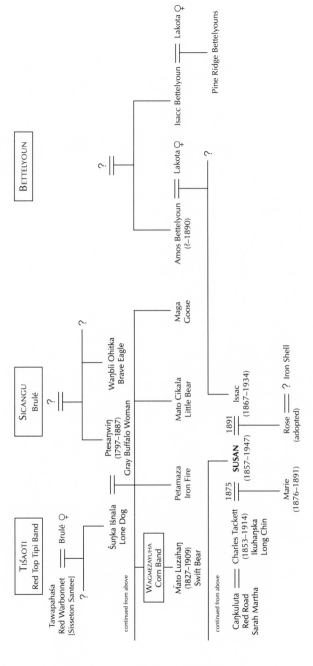

Chronology

1797 Ptesaŋwiŋ, Bettelyoun's maternal grandmother, born
1814 James Bordeaux born
1816 Iron Shell born
1821 Little Thunder born
1822 Huŋtkalutawiŋ born
1833 James Bordeaux travels to Fort Union
      Little Wound born
1834 "Fort Laramie" founded
1835 James Bordeaux and Pete at Bear Butte
1837 James Bordeaux marries Ree woman
1838 White Thunder born
1841 James Bordeaux and Huŋtkalutawiŋ marry
1849 Fort Laramie sold by American Fur Company to U.S. army
1851 Horse Creek Treaty
1854 Mormon cow incident, Grattan fight
1855 Harney attacks Little Thunder on Blue Water Creek
1856 Harney treaty at Fort Pierre (not ratified)
1857 Sumner campaign against Cheyennes
      Lakota-Omaha battle, Logan Fontenelle killed
      Mountain Meadows Massacre
      Susan Bordeaux born
1858 Gold discovered in Colorado
1862 Santee uprising in Minnesota
1863 Sibley and Sulley campaign, Whitestone Hill
1864 Killdeer Mountain fight
      Sand Creek Massacre
      Lakota/Cheyenne raids, beginning of organized defense
1865 Powder River Expedition, Sawyers' wagon road
      Two Face and Black Foot hung at Fort Laramie
      Horse Creek fight
      Attack on Julesburg, Platte Bridge fight
1866 Lakota defense of Powder River Country

War on Bozeman Trail
Fetterman fight
Susan Bordeaux to Hamburg, Iowa, to attend school
1867 War on Bozeman Trail continues
Wagon Box fight
Fort Laramie treaty council
1868 Treaty signed, war on Bozeman Trail ended victoriously
1869 Brulés to Whetstone Agency
1870 Red Cloud and Spotted Tail to Washington
Susan Bordeaux to Whetstone
1871 Brulé agency moved to White River country, Nebraska
1872 Josephine Waggoner born
1873 Lakota-Pawnee fight on Republican River
1874 Custer invades Black Hills
Susan Bordeaux marries Charles Tackett
1875 Failure of Black Hills Treaty Commission
Episcopalians come to Brulés at Beaver Creek agency
1876 Fight with Crook on Rosebud Creek
Little Big Horn fight
Army pursues Lakota and Cheyenne
Susan Bordeaux at Fort Robinson
Susan Bordeaux's daughter, Marie, is born
Spotted Tail visits Indian Territory
1877 Crazy Horse surrenders, is murdered
Brulé moved to old Ponca Agency
Dismounting of the Lakota
1878 James Bordeaux dies
Cheyenne flight north to homeland from Indian territory
1879 Cheyenne outbreak at Fort Robinson
Little Thunder dies
1881 Crow Dog kills Spotted Tail
Josephine Waggoner to Hampton Institute
1884 Susan Bordeaux and Marie to Anoka, Minnesota
White Thunder killed
Huŋtkalutawiŋ dies
1890 Ghost Dancing on Lakota reservations
Sitting Bull killed
Wounded Knee Massacre
1891 Susan Bordeaux marries Isaac Bettelyoun

1892 Little Wound dies
1894 Adopted daughter Rose is born
1896 Iron Shell dies
1909 Bettelyouns move to Winner, South Dakota
1933 Bettelyouns move to Old Soldiers Home, Hot Springs
1934 Isaac Bettelyoun dies
1943 Josephine Waggoner dies
1946 Susan Bordeaux Bettelyoun dies

Notes

1. SUSAN BORDEAUX BETTELYOUN

1. In June of 1853, at Fort Laramie, a Minniconjou shot at a soldier as he was ferrying across the North Platte. In response, post commander Richard Garnett ordered West Point graduate and second lieutenant Hugh Brady Fleming (ca. 1828–April 9, 1895) to go to the Minniconjou village and take the Indian prisoner. Fleming, with twenty-three men, proceeded to the camp; a fight ensued in which six Lakota were wounded and three killed. Fleming did not get his man but took two prisoners. The incident caused bad feelings among the Indians and was not forgotten the following year when Lt. John L. Grattan approached a Brulé camp looking for a different Minniconjou to take prisoner. Bettelyoun discusses the famous Grattan episode at length in later chapters.

2. In August 1877 the Northern Cheyennes who surrendered with Dull Knife (Mila Peśni) at Camp Robinson were sent to Indian Territory on what they believed was a trial basis. Suffering tremendously from disease and hunger in the south, the Cheyennes made known their desire to return home to their Powder River country. Denied permission to leave, close to 300 Cheyennes, led by Dull Knife and Little Wolf (Suŋkmanitu Cikala), left their Oklahoma reservation on September 9, 1878. Pursued by a huge army force, 149 Cheyennes under Dull Knife were finally captured and imprisoned at Fort Robinson in late October. Denied food and water by post commander Capt. Henry Walter Wessels (1846–

1929) in an attempt to force their submission to return south, the Cheyennes decided to escape and die fighting if necessary. On January 9, 1879, they broke out of their barracks into the frigid snow. The story of the Cheyennes' flight north and the outbreak at Fort Robinson can be found in Mari Sandoz, *Cheyenne Autumn* (New York: McGraw Hill, 1953); George Bird Grinnell, *The Fighting Cheyennes* (Norman: University of Oklahoma Press, 1956); and Peter J. Powell, *People of the Sacred Mountain: A History of the Northern Cheyenne Chiefs and Warrior Societies, 1830–1879, with an Epilogue 1969–1974*, 2 vols., (New York: Harper & Row, 1980). Extensive documentary material can be found in NARS M666, reels 428–430 and 449; see especially the "Proceedings of a Board of Officers Convened to Investigate the Arrest, Escape, and Recapture of Cheyenne Indians at Fort Robinson." See also U.S. Congress, 45th Cong., 3rd sess., 1879, S. Misc. Doc. 64, and 46th Cong., 2nd sess., 1880, S. Rept. 708.

3. See appendix 3 for information concerning the locations of these agencies.

4. See chapter 11, note 1.

5. See D. C. Poole, *Among the Sioux of Dakota: Eighteen Months' Experience as an Indian Agent, 1869–70* (New York: Van Nostrand, 1881; reprint, Saint Paul: Minnesota Historical Society Press, 1988). A rival of Spotted Tail's at Whetstone, Big Mouth (I Taŋka) was killed October 29, 1869.

6. See Garrick Mallery, "Pictographs of the North American Indians," *Smithsonian Institution, Bureau of American Ethnology, Annual Report* 4 (Washington DC: GPO, 1886): 117.

7. Logan Fontenelle (Śuŋkaska, White Horse), the mixed-blood son of French trader Lucien Fontenelle and an Omaha woman, was killed by a Brulé war party in the summer of 1855. The incident took place on Beaver Creek in northern Boone County, Nebraska. An Omaha view of the fight is given by Iron Eye in T. H. Tibbles, "Death of Logan Fontenelle," NSHS Proceedings and Collections 5(1902): 161–64.

8. Big Turkey (Waglekśuŋ Taŋka, 1841–1920) was born in the "year of snow shoes" or *Psohaŋpi* (*Psa*, "rush," *haŋpi*, "moccasins"), 1841–42. He was a man noted for his great geographical memory and knowledge who once made a large canvas map encompassing the whole Lakota territory for the Jesuit priests, who often became lost during their travels. In the early 1880s Big Turkey converted to Catholicism. He was married to "Catherine" Wazileya (Sets Pine on Fire), who converted in

1898. In addition to his geographical and cartographic skills, Big Turkey was helpful to Father Buechel and other priests at Saint Francis because of his knowledge of local native plants. A biography of "Peter" Big Turkey can be found in *The Indian Sentinel* 3, no. 5 (Jan. 1921): 237–39. Although photographs of Big Turkey working on maps can be found at the Buechel Memorial Lakota Museum, the great canvas map once housed there has been missing for many years.

9. George Hyde's Lakota sources told him that it was White Thunder who shot Fouts. See his *Spotted Tail's Folk: A History of the Brulé Sioux* (Norman: University of Oklahoma Press, 1961; reprint, 1974), 120.

10. Upon Spotted Tail's death in 1881, a struggle for Brulé leadership ensued. The rivalry between Spotted Tail's son (Sinte Gléška Cikala, or Little Spotted Tail) and White Thunder (Wakiŋyaŋska), generally considered a progressive on the reservation, escalated when the former stole White Thunder's wife. White Thunder retaliated by stealing Little Spotted Tail's horses. On May 29, 1884, Little Spotted Tail, Thunder Hawk (Wakiŋyaŋ cetan), and Long Pumpkin (Wagamuha Cetan Haŋska, Long Gourd Rattle) ambushed White Thunder and his father, killing both. Rather than elevating him in the eyes of the Brulés, Little Spotted Tail's actions ruined any chance of leadership he had. See George E. Hyde, *A Sioux Chronicle* (Norman: University of Oklahoma Press, 1956), and Rosebud agent James Wright's account in *The Annual Report of the Commissioner of Indian Affairs*, 1884, 46–47.

11. Bettelyoun is referring to Saint Stephan's Church. Her daughter attended the church's Saint Anne's school.

12. As part of the Office of Indian Affairs' assimilation policy in the late nineteenth century, the field matron program sought to educate Indian women in the domestic arena. The job of the field matron—mostly white women—was to acculturate Indians. Lisa E. Emmerich puts it succinctly when she writes that such programs were "designed to eradicate Indian culture and undercut tribal autonomy. . . . [T]he field matron program became, in the hands of these activists, [a] formidable weapon in the war against traditionalism." See Lisa E. Emmerich, "'Civilization' and Transculturation: The Field Matron Program and Cross-Cultural Contact," *American Indian Culture and Research Journal* 15, no. 4 (1991): 33–48.

13. Charles Tackett or Tackette (Jan. 18, 1853–July 2, 1914), a mixed-blood, was born on Horse Creek in Wyoming to George L. and Ellen Tackett. Episcopal Church records at the Lakota Archives and Research

Center (LARC) at Sinte Gleska University show a daughter, "Ellen," born to Charles Tacket and Susie (Bordeaux) "on the Niobrara, Holt Co. Nebraska, Oct. 5, 1876" (164–65; see also 29). She was baptized on Christmas Day, 1876, at Christ Church, Spotted Tail Agency, Nebraska. On her gravestone at the Saint Francis cemetery, Rosebud reservation, is recorded "Mary Agnes Tackett, Oct. 5, 1876–Aug. 27, 1891."

Tackett later married Spotted Tail's daughter Red Road (Caŋkuluta), who is listed in the Episcopal Church records as Sarah Martha. In 1876, according to Hyde, eighteen-year-old Red Road eloped with a warrior named Lone Elk rather than be sent to a Kansas City convent as her father had planned. Returning a year or two later, she married Tackett, who had been an interpreter at Camp Sheridan. In 1879 Spotted Tail sent the couple to Carlisle as guardians of his children and grandchildren who were attending the school. Tackett served as interpreter for Richard Pratt, founder of the school. A year later, having been told by Tackett that the children had been baptized and given white names, an angry Spotted Tail traveled to Carlisle and removed the children. See Hyde, *Spotted Tail's Folk*.

Bettelyoun gives us no clue as to what transpired between her and Charles Tackett. The Episcopal Church records contain the following confusing entry under "Families": "Charles Tacket, Sarah Martha (wf), Fannie (dau. of above), Susie (wf), Ellen (dau. of above)" (29). Reading in the records that Fannie was born in March of 1881, one could get the impression that Tackette, Red Road, Bettelyoun and the two girls were somehow living together as a family for a number of years. An explanation as to what actually transpired can be found in agent William Pollock's correspondence with the Commissioner of Indian Affairs. Writing from Yankton on September 15, 1878, Pollock laments: "The best educated and most influential half breed on the reservation having been several years lawfully married, 'put away' his wife while on the move and took unto himself with great eclat, according to the Indian custom no less a personage than the favorite daughter of Spotted Tail." Writing from Rosebud six months later, the Episcopal minister W. J. Cleveland told his bishop, "The ostensible object of his [Spotted Tail's] visit—and this explained all perhaps—was to get me to read a letter for him from Charles Tacket now at Carlisle. In this letter he was informed that those of his children who went to Carlisle and many others from here (34) had been baptized in the Church and that Charley having obtained a legal divorce had been lawfully married to his daughter (he was married by a Presbyterian) and with her confirmed by the Bishop." (Letters received, NARS 75; NSHS RG 508, roll 85.) Additionally, census records from the Rosebud Reservation in 1887 show Bettelyoun listed separately from Tackett.

Luther Standing Bear says the Indians called Tackett Ikuhaŋska, or Long Chin.

14. Joseph Alfred (Jack) Slade (1829–March 18, 1864) was born in Carlyle, Illinois, and served as a private during the Mexican War. Legend has it that around 1850 he killed a man with a rock and shortly thereafter fled west. By the late 1850s he was employed as a wagon boss, freighting on the overland trail. Again, the story goes, Slade killed one of his teamsters, Andrew Farrar. Later he worked as a stage driver and station agent at Kearney, Nebraska. In 1859 he was employed by the Overland Stage as District Superintendent, covering the region from Julesburg to South Pass.

15. Regarding Slades's murder of the Lakota family, cf. Billy Garnett: "On the Bitter Cottonwood about twenty miles above Laramie was a trading and mailing place and a stopping place for emigrants, log buildings here; was kept by a Frenchman whom the Indians called Bare Bad Hair [Pehiŋśla Śica]. His wife was an Indian. He and his wife and an Indian who was working for him were killed in the sixties by the Slade gang. Two or three of his children ran to escape; they found shelter in the brush and were frozen to death. It was winter." (William Garnett interview with Eli S. Ricker, Jan. 10, 1907. NSHS MS8, Ricker Collection, roll 1, tablet 1.)

In an undated letter to Addison Sheldon, Bettelyoun wrote (via Waggoner): "I made a mistake in the Slade narrative. Slade came on the Platte in a drunken state at a white man's ranch above Fort Laramie on the Platte in 1862. This was a way station and I have forgotten the man's name, but he was a white man married to an Indian woman. At this place Slade stayed; he sent the mail on by his escort. In his drunken state he killed this white man. There were four or five children. It was midwinter and real cold. The wife, her brother, and four children ran away into the timber and all froze to death. There was only one boy left asleep in the bed. Slade took this boy and kept him. He took this boy to raise to his Cherokee wife" (NSHS MS185, S1). This child was Mato Hiŋsma or Hairy Bear.

16. French Canadian Jules Beni, a former Indian trader, operated an Overland Stage station on the South Platte opposite the mouth of Lodgepole

Creek which, along with the surrounding accumulation of buildings, was known as Julesburg. According to the story, when Slade tried to replace Jules, the Frenchman emptied both a revolver and a shotgun into the unarmed man. Slade recovered and, with a gang of men, captured Jules at Cold Springs Station, twenty-two miles east of Laramie. Slade had Jules tied to a post and executed him. The legend says that Slade then cut off the man's ears, carrying them on his person for the rest of his short life. Fleeing north, Slade settled in the mining town of Virginia City, Montana. Unwilling to accept his lawless behavior, the townspeople hanged Jack Slade in 1863.

17. The story of Bettelyoun's great-aunt, Pretty Woman, and Red Cloud has not been substantiated.

18. Genoa Indian School, located in east central Nebraska's Nance County, was one of a number of off-reservation boarding schools established in the 1880s to assimilate Indian children into white society. Children were taught both academic and vocational skills with military regimentation. Instead of entering the white world, most of these children returned to their reservations, where they were often ostracized. See Wilma A. Daddario, "'They Get Milk Practically Every Day': The Genoa Indian Industrial School, 1884–1934." *Nebraska History* 73, no. 1 (spring 1992): 2–11.

19. Charles Percival Jordan (1851–1924) worked as clerk, acting superintendent, and trader at the Pine Ridge and Rosebud reservations from 1874 until his death. Jordan was married to Wicakawiŋ (Truthful Woman), known as Julia Walks First. Their daughter married Alexander Bordeaux Jr., the grandson of James Bordeaux and his third wife, Supiwiŋ.

20. For unknown reasons, Isaac Bettelyoun's records at the Old Soldiers' Home and his gravestone give his date of death as August 6, 1934.

2. JOSEPHINE WAGGONER

1. In her application to the South Dakota Soldiers' Home, Waggoner gives her date of birth as October 28, 1871, and in an autobiographical sketch at the State Historical Society of North Dakota, she states that she was born on Oct. 28, 1872.

2. Here as in other instances, the suffix "ya" is added to the band name Huŋkpapa. It appears that this was done by Waggoner, as her manuscript also refers to the band as Huŋkpapaya. According to native speakers as well as Buechel, this use of "ya" means "like," so what Waggoner is saying is "like a Huŋkpapa." Why she would do this is unclear. It is the

only band she refers to in this way, perhaps because she herself was a Huŋkpapa.

See appendix 2 for a discussion of Lakota social organization. In his list of Huŋkpapa bands, James Owen Dorsey translates Kiglaśka as "ties-his-own." See his "Siouan Sociology: A Posthumous Paper," *Smithsonian Institution, Bureau of American Ethnology, Annual Report* 15 (Washington DC: GPO, 1897): 213–244.

3. Waggoner's mother, Itatewiŋ (Wind Woman), had been married previously to Benjamin Monroe Connor (ca. 1844–1922), also known as Ben Arnold. The Lakota called him Waśicuŋ Tamaheca or Lean White Man. Connor served in the Civil War from Ohio and traveled to Fort Kearny, Julesburg, and Fort Laramie with that state's Eleventh Cavalry. At various times, he worked as an Indian trader, teamster, scout, wood cutter, cowboy, mail carrier, and miner throughout the northern plains and Rocky Mountains. The story of his adventures is told in Lewis F. Crawford, *Rekindling Camp Fires: The Exploits of Ben Arnold (Connor)* (Bismarck SD: Capitol Book, 1926). Crawford's book relies heavily on fourteen manuscript tablets of biographical material written by Waggoner. See SDSA H75.17, Ben Arnold Manuscript.

4. George Walter Yates (Feb. 26, 1843–June 25, 1876). In 1867, after serving as brevet lieutenant colonel of volunteers in the Civil War, Yates became a captain in the Seventh Cavalry and commanded Company F in Custer's "battle" at the Washita River. He accompanied Custer on his invasion of the Black Hills—the 1874 Black Hills Expedition—and a year later was sent with Tom Custer to Standing Rock on an unsuccessful attempt to arrest Rain In The Face (Iteomagaju) for murder. He served as a battalion commander at the Little Bighorn and was killed and buried on "Custer Hill." A year later his body was exhumed and reburied at the Fort Leavenworth National Cemetery. The military post at the Standing Rock Agency was named for Yates in December 1878.

5. After Custer's defeat at the Little Bighorn in June 1876, control of Indian agencies on the northern plains was transferred from civilian to military authority. Ostensibly as a means of denying the Lakota mobility, but clearly as a retaliatory punitive measure, Gen. Philip H. Sheridan, commander of the Division of the Missouri, instigated a policy of dismounting the Indians. Additional troops were sent to the various agencies to carry out this policy; the Huŋkpapas and others at Standing Rock had the misfortune of being assigned the Seventh Cavalry, Custer's unit. Meanwhile, the Commission of 1876 was visiting the Dakota/Lakota

agencies in an attempt to force the Indians to cede the Black Hills. At the Cheyenne River Agency, commissioners tried to allay Lakota fears that their ponies were about to be seized, assuring them that individuals and their property would be protected.

In October, after the Commission claimed ownership of the Black Hills, Gen. Alfred Terry, commander of the Department of Dakota, was ordered to disarm and dismount the Lakota at Standing Rock and Cheyenne River. Terry threatened the Indians with denial of rations when he found that, forewarned, they had removed their ponies to distant pastures. The Lakota relented. On October 23 Terry's men seized 1,222 horses at Standing Rock. When the "pony campaign" ended in May 1877, over 5,000 horses had been seized at Standing Rock and Cheyenne River. The horses were to have been sold at auction and the proceeds were to have been used to provide cattle for the Indians. Through disease, incompetent drunken herders, and corruption and outright theft, only 429 of the horses taken from Standing Rock and Cheyenne River made it to auction. Of the money received, only a portion actually went toward stock for the tribe. Standing Rock received 315 cows and 8 bulls.

The Lakota worked for years to receive compensation for their stolen horses. In 1892, the government began to pay the people at Standing Rock and Cheyenne River for over 5,000 head. Additional "pony claims" from Standing Rock and other agencies dragged on until 1944. In the end, the government paid compensation for over 8,000 pony claims totaling more than $320,000. See Richmond L. Clow, "General Philip Sheridan's Legacy: The Sioux Pony Campaign of 1876," *Nebraska History* 57, no. 4 (winter 1976): 461–77, and Forrest W. Daniel, "Dismounting the Sioux," *North Dakota History: Journal of the Northern Plains* 41, no. 3 (summer 1974): 9–13.

6. Father Jerome Hunt, O.S.B. (1849–1923), came to America from Germany in 1867 and was ordained in 1872 at Saint Meinrad's Abbey. He arrived in Dakota in June 1877 and worked among the Indians until his death. Hunt published a prayer book and a newspaper, *Eyanpaha* (The Herald), in the Lakota language. Records indicate that three sisters and one novice from the Benedictine convent of the Immaculate Conception in Indiana arrived at Standing Rock in 1878. They were M. Rose Chappele, Placida Schaefer, Maura Weyer, and Anastasia Sassel. The four log rooms Waggoner refers to served as kitchen, dining room, dormitory for the girls, and dormitory for the sisters. For a discussion of early

Catholic missionary activity at Standing Rock see Sister Mary Claudia Duratschek, O.S.B., "St. Peter and St. Benedict Missions," chap. 4 in *Crusading Along Sioux Trails: A History of the Catholic Indian Missions of South Dakota* (Yankton: Benedictine Convent of the Sacred Heart, 1947).

7. Joseph A. Stephan, born in Baden, Germany, was studying for a career in the military when a two-year bout with blindness led him to turn to the priesthood. He emigrated to the United States in 1847 and later served as an army chaplain during the Civil War. After the war Stephan was engaged in parish work in Indiana. He was appointed agent at Standing Rock in 1878. See "Monsignor Stephan," *The Indian Sentinel* (Washington DC: Bureau of Catholic Indian Missions, 1902–3), 2–5.

   James McLaughlin (Feb. 12, 1842–July 28, 1923) was born in Ontario and moved to Minnesota in 1863. He entered the Indian Service in 1871 acting as assistant agent at the Devil's Lake Agency near Fort Totten, North Dakota; he became agent in 1876. In 1881 McLaughlin was transferred to Standing Rock. His orders in 1890 for the arrest of Sitting Bull led to the Huŋkpapa chief's murder and, ultimately, to the massacre of Big Foot's (Si Taŋka) band at Wounded Knee Creek on the Pine Ridge reservation. For his view of things, see McLaughlin's *My Friend the Indian* (Boston: Houghton Mifflin, 1910).

8. Marie L. McLaughlin (nee Buisson) was born December 8, 1842, at Wabasha, Minnesota. In the foreword to her collection of Dakota stories, *Myths and Legends of the Sioux* (Bismarck SD: Bismarck Tribune, 1916), McLaughlin states that she is one quarter Dakota—her maternal grandmother, Hazahotawiŋ (Gray Huckleberry Woman) being a member of the Mdewakaŋtoŋ band of Santee. McLaughlin states that she was "born and raised in an Indian community." The couple was married January 8, 1864.

9. The Hampton Normal and Agricultural Institute was founded in 1868 by Samuel Chapman Armstrong as a school for freed African Americans. The institution began its experiment in Indian education ten years later when Richard Henry Pratt (later founder of the Carlisle Indian School) convinced Armstrong to accept seventeen men of southern Plains tribes who had been held as prisoners of war at Fort Marion, Florida. With financial support from the government Armstrong expanded the program, and, in November 1878, Pratt returned from Dakota Territory with forty boys and nine girls. During its forty-five years of operation, 1,387 Indians—mostly Sioux—attended the school. Hampton was a

brave attempt at coed, biracial education; although assimilation was the goal, both blacks and Indians were taught to value their culture. Federal support was withdrawn in 1912 when racists in Congress concluded that compelling Indians to attend school alongside blacks was humiliating and degrading to them. Enrollment dwindled and Hampton closed its doors in 1923. The school's carefully maintained archives are a treasure illuminating life at the school and preserving numerous student records and photographs, including those of Josephine Waggoner. See Mary Lou Hultgren and Paulette Fairbanks Molin, *To Lead and To Serve: American Indian Education at Hampton Institute, 1878–1923* (Virginia Beach: Virginia Foundation for the Humanities, 1989).

10. Saint Elizabeth Mission was founded in 1885; its school was built in 1890.

The Right Reverend William Hobart Hare (May 17, 1838–Oct. 23, 1909) was the first bishop in the United States assigned to minister to a race of people, serving as Protestant Episcopal missionary bishop of Niobrara and South Dakota from 1873 to 1909. The Protestant Episcopal Church was charged with serving and administrating seven Lakota/Dakota agencies. Hare was born in Princeton, New Jersey, and studied at the Academy of the Protestant Episcopal Church and the University of Pennsylvania. He was ordained in Philadelphia in 1862. In 1871 he was named secretary and general agent of the Foreign Committee of the Board of Missions, and in 1873 was consecrated as the missionary bishop of the Niobrara to serve the northern Great Plains. Arriving at Yankton, Dakota, in April of 1873, Hare established himself at that agency and set to work on his policy of assimilation, building churches and schools throughout his region.

For more information on Bishop Hare and the early Protestant Episcopal Missions see K. Brent Woodruff, "The Episcopal Mission to the Dakotas, 1860–1898," *South Dakota Historical Collections* 17 (1934): 553–603; Virginia Driving Hawk Sneve, *That They May Have Life: The Episcopal Church in South Dakota, 1859–1976* (New York: Seabury, 1977); and M. A. DeWolfe Howe, *The Life and Labors of Bishop Hare: Apostle to the Sioux* (New York: Sturgis & Walton, 1911). Papers of Bishop Hare and the Protestant Episcopal Church in the Dakotas can be found at the SDSA, MSS12 and H74.774, and at the Center for Western Studies, Augustana College, Sioux Falls SD.

11. Gall (Pizi, ca. 1840–Dec. 5, 1894) was born on the Moreau River in South Dakota and raised by a widowed mother. Along with other Huŋk-

papas, he allied himself with the Oglalas under Crazy Horse. Gall fought prominently in the battles of Rosebud Creek and the Little Bighorn, afterward fleeing to Canada with Sitting Bull. He returned to the United States in 1881, surrendering to Major Ilges at Poplar River, Montana, on January 1, 1882. He moved to Standing Rock and took an allotment next to Bishop Hare's Saint Elizabeth's Mission, where he was involved in the establishment of the school. Gall visited Washington twice, in 1888 and 1890. He was baptized at Fort Yates by an army chaplain and later confirmed by Bishop Hare. Because of his peaceable nature in his later years and his belief that cooperation was necessary for the survival of his people, Gall won the respect of agent McLaughlin and other whites who held him up as an example in contrast to Sitting Bull. Gall died at his home at Oak Creek and was buried at Saint Elizabeth's cemetery.

John Grass (1837–1918), Charging Bear (Mato Nataŋ), was a Blackfoot (Sihasapa) Lakota. A distinguished warrior against the Crows, Mandans, and Flatheads, he nevertheless opposed war with the whites. He signed the 1889 agreement breaking up the Great Sioux Reservation and for thirty years served as a judge on the Indian Court at Standing Rock. He lived his later years at Fort Yates, where he is buried.

3. CHIEF LONE DOG

1. Iŋkpaduta (Scarlet Point, ca. 1815–ca.1879), the controversial hereditary chief of the Wahpekute Santee, led his band in the Spirit Lake Massacre of March 1857 after the band was reduced to starvation by white settlers. Seen as an outlaw and renegade by whites and many of his own tribe, Iŋkpaduta and his people fled west and lived with the Yanktons. He took part in the battles of Whitestone Hill (1863) and Killdeer Mountain (1864), and later had the distinction of leading the only Santee force at the Little Bighorn. Iŋkpaduta then fled to Canada with Sitting Bull where he died sometime before 1880. See Mark Diedrich, *Famous Chiefs of the Eastern Sioux* (Minneapolis: Coyote Books, 1987). Josephine Waggoner believed Iŋkpaduta to be a great Dakota hero. Her research can be found in her correspondence with I. H. Herriott housed at the SHSI. See also Herriott's subsequent five-part article on the Spirit Lake Massacre in the *Annals of Iowa*, 18, no. 4–8 (1932–33).

4. MY MOTHER, HUŊTKALUTAWIŊ

1. Swift Bear's band was the Corn band. Hyde writes, "The Swift Bear winter count states that a white man taught this camp how to plant corn

on White River in 1823–24. . . . [A]fter that the band was called Wag-mezayuha (They Have Corn). The other Brulé bands thought it was an outrageous thing for any bold Brulés to attempt to cultivate the soil, and they forced the Corn Band to give up this practice. After 1845 the Red Lodge camp belonged to the Corn Band, and Swift Bear of the Red Lodges finally became chief of this camp" (*Spotted Tail's Folk*, 43).

2. William W. Bent's (May 23, 1809–May 19, 1869) second post near La-Junta, Colorado, on the Arkansas River was the preeminent mercantile center of the southern plains. Bent married Owl Woman, a Cheyenne, in 1837. See David Lavender, *Bent's Fort* (Garden City NY: Doubleday, 1954; reprint, Lincoln: University of Nebraska Press, 1972). One of their sons, George, who fought with his tribe against the whites, has left a valuable written record of his experiences. See George E. Hyde, *Life of George Bent: Written from His Letters*, ed. Savoie Lottinville (Norman: University of Oklahoma Press, 1968; reprint, 1987.)

3. According to Gilmore, "The Dakota formerly had a custom by which marks of recognition and distinction were publicly conferred on persons who from personal character and acts of public benefaction were esteemed worthy of honor. The custom was the institution of *Hunka*. The term *hunka* primarily means parent or ancestor. In the primary sense of the term an elder brother might be termed hunka by his younger brothers and sisters by reason of his favors and benefactions to them. The sun might be called *hunka* from the beneficent effects of his radiance. So any person who had become elevated in the esteem of the people in such a degree as to be considered in the manner of a public benefactor or parent to the community, might be given this title. Thus the term was used as a title of respect, and those on whom it was conferred constituted socially an aristocracy within a community which, in political organization was essentially democratic, for the Dakota form of government was quite democratic. . . . Recognition of any person as *hunka* was made the occasion of public ceremony. Some family of good standing, and being of this rank, having a daughter come to marriage-able age, might announce that they would hold the *Hunka* ceremony for her. . . ." Gilmore goes on to describe, in great detail, such a ceremony which he viewed as "a kind of coming-out party." See Melvin R. Gilmore, "The Dakota Ceremony of *Hunka*," in *Indian Notes*, 1, no. 1 (Jan. 1929): 75–79. See also James R. Walker, *Lakota Belief and Ritual*, eds. Raymond J. DeMallie and Elaine A. Jahner (Lincoln: University of Nebraska Press, 1980), documents 71–84.

5 . BORDEAUX

1. James Bordeaux, called Mato, or Bear, by the Lakota, was born in the French village of Saint Charles about eighteen miles northwest of Saint Louis on August 22, 1814. Biographical information on Bordeaux can be found in Charles E. Hanson, "James Bordeaux," *Museum of the Fur Trade Quarterly* 2, no. 1 (spring 1966): 2–12, and "James Bordeaux Chapter Two," *Museum of the Fur Trade Quarterly* 27, no. 4 (winter 1991): 2–9. See also John Dishon McDermott, "James Bordeaux," in *Mountain Men and the Fur Trade of the Far West*, ed. LeRoy R. Hafen (Glendale CA: A. H. Clark, 1965) vol. 5, and Virginia Cole Trenholm, "The Bordeaux Story," *Annals of Wyoming* 26, no. 2 (July 1954): 119–27.

2. Pierre (Paul) Bordeaux married Therese Petit of Saint Louis on October 13, 1795. Baptismal registers and other records in Saint Charles and Saint Louis, Missouri, show the following ten children born to the couple: Pierre, 1797; Josette, 1799; Eustache, 1801; Therese, 1803; Joseph, 1805; Jean Baptiste (John), 1807; Catherine, 1809; Rosalie, baptized 1811, died 1813; Jaques (James), 1814; and Marguerite, 1819. Other records indicate two additional children, Suzanne and Charles. It is probable that a number of these children died in infancy or early childhood and were never mentioned to Susan. The discrepancy in the names of the children may be due to a difference between baptismal names and what the children were actually called by the family.

3. According to Charles Hanson, Bordeaux was hired by the Upper Missouri Outfit in May 1830 to be a hunter at Fort Union, and in 1832 by William Sublette as a boatman (Hanson, "James Bordeaux," 3).

4. Due to a meteor shower on November 12, 1833, the year 1833–34 is recorded in almost all Lakota winter counts and in the oral history of many other tribes as "the year the stars fell," *Wicahpi okicamna*. *Wicahpi*: star, *okicamna*: storm, to shower down, snow.

5. Built in 1829 by John Jacob Astor's fur trading giant, the American Fur Company, Fort Union stood on the east bank of the Missouri River four miles upstream from its confluence with the Yellowstone. Pierre Chouteau Jr. (Jan. 19, 1789–Oct. 6, 1865) began his career in his father's fur trade business at the age of fifteen. In 1809 he worked for the Missouri Fur Company but formed his own company a few years later. Chouteau was involved in various partnerships. In 1834 Pratte, Chouteau and Company purchased the American Fur Company's Western Division, the business continuing under its original name. Chouteau was the ma-

jor figure in the Upper Missouri fur trade business. See Janet LeCompte, "Pierre Chouteau, Junior," in *Mountain Men and the Fur Trade*, ed. Hafen, vol. 9. For a complete discussion of the complex history of the American Fur Company, its rivals and mergers, see Hafen, vol. 1, and Hiram Martin Chittenden, *The American Fur Trade of the Far West* (New York: Press of the Pioneers, 1935, 3 vols.; reprint, Lincoln: University of Nebraska Press, 1986, 2 vols.)

6. No diary has ever been found. Charles Hanson maintains that Bordeaux was illiterate.

7. Complete histories of all these posts can be found in Chittenden, *The American Fur Trade of the Far West*.

8. None of these men was associated with the American Fur Company. Manuel Lisa died in 1820; the American Fur Company's Western Branch was not established in Saint Louis until 1822. He was, however, the moving spirit behind the establishment of the Missouri Fur Company in Saint Louis. Mixed-blood George Drouillard acted as interpreter (through sign) for Lewis and Clark before going to work for the Missouri Fur Company. He was killed by the Blackfeet in 1810. Francis M. Benoit, a prominent Saint Louis fur trader, had for a time a post among the Otoe and Pawnee. See Chittenden, *The American Fur Trade of the Far West*, and M. O. Skarsten, "George Drouillard," in *Mountain Men and the Fur Trade*, ed. Hafen, vol. 4.

9. Bear Butte is known to the Cheyennes as Noaha-vose and to the Lakota as Mato Paha. This especially sacred place is a laccolith or unexploded volcano at the northeast edge of the Black Hills. See Thomas E. Odell, *Mato Paha: The Story of Bear Butte* (Spearfish SD: n.p., 1942).

10. On February 20, 1940, the *Rapid City Journal* published a similar version of this story by Bettelyoun under the headline "Killing of French Trapper at Bear Butte by Ree Indians in 1836 Revealed by Aged Woman." This account is reprinted in Odell, *Mato Paha*, 57–61. A manuscript copy can be found in the Charles P. Jordan Collection, NSHS MS71.

11. Early in 1835, Pratte, Chouteau & Company (the successors to the American Fur Company, and still known as such) lent money to Fontenelle, Fitzpatrick and Company (which it served as supply agents and ostensibly controlled) to buy Fort William from William Sublette and Robert Campbell, founders of the post. The following year Chouteau bought the post outright. A readable account of the founding and many incarnations of the post; the intricate Rocky Mountain fur trading rival-

ries; and the comings, goings, and mergers of the companies involved can be found in David Lavender, *Fort Laramie and the Changing Frontier*, National Park Service, Division of Publications, Handbook 118 (Washington DC: U.S. Dept. of the Interior, 1983).

12. It is generally believed that the place name of "Laramie" in Wyoming stems from a French Canadian trapper by the name of LaRamee. His first name is disputed, but it was probably Jaques or Joseph. LaRamee came to the North Platte country in around 1815 and he and his men generally rendezvoused at the mouth of the present day Laramie River. In 1821, on that river, LaRamee was killed. Arapahos were accused, although they vehemently denied it. By the early 1820s, when Bordeaux was still a child, the name Laramie (in its various spellings) was used for the area. Bettelyoun may have heard the story of LaRamee and assumed it was her father's cousin. James Bordeaux, on the other hand, may have inserted himself into the story to impress his children. Whatever the source of the confusion, if the trapper's death took place as late as 1836, there were certainly enough people in the area by that time that it would have been remembered clearly. As John Dishon McDermott's research points out, the origin of the name is surrounded by "mystery and uncertainty." See his "J. LaRamee" in *Mountain Men and the Fur Trade*, ed. Hafen, vol. 6, and "The Search for Jaques Laramee: A Study in Frustration," *Annals of Wyoming* 36, no. 2 (Oct. 1964): 169–72.

6. AT LARAMIE

1. Jacob Herman (1827–Dec. 19, 1887) emigrated from Germany in 1844. He was the army's blacksmith both at Fort Laramie and Fort Randall, where he moved in 1874. At Fort Randall, Herman was active in building a church, library, and the Odd Fellows Hall. Gladys Whitehorn Jorgensen writes that Herman died December 19, 1887, and that his tombstone at the Fort Randall cemetery is "impressive."

2. According to Jorgensen, Herman's wife was named Mary Louise Teisen, a surname curiously similar to that of the trader Bettelyoun mentions next.

3. Concerning Mrs. Herman and the children, the holograph is confusing. Bettelyoun says there were three girls and three boys: "There was Mary, the oldest, Louisa, Theresa. . . ." The name "Sophie" is written in the margin, and inserted in the list of girls' names as if later remembered and added by Waggoner. The text has been changed accordingly. Mary Louise died November 7, 1906, and is buried at Saint Francis, South

Dakota. See Gladys Whitehorn Jorgensen, *Before Homesteads: In Tripp County and the Rosebud* (Freeman SD: Pine Hill Press, 1974), 126.

4. After receiving a boarding school education, including some years at Carlisle, Jake Herman (1893–1970) was, at one time or another, a soldier, writer, artist, trick rider, fancy roper, and rodeo clown. He rode with Jack King's "Wild West Show" and the "Rodeo Royal Circus." He wrote about himself and the Lakota people for *The Shannon County News*, *The Western Horseman*, and *Frontier Times*, illustrating his own stories. See T. Emogene Paulsen and Lloyd R. Moses, *Who's Who Among the Sioux* (Vermillion SD: University of South Dakota Press, 1988), 93. An interview with Herman conducted in 1967 appears in Joseph H. Cash and Herbert T. Hoover, eds., *To Be an Indian: An Oral History* (New York: Holt, Rinehart & Winston, 1971), 102–3.

5. Present-day Marysville, Kansas, is located on the Big Blue River, more than eighty miles from the Missouri. When asked by Sheldon to explain this discrepancy, Bettelyoun replied, "I was told that Father DeSmet founded a school at Marysville, Kansas, the exact date I could not say. At first the school was an orphanage. Many mixed-blood children were taken there to be educated. My father's brother, who was married to an Indian woman, took his son there, where he grew to manhood" (NSHS MS185, Bettelyoun Collection, S1, Nov. 23, 1938). Bettelyoun appears to be referring to Saint Mary's, a Potawatomie mission founded by DeSmet in 1838 and run by the Sisters of the Sacred Heart. Saint Mary's is located on the Kansas River, northwest of Topeka. See Hiram Martin Chittenden and Alfred Talbot Richardson, eds., *Life, Letters and Travels of Father Pierre-Jean DeSmet, 1801–1873,* 4 vols. (New York: Francis P. Harper, 1905; reprint, New York: Klaus Reprint, 1969).

6. This statement contradicts the earlier assertion that Bordeaux's Ree wife had taken both of their children with her when she returned to her country. When Sheldon questioned her about this contradiction, Bettelyoun reiterated, "My father sent his daughter Mary from his Ree wife to Saint Louis to school to his people" (NSHS MS185, S1).

7. The 1860 census of Fort Laramie provides the following information: Samuel Smith, age 30, post interpreter, born in Nebraska. Nape Śica translates as Bad Hand.

8. Joseph Robidoux: The large and confusing Robidoux family (apparently spelled as many ways as there were members) has long been a bane of scholars who have tried to sort it out. Such an exercise is not possible, or necessary, for this work. Those interested should refer to Merrill

Mattes's works: "Joseph Robidoux's Family: Fur Traders and Trail Blazers," *Overland Journal* 6, no. 3 (1988): 2–9; "Antoine Robidoux" and "Joseph Robidoux," in *Mountain Men and the Fur Trade*, ed. Hafen, vols. 4 and 6, respectively; and "Robidoux's Trading Post at 'Scott's Bluff,' and the California Gold Rush," *Nebraska History* 30, no. 2 (June 1949): 95–138.

9. Little is known of Louis Chardon, an early trader whose name, in corrupted form, was given to Chadron, Nebraska, and a nearby creek. He was born in Saint Louis and was married to a white woman named Therese before marrying Bull Tail's daughter. Chardon worked for a number of different trading companies including Pierre Chouteau & Company, the American Fur Company, and Sybille & Adams. He operated a post on the creek that bears his name just west of Chadron in northwest Nebraska.

10. Bull Tail (Siŋte Tataŋka, c. 1770–Aug. 18, 1854), chief of the Brulé Orphan band, was one of the men who counseled with Kearny at Fort Laramie during his 1845 expedition. He was the father of Iron Shell. Bull Tail died the day before the Grattan fight, which is discussed at length in following chapters.

11. French Canadian Clement Lamareaux was born September 19, 1837. He traveled to the Denver area while in his teens, later moving to Fort Laramie, where he married Louise Bordeaux. The couple settled in "French Village" near present day Hamburg, Iowa, where Lamareaux ran a freighting business to Denver and Fort Laramie. After helping to found the town of Hamburg, Clement and Louise moved to the Niobrara River in Holt County, Nebraska, in 1887. They had a ranch near the former towns of Paddock and Red Bird. In the 1890s they bought land on the Rosebud reservation along Mud Creek and continued to prosper in ranching. Clement Lamareaux died in 1895. Louise Bordeaux Lamareaux was born April 1, 1842, at Fort Laramie. A pianist, she was an accomplished musician, as were all eight of her children.

12. Joseph Bissonette (Wapahahota, Gray Hat, 1818–Aug. 1894) was born in Saint Louis of French-Canadian descent and headed west at the age of eighteen. Six years later he was a principal trader for Sybille & Adams, the owners of Laramie precursor Fort Platte. In 1843 Bernard Pratte and John Cabanne bought Fort Platte, and Bissonette was given additional responsibility. When Frémont came through the area, he was hired as a guide and interpreter. By this time he had married an Oglala woman and had had three of his seven children with her. In 1845 Pratte &

Cabanne abandoned Fort Platte, and Bissonette packed their goods and moved eight miles downriver where he established Fort Bernard. Pratte & Cabanne soon sold out to the American Fur Company, but Bissonette, with his partner John Richards, remained at the post as rivals to that company. Within a year Fort Bernard mysteriously burned. In 1849 Bissonette had a partnership with James Bordeaux and Charles Primeaux at the Fort Bernard site, but it was soon dissolved and he moved three miles upriver and opened a competing post.

In the early 1850s Bissonette diversified his trading, began raising horses, and even did some farming. He teamed up with Richards and other partners in 1853 to build and operate toll bridges on the North Platte in Wyoming, becoming wealthy in the process. The years 1854 and 1855 brought trouble for Bissonette; Indian raids and military orders to stop trade after the Grattan fight disrupted his business. Around this time Bissonette married his second wife, Nellie or Ella Plenty Brother. In 1856 Bissonette became friends with the Upper Platte Indian agent Thomas Twiss. Twiss appointed him interpreter, and Bissonette moved with his family to the Deer Creek Agency and set up a trading post, illegally dealing in liquor. Accusations of corruption were brought against the two men and, in 1861, Twiss was finally removed by President Lincoln. Bissonette remained at Deer Creek, but he suffered financially. In 1863 the new agent, John Loree, moved the agency twenty miles east of Laramie and Bissonette lost his tradership. The next year he lost a number of horses in raids; when he gave up and left Deer Creek, the Indians burned the post. McDermott says it was the following winter, in 1865, that Bissonette and his family stayed at Bordeaux's.

In 1868, he was appointed interpreter for the peace commission at Laramie following the so-called Red Cloud War. He was appointed interpreter to accompany the Brulés to the Whetstone agency in 1869. When the Brulés moved to their next agency in northwest Nebraska in 1871, Bissonette went with them, acting as subagent and assistant farmer. In 1875 he traveled to Washington with Red Cloud and Spotted Tail. Later in the decade Bissonette settled on Wounded Knee Creek on the Oglala's Pine Ridge reservation, where he farmed and received government rations. Joseph Bissonette died in 1894. Bissonette's name crops up in the writings of many who visited the Laramie and Deer Creek areas. A good biography of him can be found in John Dishon McDermott, "Joseph Bissonette," in *Mountain Men and the Fur Trade*, ed. Hafen, vol. 4.

13. Gladys Whitehorn Jorgensen says Enoch Wheeler Raymond served in the Mexican War in 1847 and 1848, and that he reenlisted at Fort Laramie on January 10, 1849, serving five years as a sergeant. Bettelyoun dates his marriage to Wiciŋcala (Young Girl) in 1851, while Jorgensen writes that he married Elizabeth (Betsy) on October 4, 1853 (88). Betsy was Raymond's mother's name, which may explain the origin of his wife's name. Church records from 1876 place the marriage at Fort Laramie by post chaplain Rev. William Vaux in 1856. In any event, Wiciŋcala was born in 1837 near Fort Pierre to Śiyoduta (Red Prairie Chicken) and Uŋpaŋtopawiŋ (Four Elk Woman). Raymond and Wiciŋcala had only one son, William, born June 24, 1856, at Fort Laramie. The children listed by Bettelyoun were born to William and his Oglala wife, Julie Pappan Menard. In 1868 the Raymond family left Fort Laramie to settle in the Keya Paha valley, a region Raymond had seen and fallen in love with as an army scout. They established a horse ranch on the road between Fort Randall and the Black Hills, receiving numerous visitors, both Indian and white. The Lakota called him Akicita or Soldier. Jorgensen says the famous golden wedding celebration occurred on October 4, 1903, and that over two hundred guests attended the all-day services at Ascension Chapel. She dates Raymond's death in October 1908. See Jorgensen, *Before Homesteads*; Winner Chamber of Commerce, *Winner, 50th Anniversary, 1909–1959* (n.p.: Sodak Printers, 1959), 12–13; and SGUA, Episcopal Church records, book A. Bettelyoun's material concerning E. W. Raymond, sent to the NSHS as a short separate section, has been incorporated into this chapter.

14. John Richards Sr. (Owaśakala: cheap, easily purchased; also known as Reshaw, April 5, 1823–1875) was born in Saint Charles, Missouri, and headed west in the late 1830s. In 1840 he trapped with his partner A. M. Metcalf in the Rocky Mountains. In 1842 he worked for Sybille & Adams, then owners of Fort Platte, where he was responsible for supplying liquor smuggled from New Mexican settlements. He stayed on when Pratte & Cabanne bought the post. In 1845 Richards abandoned Fort Platte and set up a new post, Fort Bernard, six miles downriver. With his brother Peter, Bissonette, and others (possibly Bordeaux) he continued to compete with Fort John (Laramie). While he was on a trip to Mexico to obtain liquor in 1846, Fort Bernard mysteriously burned.

Throughout the next five years Richards established a number of trading posts in the North Platte and Laramie region, but it was in 1851, with the start of his toll bridge enterprises, that he began to prosper.

His first bridge, which spanned the Laramie, lasted about two years before it was destroyed by spring floods. The second bridge, over the North Platte near the mouth of Deer Creek, was also short-lived. In 1853 Richards built a bridge over the Platte at the present site of Evansville, Wyoming. Here he settled with his family and let the money flow in. Except for a short time spent at Fort Laramie in 1855 avoiding raids after the Grattan fight, Richards stayed at the bridge until 1858. In June of that year, ever conscious of economic opportunity, Richards went to the Pike's Peak region along Cherry Creek. After spreading word of the gold discovery, he returned to Cherry Creek and established one of the area's first businesses. By the early 1860s Richards was doing well with his trading house, saloon, and store. He sold out in 1863 after his buildings were damaged by fire. After leaving Colorado he sold hay to the military to supplement his trading and bridge income. Richards sold his Platte bridge site in 1865 and set up a post at Rock Creek, twenty miles west of Laramie. At the end of the decade he was settled near Bordeaux, Wyoming, raising horses and cattle. In the winter of 1875, while on a trading trip to the north, John Richards was killed—by white outlaws or Cheyennes—on the Niobrara River. See FLNHS, file CIN-29, and Brian Jones, "Those Wild Reshaw Boys," in *Sidelights of the Sioux Wars*, ed. Francis B. Taunton (London: English Westerners' Society, 1967).

15. During the 1860s John Richards Jr. (Hehaka kiŋyaŋ, ca. 1844–May 17, 1872) was following in his father's footsteps of diversified business. Speaking fluent Crow and Lakota, he carried on a profitable trade with those tribes. In addition, he hauled trade goods to the miners of Virginia City, Montana, and held haying contracts for Forts Phil Kearny and Fetterman. It was in August 1869 that Richards mortally wounded Cpl. Francis Conrad, Company E, 4th Infantry, at Fort Fetterman. He fled to the Crows and married a captive Piegan woman, returning to Red Cloud's camp in the spring. Although a Wyoming grand jury indicted him for murder, Richards successfully pleaded his case to Washington with the help of his white, mixed-blood, and Lakota friends. Appeals were made on a June 1870 trip to the capital with Red Cloud, Spotted Tail, and others, and Richards was pardoned. Copies of petitions for the pardoning of Richards containing the signatures of eighty-seven prominent men of all races can be found in the archives at the FLNHS, files CIN-18 and CIN-29. See also Brian Jones, "John Richards, Jr. and the Killing at Fetterman," *Annals of Wyoming* 43, no. 2 (fall 1971): 237–57.

16. The deaths of Brown Eagle and John Richards occurred on May 15,

1872. All other accounts name the Lakota killed by Richards as Yellow Bear (Mato Hiŋzi), a member of the Tapiśleca or Spleen band, not Brown Eagle (Waŋbligi). The most complete account is that given by eyewitness Billy Garnett in an interview with Judge Eli S. Ricker in 1907 (NSHS MS8 Ricker Collection, roll 1, tablet 1). See also Donald F. Danker, "The Violent Deaths of Yellow Bear and John Richard, Jr." *Nebraska History* 63, no. 2 (summer 1982): 137–51; FLNHS file CIN-29; and Jones, "Those Wild Reshaw Boys." Bettelyoun's account has been reordered for clarity.

Billy Garnett (April 25, 1855 – Oct. 12, 1928), also known as Billy Hunter, was born on the Laramie River to Looking Woman, a full-blood Oglala. His father, Richard Brooke Garnett, commander of Fort Laramie from 1852 to 1854, left the region before the birth of his son and returned to his white wife and family in Virginia. Billy Garnett worked for various traders including Baptiste Pourier, Jules Ecoffey, John Richards, and Adolf Cuny. He served for many years as an interpreter and scout for the army. He married and divorced three women by Indian custom in quick succession, finally settling down with Filla Janis, daughter of Old Nick Janis. Garnett is buried in the Catholic cemetery north of Kyle on the Pine Ridge Reservation. Today he is best known for his account of the death of Crazy Horse. (See FLNHS CIN 81.)

Louis Shangreaux (1848 – Jan. 1899) married Emily Janis's sister Louise the following year. Emily Janis subsequently married Robert Pugh and, later, Benjamin Tibbitts.

17. Sefroy Iott (? – July 15, 1885) came west from Missouri and by 1834 was working for Fontenelle on the Green River. Later he worked for Pratte & Cabanne. In 1838, in Saint Louis, he married Nick Janis's sister Leonide. Records show the couple had three children: Margaret Philomena, Emilie Sophie, and Marie Felicite. Iott moved to Fort Pierre in 1846 where he worked for Pierre Chouteau & Company. During the 1850s and 1860s he lived around Laramie working as an interpreter, guide, trapper, and trader. Episcopal church records dated June 9, 1877, show a marriage between Iott and a Lakota woman named Ellen with a note by Reverend Cleveland that they "had lived together about twenty years" (SGUA, book A, 400–401). Iott had another Indian wife at Laramie named Mary. Iott was the Oglala's interpreter at the 1867 treaty council at Fort Laramie and later moved to Whetstone with the Brulés. When that agency was moved to Nebraska, Iott was employed as "assistant farmer." In 1875 he served as interpreter at the Spotted Tail agency

during the council held regarding the "sale" of the Black Hills. Sefroy Iott died in northwest Nebraska in 1885. See Charles Hanson Jr., "Sefroy Iyott," *Museum of the Fur Trade Quarterly* 7, no. 4 (winter 1971): 4–6. Hanson quotes an army colonel as saying the Lakota's name for Iott was Stands in the Prairie.

18. Joseph Knight (ca. 1834–Oct. 1931) came to Wyoming in 1849 and worked for many years as a fur trader. Later he was involved in overland freighting from Saint Joseph to Montana. He married Waŋbliśuŋ (Eagle Wing Feather, ca. 1840–April 1866) in 1856. She was the daughter of Black Moon (Wi Sapa) and mixed-blood Oglala Mary Gardner. Waŋbliśuŋ was later adopted by Gardner's husband, John Richards Sr. and became known as Mary Richards. She died in April 1866 and was buried in the Fort Laramie cemetery. Knight later became a stock raiser and married Bertie Helen Telson in Saint Joseph. He died of stomach cancer at his home in Cheyenne. See FLNHS file CIN-84.

19. One of the more fanciful tales from Fort Laramie stems from the burial of Spotted Tail's daughter Hiŋziwiŋ (Yellow Woman, ca. 1848–spring 1866). White chroniclers have created the romantic saga of Ah-ho-appa or Falling Leaf, the Indian princess who was in love with a soldier at the fort. (Bettelyoun's account is interesting in that it clearly states that it was the solider who was in love with Hiŋziwiŋ). In 1856 Hiŋziwiŋ had gone to prison at Fort Leavenworth with her father when he surrendered for the attack on the mail wagon. John Hunton writes of her, "She dressed herself as a young man, liked to carry a gun like her father and performed none of the squaws' menial tasks" (17). Hunton also qualifies his version of the legend by stating, "At least part of it is true" (15). John Colhoff, in his interview with Eli Ricker, says the story of Hiŋziwiŋ being in love with an army officer is "a fabrication" (NSHS MS8, Eli Ricker Collection, roll 4, tablet 17: 26–27).

The most accurate and detailed account of Hiŋziwiŋ's burial is Fort Laramie commander Col. Henry E. Maynadier's report to the Commissioner of Indian Affairs (*The Annual Report of the Commissioner of Indian Affairs*, 1866: 207–8; see also SDHRC file SC23). For those interested in the romantic white myth of Ah-ho-ap-pa, see John Hunton, *Diary 1880–81–82*, ed. Pat Flannery (Lingle WY: Lingle Guide Review, 1963), 15–25; Capt. Eugene F. Ware, "The Daughter of Shan-Tag-A-Lisk: A Piece of Western History," in *The Indian War of 1864* (1911; reprint, New York: St. Martin's, 1960, and Lincoln: University of Nebraska Press, 1994), 407–18; and "Falling Leaf was a Lovely Indian

Maiden" and "The Legend of the Indian Princess Ah-ho-ap-pa, Daughter of Chief Spotted Tail or Shan-tag-a-lisk," WDCR WPA file 3.

In the summer of 1876, Spotted Tail removed the remains of his daughter to his agency for reburial. The event is recorded in the Episcopal church burial records: "Monday June 26, 1876, Hinziwin, daughter of Spotted Tail.... died on the Yellowstone River. Said to have been poisoned by an Indian who wished her for his wife but she loved an officer at Fort Laramie. Burial place, hill in front of Spotted Tail Agency" (SGUA, book A, 442–43). See also Hyde, *Spotted Tail's Folk*.

20. The famous mountain man Jim Bridger (May 17, 1804–July 17, 1881) was born in the east in Richmond, Virginia, but his family soon moved to Saint Louis. Bridger headed for the Rockies at age eighteen with Ashley's first expedition in 1822 and spent the next two decades in the mountains, working at various times with Smith, Jackson & Sublette; the Rocky Mountain Fur Company (he was a partner 1830–34); and the American Fur Company. In 1843, in partnership with Louis Vasquez, he built Fort Bridger on the Green River in southwest Wyoming, selling out to the Mormons ten years later. Bridger's vast experience in the mountains led to his employment as a guide for numerous government expeditions: in 1850 with Stansbury, in 1859–60 with Raynolds to the Yellowstone, in 1865–66 with the Powder River Expedition, and, later, with Grenville Dodge's Union Pacific surveys. In 1867, suffering from failing eyesight, Bridger bought a home in Westport, Missouri, near his friends Bent and Vasquez. He had three Indian wives—Flathead, Ute, and Shoshone—and sent a number of his children east for their education. Bridger's work as a trapper, scout, and guide gained him immeasurable knowledge of western geography and Indian tribes. See Stanley Vestal, *Jim Bridger, Mountain Man: A Biography* (New York: William Morrow, 1946; reprint, Lincoln: University of Nebraska Press, 1970), and J. Cecil Alter, *James Bridger: Trapper, Frontiersman, Scout and Guide* (Columbus OH: Long's College Book, 1951).

21. Geminien P. Beauvais (Dec. 6, 1815–Nov. 15, 1878) was born to Geminien Beauvais and Placide Aubuchon in Saint Genevieve, Missouri. At age sixteen G. P. Beauvais went to work for the Chouteaus, going up the Missouri on the steamship *Yellowstone*'s maiden voyage. In 1833 he was at Salt Lake with Fontenelle, and a year later attended the Green River rendezvous. He returned to Saint Louis and in 1835 married Marie Louise Montary. His wife and son soon died, and after a stint with

the Saint Louis police, Beauvais returned to the mountains and a life of trapping and trading.

Beauvais established a road ranch five miles east of Fort Laramie in 1853 (Five Mile Ranch) and in short time was a major trader on the upper North Platte. Like many traders, Beauvais while maintaining a white family (his second) back east had an Indian wife and children in the west. To reap the benefits from Colorado mining emigration, he established a second post on the South Platte at the Old California Crossing twenty-five miles east of Julesburg. Between this Star Ranch and the Five Mile, Beauvais employed a large number of traders dealing with the Crow, Cheyenne, and Lakota. Working for him at one time or another were Samuel Deon, Tom Dorian, Leon Pallardy, and Charlie Elston.

Beginning in 1864, Indian troubles precipitated changes in Beauvais's enterprises. That year one of the buildings at the Star Ranch became the barracks for the First Nebraska Cavalry, and numerous raids on his posts and caravans caused Beauvais to sell the Five Mile to Ecoffey & Cuny, file claims for his losses, and move to Saint Louis with nearly one million dollars in profits. His Lakota wife and children moved north to their people.

Although he moved from the Laramie region, Beauvais stayed involved in U.S.-Lakota relations; he attended the 1867 Laramie council and in 1870 traveled to Washington with Red Cloud. In 1875 Beauvais was a member of the Allison Commission, the entity that failed in its attempt to pressure the Lakota into selling the Black Hills. G. P. Beauvais died of blood poisoning in 1878 in Saint Louis. For additional information see Charles E. Hanson Jr., "Geminien P. Beauvais," in *Mountain Men and the Fur Trade*, ed. Hafen, vol. 7, and NSHS MS697 G. P. Beauvais Collection.

22. Adolf Cuny was involved in a variety of trading and ranching partnerships in the Laramie region. He was married to Josephine Bissonette, mixed-blood daughter of Joseph and his wife Ella Plenty Brothers. In July 1877 Cuny, then a deputy sheriff, was killed at the Six Mile Ranch by the outlaw Billy Webster, alias Clark Pelton.

23. The great traveling Jesuit missionary Father Pierre Jean DeSmet (Jan. 30, 1801–May 23, 1873) was born in Belgium and came to the United States in 1821. He entered the novitiate at Baltimore and then went to Florissant near Saint Louis. He was ordained in 1827, taught at the University of Saint Louis, and spent the years 1833–37 in Europe. In 1837

he was sent as a missionary to the Potawatomi near Council Bluffs. DeSmet traveled to the distant Flatheads in 1840 and spent the next thirty years bringing the word of Christ to Indians of the northern plains, Rockies, and Northwest. Seen as a friend by many tribes, he attended the 1851 Laramie treaty council and met with Sitting Bull in 1868. DeSmet died in Saint Louis. The best source on DeSmet's life and work is Hiram Martin Chittenden and Alfred Talbot Richardson, *Life, Letters and Travels of Father Pierre-Jean DeSmet, S.J.*, 4 vols. (New York: Francis P. Harper, 1905).

24. The 1875 Spotted Tail census lists a "Metcalf" with no additional information. He appears in the 1886 Pine Ridge census at age 45 married to Red Road. The 1892 Rosebud census has a listing for a 79-year-old widow identified only as "Metcalfe's mother." The paragraph concerning Metcalf was sent separately to the NSHS and has been inserted in the text.

25. As in other instances, Bettelyoun uses the word "us" although she could not have been present during this incident, having been born nine years later.

7. CROW BUTTE

1. In the holograph Bettelyoun dates this event as occurring in 1859. The text has been changed to agree with her dates elsewhere and with a clarification she gave to Sheldon in correspondence. (NSHS MS185, S1; Nov. 23, 1938.)

2. *Paha akan najiŋ wica api*: made to stand on top of the hill.

3. The incident at Crow Butte (Paha Kaŋgi) is dated as 1849 in the Baptiste Good winter count and in Bordeaux's claim for losses. Bettelyoun's brother Antoine, not Louis, was then about two years old. See participant Cloud Man's account in William J. Bordeaux, *Conquering the Mighty Sioux* (Sioux Falls: n.p., 1929), 41–45.

8. THE BATTLE OF THE BLUE WATER

1. Ituhuwaŋka (*Ituhu*, forehead; *waŋka*, high) is usually translated as High Forehead. Sandoz alone calls him Straight Foretop. Other sources indicate that the cow's killer was Ituhuwaŋka himself, not a son.

2. Mato Oyuhi (*Mato*, bear; *oyuhi*, to scatter or spread; 1821–Aug. 19, 1854) was a Wajaja Brulé. His name has been variously translated as Conquering Bear, Brave Bear, and Whirling Bear. Mato Oyuhi had

signed the 1851 Laramie Treaty as government-appointed chief of the Brulés and had maintained peaceful relations with whites.

3. Auguste Lucien (Wyuse; May 1814–Aug. 19, 1854), a French Canadian–Iowa mixed-blood, was married to Ena Tiglak. All accounts agree that Lucien was drunk and belligerent toward the Lakotas during the incident.

4. Lt. John Lawrence Grattan (ca. 1830–Aug. 19, 1854) graduated from West Point in 1853 and had been at Fort Laramie since July of that year. He was, by most accounts, a rash young officer eager to prove himself against the Indians, for whom he had no respect and little understanding. No less a person than Laramie's army chaplain, William Vaux, gives the following testimony regarding Grattan's relationship with the Lakotas and the actions that cost him his life:

> [Grattan] had an unwarrantable contempt of Indian character, which frequently manifested itself in my presence and at my quarters; and often, at the latter place, have I reproved him for acts which I conceived highly improper, such as thrusting his clenched fist in their faces, and threatening terrible things if ever duty or opportunity threw such a chance his way. I have said to him again and again, "Mr. Grattan, if you choose to act in this way, I must beg you to indulge elsewhere than in my quarters." Indeed, so notorious was this trait, that it was remarked to me by a trader here, "If ever G. gets into a difficulty with the Indians, I hope he may come out safe, but I doubt it." Meaning by this remark that from his contempt of the Indians and an undue reliance on his own powers, he would be led into conflict when there was no hope of success. On the day of Mr. Grattan's departure, I saw him when about starting, and could not but notice his extreme agitation. And some days after the fatal affair, I was fishing with Mr. Renald, who was present during the whole difficulty, and he assured me most solemnly, that G. was quite intoxicated. I do not vouch for this, at the same time I do not doubt its truth. The awful consequences of the whole occurrence, with the existing state of things, and the unknown future results, I conceive to be the *effects* and not the *cause* of culpability. That cause is to be traced to the fact of the garrison being left under the command of inexperienced and rash boys.

Vaux concludes with a prophetic warning: "Behold, how great a matter a little fire kindleth!" Statement of William Vaux, Chaplain, U.S. Army,

Oct. 4, 1855, in *Report of the Secretary of War,* 34th Cong., 1st sess., 1855–56, S. Exec. Doc. 9.

For general accounts of the Grattan fight by white historians see Hyde, *Spotted Tail's Folk,* 56–62; Remi Nadeau, *Fort Laramie and the Sioux* (Englewood Cliffs NJ: Prentice-Hall, 1967; reprint, Lincoln: University of Nebraska Press, 1982) 89–110; Mari Sandoz, *Crazy Horse: The Strange Man of the Oglalas* (New York: Knopf, 1942) 9–44; and Lloyd E. McCann, "The Grattan Massacre," *Nebraska History* 37, no. 1 (March 1956): 1–25. McCann identifies the wounded soldier as Pvt. John Cuddy. He died on August 21. For documentary materials see 33rd Cong., 2nd sess., 1854–55, H. Exec. Doc. 63, and 34th Cong., 1st and 2nd sess., 1855–56, S. Exec. Doc. 91 (James Bordeaux's accounts, conflicting with Bettelyoun's contention that her father's store was "not molested," can be found in the latter document); *The Missouri Republican,* Sept. 13, 1854, reprinted in NSHS *Publications* 20 (1922): 259–60; and *The Annual Report of the Commissioner of Indian Affairs,* 1854. Of particular interest is "Narrative of Particulars of Affair of 19th August Last by the 'Man Who Is Afraid of His Horses' " (NARS RG393, Letters Received by the Dept. of the West, box 2, letter H111). Finally, of additional interest from the Lakota perspective, five drawings by Black Horse depicting the fight as told to him by his participant grandfather can be found in U.S. War Department, *The Massacre of Lieutenant Grattan and His Command by Indians* (Glendale CA: Arthur H. Clark, 1983).

5. This stream in Garden County, Nebraska, is usually referred to as Blue Water Creek, Mni To Wakpala.

6. In his report of the fight, Lt. Col. Philip St. George Cooke, commander of the mounted force, writes: "[F]ortunately our cautious approach was not discovered, and withdrawing, I succeeded under the excellent guidance of Tesson (Honore), after a march of ten or twelve miles in all, in getting a very favorable position soon after sunrise behind a slight ridge" (Selected Letters Received, 1855 and 1856, Post Records of the War Dept., Office of the Adjutant General, National Archives).

Harney himself reported: "I should do an injustice to Mr. Joseph Tesson, one of my guides, were I to omit a mention of his eminently valuable services in conducting the column of cavalry to its position in the rear of the Indian villages. To his skill as a guide, and his knowledge of the character and habits of the enemy, I ascribe much of the success gained in the engagement." (Report of the Secretary of War, 34th Cong., 1st sess., 1855, S. Exec. Doc. 1, 51).

7. Standing over six feet, Little Thunder (Wakiŋyaŋ Cikala; ca. 1821–79) is cited, along with Conquering Bear, as one of the two leaders of the Brulés after 1845. He rose to greater prominence following the Bear's murder. After the disaster at the Blue Water, Little Thunder signed Harney's unratified treaty at Fort Pierre in 1856. He moved with his band to the various Brulé agencies, finally settling on the Rosebud; he died soon after on Hay Creek.

Iron Shell (Tuki Maza; 1816–96), the son of chief Bull Tail and father of Hollow Horn Bear, was the leader of the Orphan band (known as the Aśke, or tuft of hair, band until 1844). He first distinguished himself in the summer of 1843 in a fight with the Pawnees. At the Blue Water fight, the youngest of Iron Shell's three wives was taken as a prisoner to Fort Laramie. When the soldier who was keeping her was discharged, he took this woman back east with him, never to be heard from again. In 1856, at the council at Fort Pierre, Iron Shell was appointed as a subchief of the Brulés under Little Thunder. Later, he fought in the 1865 raids and in "Red Cloud's War" to close the forts on the Bozeman Trail; he signed the Treaty of 1868 at its conclusion. Iron Shell settled in the Cut Meat District of the Rosebud Reservation and died in 1896 at the age of eighty. He was buried on a hill some miles west of the Rosebud Agency.

8. The literature concerning the Blue Water fight is extensive. See Fred H. Werner, *With Harney on the Blue Water: Battle of Ash Hollow, 1855* (Greeley CO: Werner, 1988); Richmond L. Clow, "Mad Bear: William S. Harney and the Sioux Expedition of 1855–1856," *Nebraska History* 61, no. 2 (summer 1980): 133–51; James Hanson, "Artifacts from the Battlefield," *Nebraskaland* 64, no. 5 (June 1986): 6–13; and Robert Harvey, "The Battle Ground of Ash Hollow," NSHS *Publications* 16 (1911): 152–64. A number of military officers wrote of the fight: see Eugene Bandel, *Frontier Life in the Army, 1854–1861*, Southwest Historical Series, vol. 2 (Glendale CA: Arthur H. Clark, 1932); Otis E. Young, *The West of Philip St. George Cooke, 1809–1895*, Western Frontiersman Series, vol. 5 (Glendale CA: Arthur H. Clark, 1955); Richard C. Drum, "Reminiscences of the Indian Fight at Ash Hollow, 1855," NSHS *Publications* 16 (1911): 143–51; and the papers of Nathan Augustus Monroe Dudley, NSHS MS3556, S1 (some of this collection has been edited and published by R. Eli Paul, "Battle of Ash Hollow: The 1909–1910 Recollections of General N. A. M. Dudley," *Nebraska History* 62, no. 3 [fall 1981]: 373–99). Finally, the diary of Army Corps of Engineers of-

ficer Gouverneur Kemble Warren is especially interesting; a microfilm copy can be found at NSHS MS3944.

9. Most sources cite five prisoners taken to Fort Leavenworth for the Grattan fight and the attack on the mail wagon: Spotted Tail (who had been wounded in the Blue Water fight); two brothers of Conquering Bear, Red Leaf (Wapeśa) and Long Chin (Ikuhaŋska); and two unnamed boys. One of the boys was too sick to come to Laramie, and the other had gone north with the Miniconjous. In their places, two men came forward and surrendered their freedom: Spotted or Standing Elk (Hehaka Gleśka or Najiŋ) and Red Plume (Waciŋhiŋśa). Spotted Tail, Red Leaf, and Long Chin reached Fort Leavenworth on December 11, 1855, and were released in the spring of the following year. Spotted Tail's experience at Fort Leavenworth is said to have impressed upon him the overwhelming power of the United States, and afterward he leaned toward peace. Red Leaf, on the other hand, returned from prison an advocate of war. As a leader of the Wajajas, he took part in the war to close the Bozeman Trail. In the early 1870s he made his camp at the Oglala agency, where in 1876–77 the army took his and Red Cloud's horses in the dismounting effort. Red Leaf's Wajaja camp was a focal point of the ghost dance in 1890.

10. *Hetopa waŋ ktepi*: a four horn was killed.

11. See chapter 12, note 1.

12. In a letter accompanying this chapter, Josephine Waggoner wrote to Addison Sheldon, "You know there were many war babies born after Harney left Laramie" (NSHS RG14, SG1, S1; Directors' Records, box 79, Dec. 5, 1935).

13. A. G. (Amberson or Augustus Gerry) Shaw enlisted as a private in Company B of the Eleventh Ohio Volunteer Cavalry on October 12, 1861. He was eighteen at the time. Bettelyoun must be confused about either the events that led Shaw to take Kills Eagle's wife, or the name of the soldier who did so, since the Battle of the Blue Water took place before Shaw entered Laramie country. Shaw mustered out with his company April 1, 1865. Ten years later, the first census taken at the Spotted Tail Agency records Shaw with his Lakota wife, two sons, and a daughter. At this time Shaw was running a "messhouse" near the agency so disreputable that agent Howard tried to have Shaw removed from the area. Howard had apparently fired Shaw from an agency job not long before. A. G. Shaw died sometime before 1877, as census records from that year lists his wife "Martoelar" as a widow at age fifty. See Harry H. Anderson,

"Fur Traders as Fathers: The Origins of the Mixed-Blooded Community among the Rosebud Sioux," *South Dakota History* 3, no. 3 (1973): 233–70.

9. CONDITIONS FROM 1854 TILL 1868

1. In September 1857 Mormons, dressed as Indians, and Paiutes attacked a gentile wagon train. About 120 people were killed and many more wounded. The incident occurred in southwest Utah. See Juanita Brooks, *Mountain Meadows Massacre*, new ed. (Norman: University of Oklahoma Press, 1962. Reprint 1991).

2. See pages 77–78.

3. George Bird Grinell wrote of this 1856 incident in *The Fighting Cheyennes*: "The following night an old trapper, named Garnier, who was returning to the fort, met the Cheyennes, who killed him" (108).

4. Little is known about Charles DeSersa (Estatolo, ca. 1830s–?), and Episcopal church and Rosebud census records leave a confusing trail. He married Julia Robidoux in 1874 at the second Whetstone agency (in Nebraska), but their daughter Minnette was born in 1859, indicating that the couple had been together at least fifteen years before the church-sanctioned marriage. Another daughter, Isabel, was born in 1875 on the White River in Nebraska to Desersa and Peicawiŋ (possibly Robidoux's Lakota name). In the 1887 Rosebud census Desersa is listed as married to Okiya (Help), with an eleven-year-old daughter, Tate Mani (Walking Wind) and a twenty-year-old son, Ihaŋktoŋwaŋ (Yankton); in the 1891 census he is listed as husband to Mary. Adult "DeSersas" in both censuses are, no doubt, his children. (See SGUA Episcopal Church Records, book A.)

5. Mapped by John M. Bozeman in 1863–65, the Bozeman Trail was the best route to the Montana gold fields. It originated at Julesburg, Colorado, on the South Platte, headed north past Fort Laramie in Wyoming to the Big Horn Mountains and the Yellowstone River, and there turned west to Virginia City. The army built three forts on the trail to protect the miners and immigrants: Reno, Phil Kearny, and C. F. Smith. It was the erection of these forts that angered the Lakota most, leading them into a successful war that eventually closed the Bozeman Trail.

6. Elbridge Gerry (Ištaska, White Eye; July 18, 1818–April 10, 1875) was born in Massachusetts. Gerry went to sea at an early age, but he soon found his way to the Rocky Mountains as a beaver trapper. Employed by Sublette & Bent, and later by the American Fur Company, Gerry arrived

in the Laramie region in the early 1840s. He had two Lakota wives, the twin daughters of Swift Bird. His first daughter, Lizzie, married Fort Laramie sutler Seth Ward. After living with a group of traders at Miraville City north of Denver, Gerry moved his family to the South Platte at the mouth of Crow Creek, ten miles east of present-day Greeley, Colorado. It was here that he developed his prosperous horse ranch. In 1864 Gerry made his famous ride warning stockowners of coming Cheyenne raids, thus becoming the "Paul Revere of Colorado." Elbridge Gerry is buried overlooking his horse ranch alongside one of his wives and his son-in-law Seth Ward. See Leroy R. Hafen, "Elbridge Gerry, Colorado Pioneer," *Colorado Magazine* 29, no. 2 (April 1952): 137–49, and Ann W. Hafen, "Elbridge Gerry," in *Mountain Men and the Fur Trade*, ed. Hafen, vol. 6.

7. Antoine DuBray had previously worked for Sybile & Adams and later for the government at Whetstone. Antoine LaDeau worked as a guide at Fort Laramie after his trapping days; he is listed in the Fort's 1870 census, at age fifty, as a laborer. He was married to Waŋbli sapawiŋ (Black Eagle) and had more than nine children. Edward de Moran (Morin) was born in Montreal in 1818, the son of a Saint Lawrence voyageur. Throughout the 1830s and 1840s he worked as a trapper for various companies from the Illinois River to the Rockies. He moved to Cottonwood Springs (later Fort McPherson) in 1853 and two years later established a road ranch there. During the 1860s de Moran worked as an independent trader on the Platte and Republican Rivers and served the military as a guide and interpreter. In the early 1870s he entered a trading partnership with his son-in-law Leon Palladay, and later in the decade was employed at Fort Robinson and various Lakota agencies. The Indians called him Hu Maza or Iron Legs. See Paul D. Riley, "Edward de Morin," in *Mountain Men and the Fur Trade*, ed. Hafen, vol. 9. Bettelyoun may be referring to either Lester or J. H. Pratt, both traders among the Brulés.

8. Born in Saint Charles, Missouri, Nick Janis (Waśicuŋ Haŋska, Tall Whiteman; Oct. 12, 1827–Sept. 13, 1902) joined his brother Antoine at Fort Laramie in 1845. Together they were traders with the Oglala. Janis married Red Cloud's niece Onasapawiŋ (Black Fire Woman), and the couple had nine children. On a trading trip to Colorado in 1858, Janis, his brother, and Elbridge Gerry were given a parcel of land near Box Elder Creek by the Cheyennes. After the gold strike the brothers worked as guides for prospectors, and in the early 1860s Nick served as the Cheyenne interpreter at the Upper Platte Agency. Janis established a

stage station in the 1870s some thirty miles east of Laramie, but sold out to John Hunton in July 1880, moving to Pine Ridge to be with his wife's people. Janis died there in 1902 and is buried at the Holy Rosary Mission. See Janet LeCompte, "Antoine Janis," in *Mountain Men and the Fur Trade*, ed. Hafen, vol. 8, and FLNHS file CIN-10.

9. Although Steve Estes (Feb. 15, 1840–June 28, 1912) does not appear on lists of agents for the Upper Platte Agency, he may have been one of the special agents sometimes sent to the Fort Laramie area. Estes was chief clerk at Whetstone under Poole and in 1870, when Spotted Tail and his people moved back to the White River, Estes served as subagent. He was married to a Lakota woman who is listed in church records as Sophie and in the 1891 Rosebud census as Mary. Estes is buried north of Rosebud, South Dakota.

10. Joseph Prue (ca. 1815–?) was married to Wicageluwiŋ, or Mary. They later settled on the Rosebud reservation with their children.

11. The holograph reads, "If I remember right, this was 1853, I was then about four years old." Bettelyoun was born in the spring of 1857; if she was indeed about four, the date is probably the fall of 1860 or 1861. The text has been changed accordingly.

12. This story of the Ford family was written and sent as a separate section.

13. *The Works of Hubert Howe Bancroft*, vol. 25, *History of Nevada, Colorado, and Wyoming, 1540–1888* (San Francisco: The History Co., 1890).

14. Col. Edwin Vose Sumner's (Jan. 30, 1797–March 21, 1863) famous saber attack against the Cheyennes occurred July 29, 1857, on the Solomon River, a branch of the Smoky Hill River, not the Arkansas. This engagement was the first of the campaign; Sumner had previously sent Maj. John Sedgwick and his cavalry up the Arkansas, but no Indians were found. E. V. Sumner went on to become the commander of the Department of the West in 1858 and later served in the Civil War as a general. He was relieved of duty at his own request. He died at his home in New York in 1863.

Two Moon (Ese'heoohnesese) was only ten to fifteen years old at the time of the fight; he later became a chief of the Cheyenne Kit Fox society. His father, Carries the Otter, was an Arikara married to a Northern Cheyenne woman. Old Man Afraid of His Horses (Taśuŋkopipape—"the man of whose horses they are afraid") is the Huŋkpatila Oglala chief who became leader of the Payaba, or Pushed Aside, band upon Red Cloud's ascendancy.

As these events took place in the summer of 1857, Bettelyoun could not have remembered this particular Mormon emigrant train. Military documents concerning the campaign against the Cheyennes have been collected and can be found in Leroy R. Hafen and Ann W. Hafen, *Relations with the Indians of the Plains, 1857–1861: A Documentary Account of Military Campaigns, and Negotiations of Indian Agents, with Reports and Journals of P. G. Lowe, R. M. Peck, J. E. B. Stuart, S. D. Sturgis and Other Official Papers,* The Far West and the Rockies Historical Series, 1820–1875, vol. 9 (Glendale CA: Arthur H. Clark, 1959). For Cheyenne accounts, see Hyde, *Life of George Bent,* 100–105; Grinnell, *The Fighting Cheyennes,* 111–23; and Powell, *People of the Sacred Mountain,* vol. 1:211–14.

15. The literature on the 1862 Santee uprising in Minnesota is vast; for Sibley and Sulley's 1863 and 1864 campaigns against the Santees, Yanktons, and Huŋkpapas, including the Battle of Whitestone Hill (Sept. 3, 1864), see Robert M. Utley, *Frontiersmen in Blue: The United States Army and the Indian, 1848–1865* (New York: Macmillan, 1967) 261–80. Sulley's 1864 campaign and the Battle of Killdeer Mountain (July 28, 1864) are well treated in Rev. Louis Phaller's "Sulley's Expedition of 1864, Featuring the Killdeer Mountain and Badlands Battles," *North Dakota History* 31, no. 1 (Jan. 1964): 25–77. Military records can be found in *The War of the Rebellion: A Compilation of the Official Records of the Union and Confederate Armies* (Washington DC: GPO, 1885–1901), series 1. A good popular discussion of Gen. Patrick Edward Connor's disastrous 1865 Powder River Expedition against the Sioux and Cheyennes is found in Utley, *Frontiersmen in Blue,* 322–32. Military records of this expedition have been collected in Leroy R. Hafen and Ann W. Hafen, *Powder River Campaign and Sawyers Expedition of 1865: A Documentary Account Comprising Official Reports, Diaries, Contemporary Newspaper Accounts and Personal Narratives,* The Far West and Rockies Historical Series, 1820–1875, vol. 12, 1961; the introduction is especially helpful. Additional military records are in *The War of the Rebellion: A Compilation of the Official Records of the Union and Confederate Armies,* series 1, vol. 48 (Washington DC: GPO, 1896). An interesting reminiscence of the campaign, replete with the racist views of the day, is H. E. Palmer, *The Powder River Expedition, 1865* (Omaha: The Republican Co., 1887). For a Cheyenne view, see participant George Bent's account in Hyde, *Life of George Bent,* 223–43.

16. Although Sabin authored countless books on the frontier, and a number appear in his "Boys' Book of" series, none is entitled *The Boys' Book of*

Scouts. However, Sabin's volume *Boys' Book of Indian Warriors and Heroic Indian Women* (Philadelphia: George W. Jacobs, 1918) includes a chapter on Red Cloud, "The Sioux Who Closed the Road of the Whites," which tells the story of Fort Phil Kearny, the Fetterman Massacre, and the Wagon Box Fight.

17. Referred to as the Wagon Box Fight by whites, the Piney Creek battle occurred on August 2, 1867. In his official report the commanding officer, Capt. James Powell, states that 3,000 Indians attacked his force of 32. Powell says no less than 60 Indians were killed and 120 wounded. In his *Indian Fights and Fighters*, in the fanciful chapter "The Thirty-Two against the Three Thousand," Cyrus Townsend Brady writes that 1,137 Indians were killed or wounded (1904; reprint, Lincoln: University of Nebraska Press, 1971).

Ring Bull, when interviewed by William J. Bordeaux, listed by name eight wounded and three killed. He went on to say that the only time more than 100 Lakota were killed in one fight was at the Wounded Knee Massacre. All three men Bordeaux spoke with denied that Red Cloud was even in the area during the attack (Bordeaux, *Conquering the Mighty Sioux*). Doane Robinson of the South Dakota Historical Society questioned two Lakota participants in 1904: "They were White Bear and Whitewash. They agreed it was not a very serious affair. As to the casualties, they said there were 'very few.' Asked if there were twelve hundred killed, they were highly amused at the suggestion; at suggesting five hundred lost, they laughed heartily. . . . 'Fifty?', 'No, no; very few.'" In 1923 Robinson sent Billy Garnett *The Bozeman Trail* by Grace Raymond Hebard and E. A. Brininstool, asking for his response. Garnett replied, "There is a great deal of genuine 'bull' in that account of the Wagon Box fight, for there was no particular Indian chief in charge of the Indians at that time. . . . The book says there were several hundred Indians killed there, some estimates being as high as fifteen hundred. This is very much exaggerated, for there were not fifteen hundred Indians killed by soldiers (that is Sioux and Cheyenne Indians) during the ten years from 1860 to 1870. I am told by Red Feather, who was in this fight, that there were actually only five Indians killed there and that it was not much of a fight. In addition to this there were five wounded" (Doane Robinson, "The Education of Red Cloud," *South Dakota State Historical Collections* 12 [1924]: 171). George Bird Grinnell believed only three hundred to four hundred Indians participated in the attack and that nine were killed. White Bull's account of the fight is given in Stanley Vestal, *Warpath: The*

True Story of the Fighting Sioux Told in a Biography of Chief White Bull (Boston: Houghton Mifflin, 1934; reprint, Lincoln: University of Nebraska Press, 1984).

18. Bettelyoun is quoting article 16 and article 2 from the treaty. William J. Bordeaux does the same thing in his *Conquering the Mighty Sioux* (33–34), and she is probably using that book as her source. The full text of the treaty can be found in Charles J. Kappler, *Indian Affairs, Laws and Treaties* (Washington DC: GPO, 1904), 2:998–1007. Proceedings of the treaty councils of 1867 and 1868 are published in *Papers Relating to Talks and Councils Held with the Indians in Dakota and Montana Territories in the Years 1866–1869* (Washington DC: GPO, 1904). The treaty was signed near Fort Laramie on April 29, 1868, ratified February 16, 1869, and proclaimed February 24, 1869.

19. "Afterwards he [Bordeaux] went across the country and settled on the north side of the Missouri River at Bijou Hill. . . . Old Jim was a hard drinker. There was a heavy emigrant travel up both sides of the Missouri. Bordeaux did a swelling business exchanging goods and alcohol for horses, mules, buffalo robes and peltries, and money. . . . Bordeaux's wife left him over there on the Missouri because of his drinking habit and came over to the Spotted Tail Agency where Rosebud now is, and where their son Louie was living. . . . After a while old Jim came over to Spotted Tail and got the government contracts for wood, hay and charcoal. In this business he prospered. Before he came over from the Missouri with two trains, one of horses and mules, one of oxen, nearly 30 teams in all, he had quit drinking. He had put in his bids and got his contracts before his departure. He did not live very long at Spotted Tail; he had quit drinking so suddenly after such immoderate use of the stuff that . . . it killed him" (paraphrase of Magloire Alexis Mosseau in interview notes by Eli Ricker, NSHS MS8, Eli S. Ricker Collection, roll 5, tablet 28).

20. An issue of *Nebraska History* was devoted to examining this Pawnee-Sioux battle. It includes reports by the Pawnee agent as well as those of Stephen F. Estes and Antoine Janis. See *Nebraska History* 16, no. 3 (July–Sept. 1935).

10. TWO STORIES OF HORSE CREEK

1. The "Fort Laramie Treaty" of 1851 called for the cessation of intertribal hostilities among the nations involved (Lakota, Gros Ventre, Assiniboine, Blackfeet, Crow, Cheyenne, and Arapaho). It also granted the

United States the right to establish roads and posts on Indian lands and to receive "satisfaction" arising from depredations committed by Indians. In turn, the Indians were to be protected from depredations committed by whites.

Article 5 of the treaty established territories for the participating tribes. For the Lakota, this meant the land "commencing [at] the mouth of the White Earth River, on the Missouri River; thence in a southwesterly direction to the forks of the Platte River; thence up the north fork of the Platte River to a point known as the Red Butte, or where the road leaves the river; thence along the range of mountains known as the Black Hills, to the head-waters of Heart River; thence down Heart River to its mouth; and thence down the Missouri River to the place of beginning." Finally, the treaty called for the delivery of annuities for fifty years, a stipulation that the Senate reduced to ten years. The full text of the treaty can be found in Kappler, *Laws and Treaties*, 2:594–96. Contrary to Bettelyoun's statement, the treaty council was held and the treaty signed during the administration of President Millard Fillmore. The amendment altering the number of years that annuities were to be given was added during Pierce's administration.

2. Two Face (Ite Nuŋpa) and Black Foot (Siha Sapa) were leaders of the Tapiśleca, or Spleen, band of Oglalas.

3. Seth Edmund Ward (March 4, 1820–Dec. 9, 1903), a major figure in the Laramie area, is, as his biographer has written, "the classic example of the rare mountain man who achieved both wealth and beneficent old age . . . rising from penniless trapper to the status of a merchant prince" (Merrill J. Mattes, "Seth Ward," in *Mountain Men and the Fur Trade*, ed. Hafen, 3:357). He ran away from his home in Virginia at sixteen, and a few years later, in 1838, he headed for the Rockies with Lancaster Lupton's fur trade caravan. For the next decade Ward trapped in the mountains, became clerk of a trading operation in Colorado, and served as the chief trader at Fort Saint Vrain on the South Platte. In 1848, he entered into a partnership with William Le Guerrier, an arrangement that would last ten years until Guerrier's death. Ward & Guerrier operated first at Ash Point near modern Torrington, Wyoming, later at Sand Point near Guernsey, and finally on the Laramie River opposite old Fort John. In 1857 Seth Ward became the dominant figure of the North Platte valley trading arena when he was appointed sutler at Fort Laramie. In this position and with his licensed tradership with the Lakota, Ward controlled much of the business in the area. On one of his semiannual

trips to Westport, Ward married Mary Frances McCarty. (His previous marriage to a Lakota woman is discussed later in the chapter.) Because his wife was unhappy at Laramie, Ward moved his home to Nebraska City in 1863 and left Bullock, whom he had hired in 1858, in charge. Fluent in Lakota, Cheyenne, and Arapaho, Seth Ward served as a commissioner for the 1866 Indian peace commission. In 1871, at fifty-two, he made his last trip to Fort Laramie, sold out his sutlership and his holdings in Nebraska City, and retired a millionaire to a large estate in Westport, now an affluent section of Kansas City. A patriarch of the city, Seth Ward was a bank president and a pillar of the Westport Baptist Church.

William Galt Bullock acted as Ward's general manager at the sutler's store at Fort Laramie from 1863 until 1871. Because the store was the hub of the fort and the fort was the hub of the area, Bullock's business letterbook serves as a rare window into the history of the region. Bullock was strongly opposed to the hanging of Two Face and Black Foot, and his general view of the government's military policy can be found in a July 23, 1868, entry in the letterbook: "I very much fear the treaty made here with the Indians will amount to nothing more than a renewal of hostilities as long as Govt. send such imbeciles out to treat with them as Gen. Harney and his like." Around 1870 Bullock established a ranch on the Laramie River, but he soon moved to Cheyenne with his wife. After her death in 1879, he married a Lakota woman and returned to the Laramie region. W. G. Bullock died in Virginia in 1896. In addition to Mattes, "Seth Ward," see WDCR, MSS556 and MSS782, and FLNHS file CIN-20. The editor's copy of Bullock's letterpress book is from the "Fort Laramie" vertical file at NSHS; it has been published in *Annals of Wyoming* 13, no. 4 (Oct. 1941): 237–330.

4. Lucinda Eubanks and her child were captured by the Cheyennes during the raids along the Little Blue River in Nebraska in late summer 1864. Accounts vary as to whether Col. Thomas Moonlight (Nov. 10, 1833 – Feb. 7, 1899), commander of the District of the Plains headquartered at Fort Laramie, or Lt. Col. William Baumer, commander of the fort itself, ordered the hanging. There is also evidence suggesting that Brig. Gen. Patrick E. Connor was responsible. Moonlight's special order for the hanging charges the "commanding officer of Ft. Laramie" with its execution (FLNHS, order book, special order no. 11, 56). In any event, it is generally acknowledged that both Moonlight and Baumer were drunk at the time. The hanging took place May 26, 1865. See *The War*

of the Rebellion, series 1, vol. 48, and Hyde, *Life of George Bent*, 207–8. An interesting article examining the discrepancies among the various versions of the story is Dorothy M. Johnson, "The Hanging of the Chiefs," *Montana: The Magazine of Western History* 20, no. 3 (summer 1970): 60–69. See also subsequent correspondence in that journal regarding Johnson's article. The Cheyenne hanged at Laramie was Four Antelope.

5. These events took place in 1865; Red Cloud and Spotted Tail first went to Washington in 1870. See Hyde, *Spotted Tail's Folk*, 172–81.

6. See Melvin Gilmore, *Uses of Plants by the Indians of the Missouri River Region* (1919; reprint, Lincoln: University of Nebraska Press, 1977); Kelly Kindscher, *Edible Wild Plants of the Prairie: An Ethnobotanical Guide* (Lawrence: University Press of Kansas, 1987); and Dilwyn J. Rogers, *Lakota Names and Traditional Uses of Native Plants by Sicangu (Brule) People in the Rosebud Area, South Dakota: A Study Based on Father Eugene Buechel's Collection of Plants of Rosebud around 1920* (Saint Francis SD: Rosebud Educational Society, 1980).

7. Captain W. D. Fouts was commanding a detachment of the Seventh Iowa Cavalry. Charles Elston, born in Brook County, Virginia, on March 2, 1830, was in charge of a unit of Indian police and acted as Fouts's interpreter. He had been among the Lakota since his arrival in the Laramie area in the 1840s and had a Lakota wife, recorded as Ella in the Episcopal church records. Eugene Ware, for whose unit Elston served as a guide in 1864, wrote of him: "He knew the Sioux language, and the Sioux country, and Indian manners and customs by heart. He knew them with even more intelligence than an Indian knew them. As a white man is smarter than an Indian in civilization, so he is smarter than an Indian when it comes to competing in Indian matters and things. Elston was a charming man. It was said that he had two Indian wives among the Sioux, and one among the Cheyennes, but he was a sort of high-toned fellow, and his wives were never seen at the squaw camp near the fort." See Eugene F. Ware, *The Indian War of 1864* (Lincoln: University of Nebraska Press, 1963) 201. Elston's Lakota name, as given in the 1887 Rosebud census, was Woŋpośita.

8. Hyde writes: "According to the Pine Ridge Sioux, the Indian prisoners in the wagons were Thunder Bear, son of Chief Two Face, Black War Bonnet, Calico (also called Black Shield), and a Brulé named Stand. In later years, Thunder Bear and Calico were judges on the Indian Court at Pine Ridge" (*Spotted Tail's Folk*, 120 n). Denton R. Bedford adds: "Two

Face's son was Thunder Bear (Mato-wakinyan), seized at the time of his father's execution and placed in chains. With him was his first cousin Calico (Minihuha), also known as Black Shield (Wohachankasapa). Vindictively the next year Calico became a charter member of the Sotka Yuha Sioux war society. . . . It is believed that young Black War Bonnet, seized at the same time, was Black Foot's son. . . . In 1912, these two younger Indians became chief informants of the noted anthropologist, Clark Wissler, on Sioux culture." See *Montana: The Magazine of Western History* 20, no. 4 (Oct. 1970): 76.

9. This paragraph was sent as an addition to the chapter when Bettelyoun and Waggoner returned their corrected copy to Addison Sheldon.

10. Sefroy Iott (see chapter 6, note 17) married Leonide Janis, sister of Old Nick and Antoine, in 1838; he married a Lakota woman, "Ellen," before 1857 and later a Lakota named "Mary," who may have been the daughter of Green Plum (Kaŋta Śtuŋa).

11. Red Cloud's people did not move to the agency near Crawford until 1873, and Spotted Tail did not move to the "second Whetstone" agency at Beaver Creek until 1871. See appendix 3.

12. In a note in her file on the Bettelyoun manuscript, Mari Sandoz writes, "The above [Bettelyoun's account of Wasna] is, in substance, the story as I heard it told by Old Provo to my father, and from some of the Brulés too, although there was less sentimentality in their stories, and more suggestion that Wasna was already dying of tuberculosis when she left" (UNLA, Special Collections, Mari Sandoz Collection, box 52, file 31). "Wasna" literally means lard, grease, or tallow, and usually refers to a food mixture consisting of meat or cherries and marrow.

13. One of the more interesting characters on the upper Platte was agent Thomas S. Twiss (Sept. 1802–Spring 1871). Twiss was born in New York, graduated from West Point a Brevet 2nd Lieutenant of Engineers in 1826, and went on to teach mathematics and other subjects at that academy. Resigning his commission in 1829, Twiss spent the next twenty years as a professor of mathematics, astronomy, and natural philosophy at South Carolina College. From 1847 to 1855 he held various positions in industry. He was named Indian agent for the Upper Platte in 1855, arriving at Fort Laramie on August 10 of that year. After being suspended by General Harney (without authorization) in 1856, Twiss traveled to Washington and was reappointed to a five-year term. He was seen as instrumental in obtaining the surrender of Spotted Tail, Red Leaf, and Long Chin in 1856 after the Blue Water fight. Twiss soon

moved the agency from Rawhide Butte, east of Laramie, to Deer Creek, some one hundred miles upriver from the Fort. Here he married an Oglala woman and began to raise a family. Twiss soon abandoned his policy of trying to get the Lakota to farm and allied himself with the nonagency Oglalas. Through his association with traders John Richards Sr., Joseph Bissonette, and others, Twiss was charged with corruption and theft of annuities.

When he was removed from office in 1861 by President Lincoln, Twiss and his wife went to the Powder River country to live with her people. A few years later he made a visit to Fort Laramie; Eugene Ware describes him as "an old gentleman whose hair, long, white and curly, hung down over his shoulders, and down his back. He had a very venerable white beard and moustache. . . . He was dressed thoroughly as an Indian." Ware goes on to describe Twiss's contribution to a discussion at the sutler's store concerning a comparison between Grant's Vicksburg campaign and that of Napoleon at Borodino (*The Indian War of 1864*, 210–11). In 1870 Twiss bought forty acres of land in southeast Nebraska near Rulo, where he died the following year. See Alban W. Hoopes, "Thomas S. Twiss, Indian Agent on the Upper Platte, 1855–1861," *The Mississippi Valley Historical Review* 20 (June 1933–March 1934): 353–64, and Burton S. Hill, "Thomas S. Twiss, Indian Agent," *Great Plains Journal* 6, no. 2 (spring 1967): 85–96.

14. As previously stated, Bettelyoun was not yet born when this incident occurred in 1854.

15. See Albert Watkins, "Fort Mitchell Cemetery: Some Account of the Re-interment of Soldiers Originally Buried There and the So-called 'Horse Creek Battle Ground'" in *Nebraska History* 1, no. 8 (1918): 2–3.

16. For sources of information on Connor's three-pronged Powder River Expedition with Cole and Walker, see chapter 9, note 15. Military records of James A. Sawyers's Wagon Road Expedition of 1865 (ostensibly an expedition to build a road from the mouth of the Niobrara River to Virginia City in the Montana gold fields but in actuality a military escort for a private mining party) are collected, along with a good introduction, in Leroy R. Hafen and Ann W. Hafen, *Powder River Campaigns and the Sawyers' Expedition of 1865*, 219–354. Fort Fetterman, at the junction of LaPrele Creek and the North Platte River, about seventy-five miles northwest from Fort Laramie, was not established until July 19, 1867. It was never burned.

17. On December 21, 1866, under orders from Col. Henry B. Carrington,

Bvt. Col. William Judd Fetterman—who had once claimed that with eighty men he could ride through the whole Sioux Nation—rode out of Fort Phil Kearny with just that many men to relieve a woodcutting party besieged by a small group of warriors. The warriors were decoys and Fetterman rode into a trap; he and his entire command were killed. See Dee Brown, *Fort Phil Kearny: An American Saga* (New York: G. P. Putnam's Sons, 1962). Cheyenne accounts of the fight can be found in Hyde, *Life of George Bent*, 341–46; Powell, *People of the Sacred Mountain*, 1:451–61; and Grinnell, *The Fighting Cheyennes*, 230–44. Lakota accounts include that of Fire Thunder in Raymond DeMallie, *The Sixth Grandfather: Black Elk's Teachings Given to John G. Neihardt* (Lincoln: University of Nebraska Press, 1985), 103–4; White Bull in James A. Howard, ed. and trans., *The Warrior Who Killed Custer: The Personal Narrative of Chief Joseph White Bull* (Lincoln: University of Nebraska Press, 1968); and Vestal, *Warpath*, 50–69. See also Carrington's account in 50th Cong., 1st sess., 1887–88, S. Exec. Doc. 33.

18. As part of the great raids after the massacre at Sand Creek, the Cheyennes, with their Lakota allies, attacked the Platte bridge on July 25, 1865. See especially George Bent's eyewitness account in Hyde, *Life of George Bent*, 214–22. A popular treatment of the battle is J. W. Vaughn, *The Battle of Platte Bridge* (Norman: University of Oklahoma Press, 1963).

19. Although this paragraph is lightly crossed out in the original holograph and Bettelyoun contends later in the chapter that "there was no such a thing," her original assertion that Capt. John Wilcox attempted to pursue the Indians corresponds with his own report of June 21, 1865, in *The War of the Rebellion*, series 1, vol. 48, 322–24. Bettelyoun implies, and Wilcox confirms, that his pursuit was quickly aborted.

20. When Colonel Moonlight and his force of 234 volunteer cavalry had their horses taken by the Lakota on June 19 after the fight at Horse Creek, they were forced to walk the 120 miles back to Fort Laramie carrying their saddles. "These horses were offered to Mr. Bordeaux, but he would not take them" (Waggoner to Sheldon, March 10, 1936, NSHS MS185, S1). The loss of his mounts, coupled with the hanging of Two Face and Black Foot, resulted in Moonlight's being removed from command. It is said that he was saved from a court-martial only by political influence. Moonlight went on to become active in Kansas politics, served as governor of Wyoming, and was later ambassador to Bolivia.

21. Good Voice later became a subchief of the Oak Creek (Okreek) District

of the Rosebud reservation. He served as a scout for the army, opposed
the Ghost Dance movement, and helped establish the first school and
church at Okreek.

22. Susan Bettelyoun's account of the fight at Horse Creek is probably
the best available on this important yet often neglected incident when
"friendly" Lakota rebelled against the army. For the military's view-
point, see *The War of the Rebellion*, series 1, vol. 48.

23. Tom Dorion was a mixed-blood Brulé.

11. MY EARLY DAYS

1. In the late 1830s, a number of French Canadian trappers and traders
settled on the east side of the Nishnabotna River in southwest Iowa. As
the settlement grew during the 1840s, it became known as French Village. Bettelyoun's older sister, Louise, and her brother-in-law, Clement
Lamareaux (Lamoureaux), settled here by 1865. At around the same
time, her brothers Antoine, Louis, and John arrived to attend school. In
a letter to Addison Sheldon, Bettelyoun writes that she went to school
at Hamburg from 1866 to 1871, arriving two years after her brothers
(NSHS MS185, S1, Nov. 23, 1938). In 1867 Lamareaux signed the peti-
tion incorporating the city of Hamburg, and in 1874 he was instrumental in founding the town's Saint Mary's Church. For information on
French Village and Hamburg's beginnings, see *St. Mary's Church, Hamburg, Iowa* (n.p., n.d.) and the "James Bordeaux" vertical file, WDCR.

2. Book A of the Episcopal Church Records gives us the following history:
"Work begun at the Spotted Tail Agency near Camp Sheridan, Beaver
Ck. Neb. June 15, 1875. Rev. W. J. Cleveland Missionary. Mrs. W. J.
Cleveland: Miss Mary Jane Leigh & sister Sophie (Sophia C. Pendleton)
teachers. Agency removed to Ponka Agency mouth of Running water
summer of 1877. . . . Agency removed to Rosebud Creek D.T. Fall of
1878. Rev. H. Burt & Sister Sophie with W. J. Schmidt catechist. Joined
Jan 1st 1879 by Rev. W. J. Cleveland. Mrs. C & Miss Leigh returned in
Spring. Rev. H. Burt removed to Crow Creek Agency. Church Mission
house (frame) built that winter (1879)" (SGUA, Episcopal Church Records, book A, "History," 6). William J. Cleveland was ordained at Santee Mission in August 1873 by Bishop Hare. Sister Sophie Pendleton
had previously run a small girls' school at Crow Creek and Mary Jane
Leigh directed a boys' school at the Episcopal Cheyenne Mission. See K.
Brent Woodruff, "The Episcopal Mission to the Dakotas 1860–1898,"
South Dakota Historical Collections 17 (1934): 553–603.

3. Bettelyoun's contention that "everyone enjoyed" the march to Ponca Agency is refuted by the fact that a number of Indians fled the column near Wounded Knee Creek. Some Sans Arcs, led by Red Bear, and possibly some Miniconjous, took off for the north, descending on Red Cloud's column, which was moving parallel to the Brulés along the White River. Crazy Horse's parents were with those who left the Brulés, supposedly taking the body of their son with them. Officials with Red Cloud's people were afraid that these northern Lakotas would cause trouble as the Indians under their charge were having a much harder march than the Brulé, poorly clothed and short of rations. But the Sans Arcs and others just continued their flight north. See *The Annual Reports of the Commissioner of Indian Affairs*, 1877 and 1878, and Hyde, *Spotted Tail's Folk*, 287.

4. Episcopal Church records list the following burials: "Monday Oct. 14th 1878, James Bordeaux, age 63, baptized Roman Catholic, residence Rosebud Agency, dated death Oct. 14th, cause of death: Bronchitis." Bordeaux was originally buried on the "side hill N.E. of Agency." On April 22, 1879, the body was "removed to the Church Burying Grounds." "Saturday July 12, 1884, Mrs. Jas. Bordeaux, age 70, date of death July 11th, cause of death: Dropsy, place of burial: church burial grounds" (SGUA, Episcopal Church Records, book A, "Burials," 442–43 and 448–49). On September 15, 1940, both were reinterred at the Saint Francis Church Cemetery, Saint Francis, South Dakota.

5. Article 10 of the 1868 "Laramie Treaty" refers to "persons legally incorporated" with the Indians. This was generally taken to mean those white men married to Indian women and with Indian families at the time of the treaty.

12. CRAZY HORSE, TAŚUŊKA WITCO

1. After the fight at the Blue Water, Harney traveled on to Fort Laramie and then to Fort Pierre, Dakota Territory, arriving on October 20, 1855. The following spring, on March 1, Harney met in council with members of the Brulé, Sans Arc, Huŋkpapa, Blackfeet, and Two Kettle bands of the Lakota, and representatives of the Yanktons and Yanktonais. On the last day of the council, the Indians signed a treaty acquiescing to Harney's demands, but the Senate never ratified it. For a detailed account of the council, see "Council with the Sioux Indians at Ft. Pierre," 34th Cong., 1st sess., 1855–86, H. Exec. Doc. 130. Bear Ribs (Mato Tucuhupi) was killed in June of 1862. See Stanley Vestal, *Warpath and*

Council Fire: The Plains Indians' Struggle for Survival in War and Diplomacy, 1851–1891 (New York: Random House, 1948), 34–45.

2. Spotted Tail and others did not visit Indian Territory (Oklahoma) until October of 1876. The trip was forced on the chiefs as part of the threat to move them south employed by the 1876 "commission appointed to obtain certain concessions from the Sioux," i.e., the group charged with the responsibility of taking the Black Hills and other land identified as Lakota territory in the 1868 treaty. An "agreement" giving up the lands was eventually signed by those Indians who were at the agencies; the so-called hostiles were still up in the north defending their country. (The U.S. ceased "treaty" making with Indian tribes in 1871; hence the use of the term *agreement*. The agreement has been challenged by the Lakotas as part of their ongoing claim to the Black Hills because it does not contain the signatures of three-quarters of the adult male population, a requirement specified by the 1868 treaty.) For information on the trip to Indian Territory and the 1876 commission, see *The Annual Report of the Commissioner of Indian Affairs*, 1876; "The Report and Journal of Proceedings of the Commission Appointed to Obtain Certain Concessions from the Sioux Indians," 44th Cong., 2nd sess., 1876–77, S. Exec. Doc. 91; and Richmond L. Clow, "The Sioux Nation and Indian Territory: The Attempted Removal of 1876" *South Dakota History* 6, no. 4 (fall 1976): 456–73.

3. At this point in the manuscript, Bettelyoun begins to rely heavily on George W. Kingsbury, *History of Dakota Territory* (Chicago: S. J. Clarke, 1915). The issue of civilian versus military control of Indian affairs is a recurring subject in his chapter 59, "Instituting the Sioux Indian Peace Policy."

4. "In the latter part of August, under the direction of the President a commission . . . was appointed to go up the Missouri to endeavor to meet and negotiate with these Indians. . . . Treaties cannot, however, be completed at this time with all who are anxious for peace. This is owing to the lateness of the season, and the very widely scattered position of the Indians" (*The Annual Report of the Commissioner of Indian Affairs*, 1865, 28). See also the "Sub-Report of Mr. Hubbard" in "Condition of the Indian Tribes," 39th Cong., 2nd sess., 1866–67, S. Exec. Rep. 156. Bettelyoun is relying here on Kingsbury, *History of Dakota Territory*, 747–48.

5. Bettelyoun is, unfortunately, relying heavily on Kingsbury in this passage. Following his book, she gives the date of the trip to Washington as

1867; I have corrected it in the text. Her use of the term "Sheridan Treaty" has no foundation. Because Kingsbury dates the trip as 1867, he follows his discussion of it with the 1868 Laramie treaty, which he calls the "Sherman Treaty." Perhaps this is the origin of Bettelyoun's confusion. Her list of the locations of the various Lakota bands comes from Kingsbury (746, 768) and is not completely accurate for the year 1870. An excerpt from Kingsbury may serve to clarify Bettelyoun's list of agents: "There were forty-two Indian chiefs and renowned warriors in the company representing all the Sioux tribes except the Yanktons, who had just returned from a similar visit. The Indians were accompanied by Maj. Joseph R. Hanson, agent of the Upper Missouri Sioux, and also those at Fort Thompson, as the Crow Creek Agency was called; also by Maj. Patrick H. Congar, the Yankton agent" (750–51). Likewise, it is because Kingsbury erroneously names the Honorable Wm. P. Dole as commissioner of Indian affairs during the time of the trip (see Kingsbury, 750–51) that Bettelyoun does so. William P. Dole served in that position from 1861 to 1865.

Narcisse Narcel, a mixed-blood stockraiser, was from the Cheyenne River Reservation. Alex Rencontre, born ca. 1840 at Fort Pierre, was the son of trader Zephyre (Xavier) Rencontre and a Lakota woman. He was educated at Saint Louis University and lived with the Lower Brulés (NSHS MS3626, Rev. Allen Shine Collection, s1, box 3). Basil Claymore (Clement), son of a Frenchman and a mixed-blood woman, worked as a trader, hunter, guide, and boatman for the American Fur Company for over two decades. In addition, he served the government as a guide for a number of expeditions in the Rockies and northern plains. The story of his life can be found in his autobiography, edited by Charles E. Deland, *South Dakota Historical Collections* 11 (1922). Charles Galpin, who was married to a Yanktonais woman, was engaged in trading at Fort Laramie (John) in the early 1830s. He later settled into trading on the upper Missouri. He is remembered for his rescue of a group of white women and children during the Dakota's Minnesota uprising in 1862, and for his part in DeSmet's peace envoy to Sitting Bull in 1868. His wife was instrumental in both events. Louis Agaard arrived on the Upper Missouri in 1844 and lived at Fort Pierre for many years. He clerked for Galpin at that trader's Wakpala post and eventually settled at Fort Yates.

6. Again, inaccuracies are due to the reliance on Kingsbury (799–802). For their own convenience in delivering treaty-stipulated annuities, the government wanted the Brulés and Oglalas located at the Missouri River.

Although the 1868 treaty states that the agent shall reside at the Missouri, it does not require the Lakotas to relocate there. In any event, the first attempt at moving the two bands east in 1869 was a failure. Removal was forced upon them again as part of the 1876 agreement—the taking of the Black Hills. Bettelyoun's statement that "From 1875 to 1878, the government had not been insistent to remove the Indians to points along the Missouri River" may stem from the subheading of the Kingsbury chapter Bettelyoun is relying on, "Indian Chiefs Visit Washington: 1875–78." Kingsbury writes: "At this time (1875, '76) negotiations were pending that looked to a cession of the Black Hills region to the Government. The Indians were, already, under the treaty of 1868, required to remove to the Missouri River and receive their agencies at Beaver Creek and Ft. Robinson, and were strongly opposed to the proposed removal" (799). The 1877 *Annual Report of the Commissioner of Indian Affairs* and Hyde's *Spotted Tail's Folk* give a clearer picture of the 1876 agreement, the 1877 trip to Washington, and the removal to the Missouri than does Kingsbury.

7. Bettelyoun's account is the most detailed source on this incident. The only government record is a brief mention in a list of "White Men Killed By Indians." It states only "DeKalb" killed "near Ash Creek" in 1873. (NARS RG75, M1282.) This date conflicts with Bettelyoun's information, which would date the killing as having occurred in 1876.

8. François C. Boucher, Bordeaux's successor at his post in the White River valley, was known to have traded guns and ammunition to the "hostiles" in 1876. See Charles E. Hanson, "The Post War Indian Gun Trade," *Museum of the Fur Trade Quarterly* 4, no. 3 (fall 1968): 1–11.

9. Spotted Tail's peace envoy left Camp Sheridan on Feb. 13, 1877, and returned April 5. The Lakotas who had been fighting for survival in the north began to drift into the agencies throughout the following month. Touch the Cloud, a Miniconjou, was not a member of the delegation but came in from the north on April 14, surrendering to General Crook at Spotted Tail Agency. On May 2 Crazy Horse and his people stopped about thirty miles from Red Cloud agency, where they were issued rations and cattle. On May 6, at the head of a stately procession of about one thousand people, Crazy Horse rode into the agency. For a discussion of the various peace delegations to the Indians in the north, see Harry H. Anderson, "Indian Peace-Talkers and the Conclusion of the Sioux War of 1876," *Nebraska History* 44, no. 4 (Dec. 1963): 233–54.

10. Bettelyoun's manuscript implies that George H. Jewett had a store at

Fort Robinson in 1877. Tom Buecher, NSHS historian at the fort, knows of no such enterprise. In testimony before a federal commission in 1875, Jewett states that he had been a trader at the Spotted Tail Agency for over two years.

11. Red Feather's sister was Black Shawl (Śinasapawiŋ); she and Crazy Horse had one child, They Are Afraid of Her (Kokipapi). Hardorff maintains that it was Black Shawl, the first wife, who was suffering from blood poisoning, which caused great swelling in her arm. She never remarried and died at eighty-four in an influenza epidemic that swept the reservation in the 1920s (34). Crazy Horse married Nellie Laravie (Iśta Gi, or Brown Eyes) when he came down to the agency. She later married a Brulé named Greasing Hand (Nape Slakiya) and settled near Eagle Pass on the Pine Ridge reservation. See Richard G. Hardorff, *The Oglala Lakota Crazy Horse: A Preliminary Genealogical Study and an Annotated Listing of Primary Sources* (Mattituck NY: J. M. Carroll & Company, 1985).

12. Frank Grouard (1850–1905) claimed to be the son of a Mormon missionary and a Polynesian woman, and the journals of missionary Addison Pratt support this. However, Billy Garnett, whose sister was married to Grouard, told Ricker that while Grouard claimed to be from the Sandwich Islands, Garnett believed his mother was a Huŋkpapa and his father a black man named "Prazost" or "Brazo." And in 1907 Mrs. Nettie (Brazeau) Goings told Ricker that she and Grouard were children of the same father by different mothers, and that their father, John Brazeau, was a French Creole from Saint Louis who worked for the American Fur Company. She said that Grouard's real name was Walter Brazeau and that the Lakota called him Grabber (NSHS MS8, Eli Ricker Collection; roll 1, tablet 1 and roll 3, tablet 13). Whatever his background, while engaged as a mail carrier in Montana, Grouard was captured by the Lakotas and adopted by Sitting Bull. In 1873 he fought with the Lakotas against government forces on the Yellowstone. Later, after quarreling with Sitting Bull, Grouard joined Crazy Horse's camp. He soon left and went to Fort Robinson, where he served General Crook as a scout. See Joe DeBarthe, *Life and Adventures of Frank Grouard* (Norman: University of Oklahoma Press, 1958), which is informative though fanciful in many regards. For evidence supporting Grouard's claims concerning his parentage, see S. George Ellsworth, ed., *The Journals of Addison Pratt* (Salt Lake City: University of Utah Press, 1990).

13. Bettelyoun, or perhaps Waggoner, is confusing Mrs. Victoria DeNoyer

with Victoria Conroy, granddaughter of Crazy Horse's aunt. Records indicate that Victoria Conroy was a resident at the Old Soldiers' Home (though her file is missing), but no such records exist for Victoria De-Noyer. Furthermore, it was through Josephine Waggoner that Conroy sent a letter to the Pine Ridge superintendent regarding Crazy Horse's burial. DeNoyer was not born until 1883, whereas Conroy was eleven at the time of Crazy Horse's death and camped at Ponca with his family in 1877. Victoria DeNoyer was the daughter of Charles DeNoyer and Pteska (Gray Buffalo). They appear in the 1887 Rosebud census among the Loafer band. Her Lakota name is given as Oheyaŋ.

14. Bettelyoun's brother Louis was an interpreter, along with Grouard, in the meeting between Crazy Horse and Lieutenant Clark. The deceit and treachery that led to the death of Crazy Horse is covered in Robert A. Clark, ed., commentary by Carroll Friswold, *The Killing of Chief Crazy Horse: Three Eyewitness Views by the Indian, Chief He Dog; the Indian-White, William Garnett; the White Doctor, Valentine McGilly-cuddy* (Glendale CA: Arthur H. Clark, 1976; reprint, Lincoln: University of Nebraska Press, 1988), and Edward and Mabel Kadlecek, *To Kill an Eagle: Indian Views on the Death of Crazy Horse* (Boulder CO: Johnson Publishing, 1981). See also Sandoz, *Crazy Horse*; Eleanor Hinman, "Oglala Sources on the Life of Crazy Horse," *Nebraska History* 57, no. 1 (spring 1976); and E. A. Brininstool, ed., "Chief Crazy Horse, His Career and Death" *Nebraska History* 12, no. 1 (1929). Bettelyoun's nephew's account is found in William J. Bordeaux, *Custer's Conqueror* (n.p.: Smith & Co., n.d.). The stories of how and where Crazy Horse was buried are as numerous as the tellers; Bettelyoun's account is only one of many.

15. The long feud between Crow Dog (Kaŋgi Śuŋka) and Spotted Tail ended on August 5, 1881. Crow Dog was tried in Deadwood, South Dakota, and sentenced to be hanged, but the Supreme Court pointed out that the United States had no jurisdiction on Indian reservations (*Ex Parte Crow Dog*, 109 U.S. 556), and Crow Dog was set free. (This judgment was the incentive for the passage of the Major Crimes Act, which gives federal courts jurisdiction over certain crimes committed on Indian land.) See Hyde, *Spotted Tail's Folk* and *A Sioux Chronicle*; William Seagle, "The Murder of Spotted Tail," *The Indian Historian* 3, no. 4 (fall 1970): 10–22; and Rosebud agent John Cook's report of the murder in *The Annual Report of the Commissioner of Indian Affairs*, 1881, 54–55.

13. ON THE RESERVATION

1. Ezra Ayres Hayt (Commissioner of Indian Affairs, 1877–80) met with Brulés at the old Ponca agency in July of 1878 as part of the Stanley Commission. Here Bettelyoun continues to rely on Kingsbury, *History of Dakota Territory* (802–8), repeating his mistake of calling Hayt E. C. instead of E. A. (corrected here). Her reference to Hayt's attempt to prohibit the Brulés' cultural practices echoes Kingsbury: "[H]e accordingly issued an order prohibiting the sale of beads, paints, shells, etc., to the Indians; these beads he regarded as one of the most serious hindrances to their rapid moulding into civilized beings; they linked the Indian women with the wild life of the past which they had pursued, and Hayt was anxious that the Indians should become oblivious to their old savage ways. . . . Spotted Tail was very much offended at the order and openly rebelled against it. He declared to Major Lee, the agent at Rosebud, that the Indians would not submit to such foolishness. He claimed that the young men and women of the Sioux had the same right to purchase ornamental articles and use them to adorn their persons as whites had. The old chief said that white women painted and powdered, bought beads, and fancy articles; and he claimed further that if the young Indian women were forbidden to manufacture their various articles of bead work which were freely purchased by the whites, they would have nothing to do, and great evils would result from such enforced idleness" (802).

2. Commissioner Hayt's visit was part of D. S. Stanley's 1878 Commission. Secretary of the Interior (not commissioner) Carl Schurz did not visit the Rosebud agency until August 1879. For information on the commission, the council with the Indians, and the choosing of the new agencies' locations, see both Hayt's report and that of the Commission in the 1878 *Annual Report of the Commissioner of Indian Affairs*. See also agents James Irwin's and William J. Pollock's reports in the same volume for discussion of the move west and the establishment of the new agencies. Cf. Kingsbury, 806–9.

3. Here, going back in time, Bettelyoun fortunately leaves Kingsbury's *History of Dakota Territory* behind and recalls events from her own memories. John Hunton relates the following story of the murder of Antoine LaDeau's son, whom he calls Baptiste: "In the winter of 1867 . . . Mr. James Bordeaux permitted two men, 'Cy' Williams and Swalley [Ben or Eli Swallow], to occupy the ranch [south of Fort Laramie on Chugwater Creek] and use it for themselves. They had in their employ a

half-breed boy about eighteen years old, named Baptiste LaDeau. About the first part of March 1868, he told them he was going to quit and go to Ft. Laramie to his father. After breakfast one morning he saddled his pony and, calling his pet dog, mounted and started for the Fort. There were three or four men (hard characters) loafing about the ranch, and after the boy started Williams remarked to one of them, 'He will never get there. Come on and go with us.' So Williams and Swalley and the men started on horse back. They overtook the boy just south of Chug Spring and as soon as he saw them coming he started his horse on the run for the bluff, but they, having much better horses than the boy, came up with him on top of the bluff about a quarter of a mile west of Chug Spring and shot and killed the boy, horse and dog, and left them where they fell. . . . About a month had elapsed after the boy was killed when General Adam J. Slemmer, on his way home from Cheyenne to Fort Laramie with an escort of 25 Infantry soldiers, camped at Chug Spring for the night . . . and discovered the remains of the boy, the horse and the dog. As soon as General Slemmer got to the fort the next morning he told of the discovery his men had made. . . . A great howl went up from the half-breed and Indian camp. The next morning a party of half-breeds went to Chug Spring and buried the boy where he fell. The murderers denied the killing and were never arrested. . . . In the spring and early summer of 1868 the Government . . . induced the Indians to consent to be moved to White Clay River. . . . This mobilization included all white men with Indian families who cared to make the move. Cy Williams, having an Indian wife, abandoned Bordeaux late in March or early April and moved to the Indian camp east of Fort Laramie so as to be ready to start with the Indians. After his wife had been interviewed by the relations of the murdered LaDeau boy, Williams was openly accused of the killing, which he denied, and was secretly and closely watched to see that he did not attempt to leave the camp. This condition of affairs lasted about a week, or when some drunken half-breeds precipitated a gunfight. Williams was killed, but not before he had killed one half-breed, Charley Richard, and wounded two other half-breeds, Joe Bissonette and one whose name I have forgotten. Oliver P. Goodwin, an innocent spectator, was wounded, but not seriously" (WDCR, 479B, Hunton Collection, folder 5).

4. The eldest son of a man who worked for trader Andrew Dripps near Scottsbluff in the 1850s and a Lakota woman named Medicine Eagle (Waŋbli Wakaŋ), James McClosky served as a guide and interpreter at

Fort Laramie from 1861 until his death. He was killed at Six Mile Ranch on October 27, 1870, by William Boyer, who was hanged for the crime. McClosky was twenty-five (FLNHS, CIN-25).

5. According to military reports and newspaper accounts, on December 25, 1872, a fight broke out at Nick Janis's place on Kiowa Creek, in which the old trader's sons, Peter and William, were killed. The killers were Charles and Joseph Richards—sons of John Richards Sr.—and Paddy Miller, "full blooded Sioux, but looked upon as a civilized Indian." (He may be the Indian Bettelyoun refers to as Big Head.) News of the murders was brought to Laramie by mixed-blood Baptiste Jewette, and he, in turn, was shot and killed by John Sr.'s widow. Of the affair, the *Cheyenne Daily Leader* wrote: "No regret at the fatal result of these Indian amusements is felt in this community. On the contrary, our people are disposed to consider these brawls blessings in disguise, as they free us from a set of hangers on to the Indian reservation, who are and have been the cause of our Indian troubles. We do not object to their continuing this pastime, and are satisfied to leave the half-breeds among the full-breeds, as an element of discord, disseminating feuds among their brethren, the Indians. With the half-breeds among the Sioux and the epizootic among the Indian ponies, the white man is content to abide the result" (Jan. 13, 1873). Military reports of the incident and typescripts of related articles from the *Cheyenne Daily Leader* are compiled in FLNHS, file CD-6. Testimony gathered at the time can be found in NARS Letters Received by the Office of Indian Affairs, M234, reel 717, Red Cloud Agency, 1873. See also Jones, "Those Wild Reshaw Boys."

Index

Chouteau, Pierre, 26, 28, 139 n.5
Clark, Lt. William, 109, 174 n.14
Clark, Rev. C. B., 111
Claymore, Basil (Clement), 105,
    171 n.5
Clement, Basil. *See* Claymore, Basil
Cleveland, Rev. W. J., 103, 130 n.13,
    168 n.2
Coarse Voice, 100
Cokawiŋ, 57–58, 62–64
Cold Springs Station, 87, 132 n.16
Conger, Maj. Patrick H., 105, 171 n.5
Congregational missions, xix, 14
Connor, Benjamin Monroe (Ben Ar-
    nold), xix, 12, 133 n.3
Connor, Marcella, 12
Connor Expedition. *See* Powder River
    Campaign
Conquering Bear. *See* Scattering Bear
Conrad, Corp. Francis, 146 n.15
Conroy, Victoria, 173 n.13
Corn Band, 137 n.1
Crawford, Lewis F., xix
Crazy Hawk, 31
Crazy Horse, 3, 78, 85, 105, 107–
    10, 169 n.3, 172 n.9, 173 n.11,
    174 n.13 n.14
Crow Butte, 51–52, 151 n.1 n.2 n.3
Crow Dog, 110–11, 174 n.15
Crow Indians, 50–52, 60
Cuny, Adolf, 43, 150 n.22

DeCalb (mail carrier), 106, 172 n.7
de Morin, Edward (de Moran), 73,
    89, 157 n.7
DeNoyer, Charles, 174 n.13
DeNoyer, Victoria, 110, 173 n.13
Deon, Samuel, 150 n.21
DeSersa, Charles, 69, 73, 156 n.4

DeSersa family, 164 n.4
De Smet, Father Pierre Jean, 35, 44,
    92–93, 142 n.5, 150 n.23
disease among Indians. *See* Lakota In-
    dians, disease
Dole, William P., 105, 171 n.5
Dorian, Tom, 101, 107, 150 n.21,
    168 n.23
Drouillard, George, 26, 140 n.8
DuBray, Antoine, 73, 89, 157 n.7
Dull Knife (Cheyenne), 4, 127 n.2

Elston, Charley, 88, 97–98, 150 n.21,
    164 n.7
Episcopal missions, xix, 14, 103,
    136 n.10, 168 n.2
Estes, Stephan, 73, 80–81, 158 n.9

Farrar, Andrew, 131 n.14
Federal Writers Project, xxi, xxiv
Fetterman, Lt. William Judd, 94–95,
    167 n.17
Fetterman fight, 79, 94–95, 167 n.17
Field Matron Program, xvii, 7,
    129 n.12
Fleming, Lt. Hugh Brady, 4, 54, 83,
    127 n.1
Flood, Thomas, 105
Fontenelle, Fitzpatrick and Company,
    140 n.11
Fontenelle, Logan, 6, 128 n.7
Ford family, 74–75, 158 n.12
Fort Berthold, 26
Fort Clark, 26
Fort Fetterman, 166 n.16
Ft. John. *See* Fort Laramie
Fort Laramie: as fur trading post, xv,
    3, 30–32, 140 n.11; life at, 91–92;
    as U.S. military post, xv, 3, 65